"Sawhney and Zabin illuminate the pathway with the bright and steady light of a customer-centered business model, rather than the flash of the tech revolution."
— Michael A. Volkema, Chairman, President, and CEO, Herman Miller, Inc.

"After reading *The Seven Steps to Nirvana*, I now know this is much more than an e-business book—it is an innovative blueprint for all managers confronting the new challenges of the Internet economy from the reality of their existing company."
— James J. O'Connor, Retired Chairman and CEO, Unicom Corporation

"Using rich metaphors and an engaging style, this book gives wise counsel to established companies on thinking strategically about e-business. The authors shatter many popular misconceptions and myths about e-business, and show how to place customers at the front and center of your e-business strategy."
— Earnest W. Davenport, Jr., Chairman and CEO, Eastman Chemical Company

"Mohan Sawhney has emerged as a true e-business visionary. He and Jeff Zabin have written a must-have book for anyone intent on winning in the changing business environment…. It's clear, comprehensive, and compelling."
— Paula Sneed, Group Vice President and President of E-Commerce and Marketing Services, Kraft Foods

"*Seven Steps* is at once deeply insightful and immensely practical. It beautifully illustrates, with many real-life examples and lasting images, how to seamlessly blend the 'hard' business issues with the 'soft' people and leadership issues. The wisdom in this book hit me like a ton of clicks!"
— Deepak Sethi, Vice President, Executive & Leadership Development, The Thomson Corporation

THE
SEVEN STEPS
TO
NIRVANA

THE SEVEN STEPS TO NIRVANA

Strategic Insights into
e-Business Transformation

Mohan Sawhney

Jeff Zabin

McGraw-Hill

New York   Chicago   San Francisco
Lisbon   London   Madrid   Mexico City
Milan   New Delhi   San Juan   Seoul
Singapore   Sydney   Toronto

Library of Congress Cataloging-in-Publication Data

Sawhney, Mohanbir S.
    The seven steps to nirvana : strategic insights into into ebusiness transformation /
    Mohan Sawhney and Jeff Zabin.
        p. cm.
    Includes bibliographical references.
    ISBN 0-07-137522-8
        1. Electronic commerce.   2. Business enterprises—Computer networks.
I. Zabin, Jeff.   II. Title.

HF5548.32 .S2 2001
658.8'4—dc21

                                                                    2001030387

McGraw-Hill

A Division of The McGraw-Hill Companies

ISBN 0-07-137522-8

Printed and bound by Quebecor World/Martinsburg.

McGraw-Hill books are available at special quantity discounts to use as premiums and
sales promotions, or for use in corporate training programs. For more information,
please write to the Director of Special Sales, Professional Publishing, McGraw-Hill,
Two Penn Plaza, New York, NY 10121-2298. Or contact your local bookstore.

 This book is printed on recycled, acid-free paper containing a minimum of
50% recycled, de-inked fiber.

To my late father Harvinder Singh Sawhney, who would have been so proud.

M. S.

To my parents Harold and Phyllis, my soulmate Jacqueline, and my e-boys Ethan and Elan.

J. Z.

CONTENTS

FOREWORD

WELCOME to the post-dotcom era. It's been more than a year since the Nasdaq imploded. Today many dotcoms are on life support or have gone under, and the market values of many technology companies have tanked.

Much can be learned from picking through the rubble. To my amazement, some people have come to an extraordinary conclusion: e-business is a bust—summed up in the view that there is no new economy. I can understand the argument's appeal. Managers can stop worrying that some dotcom startup will crush them overnight. While this is probably true, it is no excuse to relax.

Today, smart companies are using the Net to achieve goals they have striven toward for the past 25 years: Focusing on core competencies, reducing transaction costs, innovating more effectively, and gaining new ways to achieve deep customer relationships. Some established companies are turning entire industries upside down. As Mohan Sawhney and Jeff Zabin rightly point out, the danger of being "Amazoned" has been replaced by the danger of being "Enron-ed" or "GE-ized."

Despite claims to the contrary, there *is* a new economy, with the Internet at its heart. As Sawhney and Zabin so ably articulate, the Net is totally transforming the business environment. Every business will be an e-business or die. If you run your company on the basis of conventional wisdom, your failure is only a question of time.

It is particularly nonsensical to look, as some do, at the dotcom boom/bust and then equate the Internet to previously hot-then-cold sectors such as biotechnology. Biotechnology mutual funds exist today, and no doubt they will continue to exist 10 years from now. But I don't know of any mutual funds targeting companies that deftly exploit the power of electricity or the telephone. The notion sounds pretty dumb. And in 10 years time it will be equally dumb for a mutual fund to claim it targets Internet or e-business companies. As Sawhney and Zabin show us, *all* companies will be Internet or e-business companies. Any others will have gone bankrupt.

This is the error pundits make when they try to equate the new economy to the technology sector. Technology is much more than a sector; it is becoming the basis of all sectors. It is creating a new infrastructure that is shaking the foundation of banking, manufacturing, health care, distribution, agriculture, construction, and every other sector in the economy.

Whether or not we are in a new economy is not a question of semantics. An economy is a system in which goods and services are created, distributed, and consumed. Throughout the twentieth century, almost all this activity was based on the corporation—vertically integrated in the manner devised by Henry Ford. It was based on an infrastructure that included the electrical power grid, the roads, and primitive analog networks like the telephone.

Now there is the addition of a new infrastructure—the Internet—that is dropping costs of transactions and collaboration among people, firms, organizations, and other entities. This development is giving rise to new business models that are more effective than the industrial-age corporation. In turn, the nature of products and services, distribution channels, the dynamics of competition, and virtually every institution in society are being subjected to discontinuous change.

Companies are functioning in an unprecedented environment. The markets for industrial-age goods and services are evaporating as consumers demand more. Products and services, from soapboxes to refrigerators and cars, are becoming Internet appliances—infused with knowledge and services. And the only way to meet these heightened expectations is for business leaders to lift their productive capabilities to new heights. The trusty logic of the B-school wisdom or case studies from ten or five years ago no longer applies. Fresh solutions are needed for fresh challenges. And no part of the economy is untouched. New illustrations pop up daily. This morning's paper talks about the terror in the boardrooms of Hollywood studios: Horrified at the prospect of having their industry turned upside down by some

Napster-like video software, studio executives are scrambling to put an Internet distribution system into place that will stave off movie piracy.

So if all this is happening, then why isn't the Nasdaq at 7500? Because Nasdaq and the new economy are not interchangeable terms. Many companies on Nasdaq are old economy, and many companies on the New York Stock Exchange (NYSE) or Tokyo Stock Exchange (TSE) are new economy. As the authors note, this book "focuses on real people within mundane sectors of the economy," and by so doing, it shows us that any company can choose the economy it wishes to be part of. It doesn't depend on what product it sells or what stock exchange it is listed on. It depends on the business model it embraces to create customer value and shareholder wealth.

Examples abound. Federal Express is listed on the NYSE and is not part of the technology sector. It delivers parcels from A to B. Nevertheless, FedEx is a new-economy company. It has totally redesigned its business processes around the Web. The vast majority of its shipments are ordered, tracked, and managed via the Internet. FedEx customers can use the Web 24 hours a day to pinpoint the whereabouts of their parcels, and they love it.

In 1998 FedEx declared that its physical distribution system of trucks and airplanes was less valuable than its internetworked information resources. FedEx decided to focus on value-added context services, such as online package tracking and logistics outsourcing, and leave the "driving" to other companies. But the business processes of FedEx and these new partners are seamlessly meshed via the Internet. The new FedEx is a perfect example of the new platform for wealth creation and the product of e-business: the *business web,* which describes a system of meshed entities—suppliers, distributors, service providers, infrastructure providers, and customers—that use the Net as the basis for business communications and transactions. Usually one company choreographs the activity (e.g., FedEx), and that company sometimes enjoys the lion's share of the business web's profits. But the other participants are essential, contributing according to their core competencies.

I meet many executives moving their companies incrementally (and often unconsciously) in the business web direction. They talk of closer links with customers via the Net, and how they can now outsource more functions to suppliers because the Internet enables close collaboration. But, as the authors note, "Only after gaining a deep understanding of its own distinct assets and priorities can a company gaze into the crystal ball and begin to see its digital future." Resolve your fundamental customer value proposition, and the business processes will follow.

We are in the early stages of transforming to the new economy. Despite the Net's dramatic growth in functionality, ubiquity, and bandwidth, it is still primitive. Nevertheless, without fail, any business that has tasted the Net's benefits is hooked. No company has integrated the Internet into its business model and concluded that the predigital way of doing business was better.

The authors explain that e-business is not a "bolt-on to your business." It must be an integral component. To be sure, many companies—of both the old and new economies—have simply set up websites and been disappointed by the results. But as I have said many times before, a website is the digital-era equivalent of a business card, and nothing more. Businesses that obsess about having "sticky" sites with an elaborate multimedia content miss the point.

The Web has created an extraordinarily fecund environment for entrepreneurship. Never has it been so easy or simple to take an idea to market. From 1997 to early 1999 we saw an explosion of business model innovation. Unfortunately, the get-rich-quick mentality that followed began to distort the assertion that "the Internet changes everything" (which is true) into the hope that "all things done on the Internet will prove lucrative" (which is rubbish). During this period, we saw outrageous excesses and spectacular market capitalizations based on absurd or nonexistent business models. Pundits offered every conceivable theory on where the smart money should be going, and everybody claimed credibility because the rising stock market tides lifted all boats. Momentum investing set in.

But, thankfully, those times are past and sanity is returning. Many high-profile dotcoms have either gone bust or are in tatters, while a few have prospered. In their defense, some of the failed dotcoms were simply ahead of their time. It's happened before. Aside from the Edsel, it is hard to think of a commercial product that suffered as much scorn as Apple's ill-fated Newton, introduced in 1993. But as the wildly popular Palm products show today, the idea of a small electronic memo taker, address book, calendar, and to-do list keeper was a helluva good idea.

What's important to understand at this time is that the headline-grabbing dotcom fireworks were largely a distraction, and they represented only a thin sliver of the businesses beginning to exploit the power of the Internet. In every sector of the economy the competitive ground has shifted, and new business models are clearly being established as the new mechanism for winning in the marketplace. As Sawhney and Zabin write, "the new economy was the best thing to have happened to the old economy."

The implications for investors are obviously dramatic. Naysayers talk nonsense when they suggest investors should simply go back to decade-old tried-and-true valuation methods to guide their portfolios. They want to go back from irrational exuberance to irrational orthodoxy. But much better lenses are needed. In the new economy, companies can grow at a previously unimaginable pace. Wal-Mart had to wait 12 years and build 78 stores before it reached annual sales of $150 million. Amazon achieved the same sales in two years with no stores, one website, and a warehouse. In the new economy, growth potential must be the overriding consideration with respect to any investment opportunity, yet assessing that potential has never been more difficult.

The upshot of irrational orthodoxy is that many companies are being unfairly punished. They have good business models and are poised for growth, but their share values languish. As investors develop the new lenses that are required in this economy, these companies will be recognized for the excellent values that they are. It is unlikely that these babies will be stuck in the drain with the dotcom bathwater for long. Those investors that stick simply to P/E ratios and similar metrics will suffer.

Even though we are in the post-dotcom era, we are about to see unprecedented creative destruction, courtesy of the Net. Want to know which companies will succumb? Listen to the doomed corporation's management. Their strategies are based on the company acting as a distinct entity, separate from its suppliers and customers. They think they can still operate with old-economy methods. Want to know which companies will succeed? Look to those that, as Sawhney and Zabin explain, are focused on the customer and on creating new customer value propositions. In envisioning such new value for your customers, don't be constrained by what you think you are capable of doing. In this new world, the art of the possible is changed. E-businesses can partner to create value previously unimaginable by the old corporation.

Skeptics dream up all sorts of reasons to dismiss the early indicators of the greater turbulence ahead. Apparently, Napster is meaningless because the company is "founded on the theft of someone else's product." Really? Let's look at Linux. IBM spent more than $1 billion developing an excellent operating system called OS/2 that failed miserably in the marketplace against the well-entrenched Microsoft Windows. It was a clash of titans, and Microsoft won.

Then came Linux, cobbled together by tens of thousands of digital Rotarians voluntarily collaborating on the Net. They weren't motivated by profit; they simply want a superior and stable operating system that would make their jobs as computer technicians easier. They created a highly integrated "good" that provides value to themselves and to others. This process itself isn't all that radical. In the past, many of humanity's highest achievements—including language and science—have resulted from open and collaborative models of innovation and value creation.

Linux is making inroads everywhere. Witness the National Center for Supercomputing Applications' recent announcement that its newest IBM supercomputer, capable of 2 trillion calculations per second, would use Linux. "We believe that Linux clusters will soon be the most widely used architecture for parallel computing," said the Center's director. The only arena in which Linux has failed to make dramatic gains is on the desktop, but that day may come.

Imagine the open-source spirit moving into the manufacturing arena. General Motors collaborates within its business web participants to design cars using three-dimensional visual prototypes distributed via the Internet. Participants could include style-conscious customers, fleet buyers, knowledgeable service technicians, supply chain partners, dealers, car buffs, and industrial designers. These participants are motivated to provide the "gift" of their advice because they love cars, enjoy interacting with the business web community, and gain pleasure from influencing the design of a future car. When GM adopts an idea, it publicizes the news to the community, enhancing the contributor's reputation. The manufacturer returns the favor by providing buyer rebates based on quality and quantity of contributions.

In this scenario, the entire value proposition for GM's customers can be transformed through a new business model. The car would become a place for work, learning, and entertainment, with customers creating much of the value. The entire industry would be restructured with a new division of labor, and customers would become part of GM's business web.

I encourage you to approach *The Seven Steps to Nirvana* with this big picture in mind. The book is a feast of down-to-earth helpful advice on how to evolve your firm into an e-business and thrive in the new economy. The authors talk evolution and provide reams of practical advice on making it happen in your company. But they also keep their eyes on the prize—the fundamental and ultimately "radical" transformation of the firm to create value for customers and shareholders for a new environment. The book will help you think differently for this post-dotcom world.

The authors tell a great story of how they taught many of the book's principles at a seminar and then asked the students what changes they would make in their companies. Most responses were timid. At a subsequent seminar, the authors asked students to take the same insights and create a competitor that would be their worst nightmare. The difference was profound. Starting with a cleaner slate, the students were much bolder and innovative.

Believe me, this is no time to be timid. Your company's survival is at stake.

Don Tapscott

Don Tapscott is Chairman of Digital 4Sight and author of eight widely read books on business strategy. Recently he co-authored the bestseller Digital Capital: Harnessing the Power of Business Webs.

PREFACE

THIS BOOK has its genesis in a highly successful executive education program called *Winning Strategies for e-Business* that Mohan Sawhney has been teaching at the Kellogg Graduate School of Management since 1998. In designing this program, we followed Willie Sutton's philosophy of "robbing banks because that is where the money is." Kellogg is located in the Midwest, the bastion of the old economy. To many of the executives who attended the program, Silicon Valley and the new economy are far removed from their day-to-day realities. The question they posed was: "What does all this e-business stuff mean to *us*? We don't sell books over the Net, and we're not highly evolved species like Cisco."

One executive even warned us: "Don't show us Mount Everest, and then laugh at us because we are never going to get there. Instead, show us the base camp, and explain how to get from there to the top of the mountain." Clearly, e-business is a journey. And a traveler embarking upon the journey is interested in milestones that he can see rather than stories of a distant promised land. Taking the challenge to heart, Mohan set out to create a systematic roadmap for an established company seeking to transform its business into an e-business. Of course, the ideas evolved over time and matured with the insights of hundreds of executives who suffered through early iterations of the program.

Enter Jeff Zabin, who shared Mohan's passion for bringing clarity around the nebulous topic of e-business transformation. For several years leading up to that point, Mohan and Jeff had talked about collaborating on a business strategy book that would be called *Metaphors for Management.* The idea was to take ancient wisdom rich in metaphors and stories and apply it to modern-day business issues. By late 1999, it became clear that the contemporary context we had been looking for was e-business transformation. At the intersection of our love for Zen koans and Aesop's fables, and our insatiable appetite for new insights into the new world of business, was born the idea for this book. After that, it was just a matter of writing it!

We have benefited immensely from the hundreds of executives who have challenged, inspired, and taught us. While they are too many to name individually, we would like to thank a few who played an integral role in advancing our thinking. They include Phil Condit and Anil Shrikhande (Boeing), Ed Liddy and Tom Wilson (Allstate), Paula Sneed (Kraft Foods), Hemant Dandekar (Eastman Chemical Company), Dave Knibbe and Gary Vanspronsen (Herman Miller), Mats Lederhausen (McDonald's), Deepak Malik (Cargill), Jonathan Greenblatt (Homestore.com), Jeffrey Ritz (Industrial Risk Insurance), Dan Tiernan (Atlas Commerce), Bryan Stolle (Agile Software), Bob Crowley (Bowstreet), Pauline Garris (Estée Lauder), Ashok Pahwa (Mary Kay), Mike Winkel (R.R. Donnelley), Rakesh Kaul (formerly of Hanover Direct), Alice Peterson (formerly of Sears, Roebuck & Company), and Shawn McCarthy (Cordis Endovascular).

We wish to acknowledge the generosity of Chris Miller and the Corporate Executive Board, which made available to us several valuable research studies for benchmarking best practices. Other companies, including Boeing, Eastman, and Herman Miller, were also kind to share with us materials that helped shine light on key topic areas.

We are especially grateful to Tia Sawhney for her countless contributions, from coordinating—and even conducting—many of the interviews, to dealing with the continuous avalanche of bureaucratic matters, to keeping us on track in view of the ever-looming deadlines. She acted as a sounding board, critic, proofreader, and business manager from start to finish.

Thanks to John Rheinfrank, Ranjay Gulati, Nick Carr, Cathy Brillson, and Ruben Shohet for taking the time to review the manuscript and provide thoughtful feedback. Thanks also to Philip Kotler and Mohan's other colleagues at the Kellogg School; to Don Jacobs, the Dean of the Kellogg School, for his unwavering support; and to David Ormesher, the CEO of closerlook. We take our hats off to Jeffrey Krames at McGraw-Hill, whose persistence, enthusiasm, and professionalism is unparalleled, and whose flair for drama has kept us entertained. Our heartfelt thanks to Ela Aktay, Scott Amerman, Kelli Christiansen, and the rest of the first-rate editorial, production, and marketing teams in the Professional Division at McGraw-Hill.

Finally, and most important, we wish to thank our families—our wives Tia and Jacqueline, as well as our children, for their sacrifices, patience, and support during the writing of this book. You are truly the wind beneath our wings, and we could never have done it without you.

Mohan Sawhney
Jeff Zabin

THE
SEVEN STEPS
TO
NIRVANA

INTRODUCTION

AN OLD CHINESE adage says: "May you live in interesting times." To say that we live in interesting times is clearly an understatement as corporations find themselves at the threshold of a discontinuity of such epic proportions that its hurricane-force winds promise to leave no company untouched—and many no longer standing—as they sweep across the business landscape. Of course *interesting times* are not necessarily something that are ordinarily sought after by large, profitable companies already in business with a legacy business architecture, legacy marketing channels, and a legacy set of customers. Indeed, precious few of them would choose to view this old Chinese adage as a blessing and not a curse.

Today an urgent challenge echoing around boardrooms across America and around the world is, "What does e-business mean for *our* business? How do we e-enable our firm? What opportunities does e-business present for us, and what threats does it pose to our current business?" For a vast proportion of established companies with long histories—the so-called incumbents—the challenge looms large. In some cases, it threatens their very survival.

Never in history has incumbency been more perplexing. Traditional competitive forces such as the good old *barriers to entry* and *competitive advantage*, once venerated by every blue chip as its own Manifest Destiny, have all but gone out the window as guarantees of future success. With market leadership no longer protected by these barriers, executives find themselves under enormous pressure to create new offerings, open new revenue streams, and push their businesses in new, profitable directions. Unfortunately, size begets rigidity—which in turn becomes a noose around the neck in times of rapid change. So while change may come easily with a handful of employees and an equally small base of customers, quite the opposite rings true when the equation includes tens of thousands of employees, millions of customers, and a complex infrastructure that for years has kept the money machine firing on all cylinders but now teeters on the brink of irrelevance. As computer industry veteran Enzo Torresi once observed: "The only reason God was able to create the Universe in six days was because *He* didn't have to worry about the installed base." Having to contend with a legacy business presents monumental constraints in terms of the ease and speed with which a company can reinvent itself.

Due to a combination of factors, both genetic and environmental, established companies are generally slow to reinvent themselves. They tend to go through life making only small, incremental innovations, leaving the introduction of truly disruptive businesses to a breed of smaller, faster, and nimbler outsiders. Traditionally, established companies have also been inexplicably slow to respond to radical change once it comes about, or at least that was the case when the pure play Internet business models first washed ashore. In that initial wave, a dotcom could unveil an entirely new business architecture, one that promised to destroy every last vestige of business as usual, and only gradually would the established companies competing in that marketplace come to grasp the implications of the change in their environment. Short term, their response might have been nothing more than a collective muttering of incredulity: "It doesn't exist, it can't be real, this is not the way *we* do business." What a difference a few years can make! By now, established companies across a broad spectrum of industries have witnessed firsthand how e-business makes possible disruptive business architectures that *do* exist, that *are* real, and that *can* completely change the basis of competition. Even the sleepers have awoken to the realization that it's time to march.

That said, much uncertainty remains as to where to line up the troops and in which direction they should advance. The good news: Despite the enormity of the challenges before them, the captains of industry are coming to recognize that their vast collections of assets, both tangible (resources, products, infrastructure, etc.) and intangible (brand equity, intellectual capital, channels, etc.), can afford tremendous opportunities for leverage. So, while the dotcoms may not have lived up to their promise of disruption, their barks being bigger than their bites, they have done valuable service by opening new pathways to business innovation and infusing a new sense of urgency among the established players.

What This Book Does

To date, e-business elightenment has been confined for the most part to Internet startups, technology companies, and the so-called early adopters among the Global 2000. But soon — just as all disruptive innovations tend to experience a lag time to mainstream acceptance — the *real* revolution will begin, with the lion's share of low-tech, smokestack businesses finally getting religion! Rather than preach to the converted, this book is targeted at senior managers and leaders of these latter companies. To borrow a phrase from Apple Computer, this book is "e-business for the rest of us." There are no Ciscos and Dells here. Everyone knows what these superheroes of e-business have accomplished, and managers' bookshelves creak with success stories of the few poster boys of e-business. In this book, we focus on real businesses and real people within mundane sectors of the economy. Accounting for the bulk of all economic activity, these are companies that, although endowed with large organizations and new technologies, are seldom seen as the movers and shakers of organizational and technological change. For them, this book lays out a systematic approach for exploiting the new possibilities of e-business. Armed with useful frameworks for sense-making and decision-making, and the ability to ask the right questions, readers of all ranks will be better positioned to take action when commanded by their CEOs to "go out and do e-business." For their part, CEOs and senior managers will be better positioned to give the right commands. If we are successful in our endeavor, this book will leave the reader with concrete insights into how to energize the core business through e-business, and how to leverage the core assets and capabilities of the firm into new directions.

This book is *not* a tactical field guide. Nor does it concern itself with sorting out the relative merits of the various technology solutions, other than to mention a few of the leaders in each category. A visit to the neighborhood megabookstore reveals a proliferation of "how-to" books focused on the nitty-gritty of technology implementation. At the same time, a sizable cottage industry of market research and consulting firms has sprung up with the express purpose of recommending product vendors and service providers based on specific client needs.

Rather than delve into tactics and implementation, this book takes a high-level view of the trenches, with the modest goal of providing a few key insights into strategy and vision. In the realm of insights, brevity indeed is the soul of wit. Written at 30,000 feet (and likely to be consumed by business travelers at the same altitude!), the book is a parachute that organizations can strap onto their backs as they make their initial descents through the upper strata of strategy formulation and into the more context-sensitive layers of their specific business situations. The *big idea*—and every product and service offering ought to be grounded in a *big idea*—is to pause for a moment and ask, "What is happening?" and, furthermore, "Why is it happening?"

Invariably these questions touch upon the interrelated arenas of marketing, strategy, organization, and technology and impact audiences that span a wide range of functions and industries. Given the scope, the book makes no apologies for being an inch thick and a mile wide. We paint many topics with broad brushstrokes out of sheer necessity. In an ideal world, there would be numerous versions of this book, each tailored to a specific industry and market niche. Moreover, each book would be continuously updated to reflect the dynamic nature of our evolving framework—as well, of course, as the constantly shifting and colliding tectonics of the business landscape itself.

Timeliness Versus Timelessness

Writing about e-business is akin to drawing a line in water. With investor trends, business models, and actual companies coming and going like planes at O'Hare Airport, any book on the subject is bound to have suffered some degree of obsolescence even before the ink can dry. With that in mind, our approach to writing this book has been to de-emphasize case studies and best practices that may rapidly lose their currency and search instead for the underlying frameworks that might better stand the test of time. Long after the "e" in "e-business" has returned to its rightful place as the fifth letter in the alphabet, we hope that the lessons from this book will still be relevant. In our quest for timeliness, we have tried to generate insights that transcend specific industry contexts, in order to be useful to companies regardless of their heritage and domain—high-tech or low-tech, large or small, old or new economy.

So while e-business may be a turbulent ocean buffeted by the waves of change, we have tried to dive beneath those waves. Here, below the surface of the storm, one finds concepts and patterns with longer-term implications—and of course it is on the ocean floor that rest the genuine pearls of wisdom! Data are ephemeral; knowledge, too, comes with an expiration date. Wisdom, however, is enduring. For that reason, in driving toward deeper meaning and longer applicability, and also subscribing to Sophocles' observation that "a short saying oft contains much wisdom," this book occasionally harks back to classic fables and ancient parables in its effort to communicate key concepts.

What's in a Name

The title of the book—*The Seven Steps to Nirvana*—contains three key concepts. First, the importance of *Steps* is that the transformation from business to e-business is not a one-shot process. Rather, it is a journey. It is a series of stages that progress in a cumulative fashion as an organization steps up its level of readiness. The notion of *Nirvana* is enlightenment. It is the sense of gaining eternal liberation, or total consciousness, and it becomes manifest as a result of having reached the highest plateau of inner harmony. As for the number *Seven*, cognitive research suggests that seven chunks of information is the maximum amount that can be processed by humans in their short-term memory.[1] Of course, the number also features prominently in a whole host of universal truths: from the seven wonders of the world, the seven seas, and the seven deadly sins to the seven colors of the rainbow, the seven notes of the musical scale, and the seven days of the week. Perhaps more importantly in this context is the fact that authors of popular self-improvement books—*The 7 Habits of Highly Effective People*, *The 7 Spiritual Laws of Success*, *The 7 Principles for Making Marriage*

Work—tend to favor seven as the requisite number of steps leading to personal change. Therefore, if this book is to serve as a self-help book for companies in need of improvement, as is the intention, then it only makes sense to go with the universal self-help standard!

How This Book Is Organized

Because it is important to know the destination before setting out on the journey, we begin with a chapter that defines what a company should seek to accomplish in terms of an overarching vision for e-business. In the next chapter, "E-volution," we discuss the process of stepping through the stages of readiness as a company gradually matures in its e-business initiatives. This requires an understanding of the various levels—from incremental to transformational—at which a company can create e-business interventions. It also requires an understanding of how to manage the paradox of duality between incremental and transformational initiatives.

Continuing the top-down approach, we next drill into the strategy layer. We articulate the need to think like an architect, not an engineer. We suggest that strategy formulation involves thinking about the scheme by which the business is configured, rather than focusing on the individual components or business processes. From this vantage point, e-business strategy simply becomes the approach you take to capitalize on the new choices that e-business opens up for configuring the business. Business innovation is innovation in business architectures. The business architecture maps into a technology infrastructure that is required to actualize the potential of e-business. In the next chapter we therefore "open the hood" to look at how the technology infrastructure that supports e-business is changing from a function-centric organization to an entity-centric organization. We outline the new building blocks of the e-architecture and explain how they connect to the various business processes.

Even more important than thinking about vision, strategy, and processes is the drive to actually get initiatives implemented. The second half of the book tackles some of the barriers that arise in implementation. This is the "Monday morning" part. It begins with a chapter on an issue that paralyzes many boardrooms into inaction: channel conflict. This paralysis stems from the fact that implementing electronic channels that reach customers directly tends to create tremendous dissension among the existing institutions that mediate the transactions. The chapter, "E-Synchronization," suggests some creative ways to think beyond disintermediation, by approaching the Net not as simply another channel, but as an enabler of a seamless multiple-channel strategy. We explode the myth of channel disintermediation by showing how the Net is turning out to be a complement, not a substitute, to the existing channels. We illustrate several interesting hybrid channel designs that are emerging, and discuss how the notion of synchronization also impacts other key aspects of e-business transformation.

The final two chapters mainly focus on putting your money where your mouth is, and getting people in the organization to embrace the often-threatening new world of e-business. In "E-Capitalization," we wear the hat of the CFO who faces difficult questions from investors and shareholders on measuring and justifying the financial returns from e-business initiatives. We find that the systemic nature of e-business prevents neat return on investment (ROI) or net present value (NPV) calculations for measuring e-business outcomes. Somewhat heretically, we propose that investing in e-business projects is often more about evangelization and keeping the faith than calculation and bean counting. However, we emphasize the importance of thinking in terms of investments as a real options portfolio—an internal portfolio geared at driving productivity and change through enabling initiatives; and an external portfolio geared at driving growth and capital appreciation through venturing activities. The final chapter, "E-Organization," focuses on the oft-ignored "peopleware" aspect of e-business. No e-business initiative, no matter how advanced the technology or how compelling the value proposition, can succeed without the cooperation of employees, suppliers, and trading partners. We examine how to create a culture that rewards and motivates change. We also examine the tension between centralization and decentralization of e-business initiatives, as well as separation versus integration of the e-business organization. We offer concrete suggestions on how to organize for e-business, and we explain how over time e-business promises to dramatically change the way in which organizations are currently structured.

Conclusion

During these "interesting times," companies of all shapes and sizes must move quickly and decisively to solidify their strategic directions within the context of an expanded set of choices for configuring their businesses. While lacking some of the topographic detail of a Michelin road atlas, the book nonetheless aims to provide some critical landmarks that will enable its readers to better chart which routes to take along the journey, and also identify which to avoid. Ultimately, the "big idea" is to simply shed some light along the critical path, for the benefit of those straining their eyes to see around the bend. Niccolò Machiavelli said it best 500 years ago: "In the land of the blind, the one-eyed man is king."

1

E-VISION: BROADENING THE VIEW

You must scale the mountain if you would view the plain.
—Chinese proverb

WE LOOK AT THE WORLD through lenses. Our vision is clouded by a residue of assumptions that has built up over time due to continuous exposure to our own sets of experiences and observations. Our bias is unavoidable; in a sense, we are prisoners of what we know. So while it may be true that "seeing is believing," also bear in mind that what we believe constrains what we see. Consequently, we must not only become keenly aware of our lenses, but we must make sure that they are cleaned. By removing the residue, we can reduce the risk of confusing lenses with eyes and assumptions with facts.

As firms grow, their mental models become deeply entrenched, and the business models that have worked for them in the past can become gospel that is never questioned. However, to observe a new phenomenon like e-business, it becomes necessary to break free from the mental models upon which these firms have come to rely and that guide them in their day-to-day understanding of how customers, businesses, and suppliers interact and transact with one another. A classic Zen story tells of a scholar and a Zen master meeting over a cup of tea. Before the two men even sit down, the scholar launches into a recital of lengthy passages from old lectures. He talks, on and on, and meanwhile the Zen master pours. And pours. And pours. Finally, his legs and feet soaked with tea, the scholar pauses long enough to look up and see that the Zen master is smiling. "Why do you continue to pour when my cup is overflowing?" asks the scholar. The Zen master replies: "How can I teach you anything about Zen when your cup is already full?"

To empty our cups is to not only discard an accumulation of age-old notions around success factors for creating value and achieving operational excellence, but to actually promote the questioning of assumptions and the killing of sacred cows. Given the inescapable hype about how "the Net changes everything," it should come as a revelation to nobody that for many companies the lessons of history—the time-proven approaches to capturing customers and revenues—no longer apply. The very notion of "time-proven" is fast becoming an anachronism. Even the most casual observer of contemporary business trends, as reported in the mainstream press, knows that the laws that govern "what works and what doesn't" are today very different from what they were yesterday, and that the gap is certain to widen over time.

Cleaning the lens means looking at a legacy business and being able to see a whole new set of possibilities, many of which exist, at least for the moment, only within the realm of the imagination. But besides *seeing differently*, which is to embrace Marcel Proust's contention that "the only real voyage of discovery consists not in seeking new landscapes but in having new eyes," it also becomes important to *see different things*, which means also seeking new landscapes. How? By broadening the field of view, or expanding the range of the radar screen, by thinking broadly in terms of the scope and magnitude of the impact that will result from e-business initiatives. Finally, because growth commonly breeds bureaucracy and dilutes the incentives for individuals to innovate and take risks, cleaning the lens and broadening the field of view means wiping away the organizational myopia that often comes as a by-product of success, and rekindling the entrepreneurial spirit that will help the elephant remember how to dance.

The creation of an *e-vision* is the first step in making the transformation from business to e-business. As *Alice in Wonderland*'s Cheshire Cat so deftly observed, if you don't know where you're going, any road will take you there. In the end, the new vision—if truly visionary!—may bear little resemblance to the existing business architecture. And bringing it to fruition may require more than just an incremental upgrade. In many cases the journey from here to there, from vision to implementation, may mean dismantling and rebuilding from the ground up core business processes and technology architectures, as well as channel structures, departmental functions, and employee performance incentives.

E-Business Is Business

Recently coined, yet already clichéd, the expression "e-business is business" speaks the truth—despite an opportunistic Big Five consulting firm having registered it as its own service mark! In fact, as pundits the world over have well observed, the word *e-business* stands to enjoy a life span perhaps only slightly longer than that of your average goldfish. To speak of e-business a few years down the road will sound foolish; the "e" will simply stand for *enhanced* or *everyday*. At that point, e-business will have become ubiquitous—and invisible. Until then, however, during this somewhat confusing and unsettling period of transition, as companies everywhere scramble to gather their bearings and find their new place in the world, "e-business" is a verbal crutch—in much the same way that "horseless carriage," a term that came into popular usage at the dawn of the last century, created a cognitive bridge before the concept of the automobile could fully take root in the American psyche.

Like the impact of the automobile, which revolutionized far more than just the transportation industry, e-business is anything but an isolated event, touching a smattering of companies in a handful of markets. If its impact has yet to be felt close to home, be forewarned: It's coming soon to a business near you. Moreover, it's not a comedy. The director Alfred Hitchcock once remarked that his mission in life was "to simply scare the hell out of people." This, in essence, has been the effect of e-business on a massive audience of corporate executives. Following years of discounting, ignoring, and even dismissing the potential threats posed by fast-moving companies unconstrained by clouded lenses and legacy businesses, few among them have not by now come to understand that the equivalent of a Travelocity (travel), Wells Fargo (retail banking), Enron (energy), or Charles Schwab (financial services) may well lurk somewhere in *their* industry. Make no mistake: The genie is out of the bottle. E-business tools are everywhere that you want to be, to borrow a phrase from Visa, available to current competitors as well as to new players in the wings, awaiting their grand entrance onto the stage.

Timing is everything. At least so it seemed until the spring of 2000, when the tables abruptly turned on the dotcom insurgents, bringing their boisterous party to an eventual halt. For the several years leading up to that point, conventional wisdom had been that a lead time of even a few months could make for an enormous head start, to the point that catching up would pose a nearly impossible challenge for those who trailed behind. Pointing to rising stars like eToys (toys) and E*Trade (investing), analysts predicted that the slow-moving bricks-and-mortar incumbents would simply have to learn the hard way about the dynamics of increasing returns—that is, successes that continue to mount at a disproportional rate—that supposedly went with being the first to market. Lending credence to the contention that slow and big *lose* the race, author Kevin Kelly put forth the notion that significance precedes momentum.[1] Using the metaphor of lily leaves on a pond, he asked his readers to compress a season into four days, while imagining that the number of lily leaves doubles every day. The first day you venture out to the pond, no more than an eighth of it is covered with lily leaves. Naturally, you barely notice. The next day a quarter of it is covered; still, you pay no attention, except perhaps to note the beauty! The day after, half of it is covered, and at this point it finally dawns on you that a major transformation is under way. Before you can even think to react, let alone mobilize your forces, another day has gone by, and now the entire pond is covered with a blanket of lily leaves. Kelly suggested that by the time a company became aware of the severity of the change disruption unleashed in its environment, it was already too late to do a whole lot about it.

However eloquent the insight, it fails to adequately predict the reality of who wins and who loses in e-business. With all due respect to *Poor Richard*, it is *not* always the early bird that catches the worm, which in this case amounts to an ability to generate sustainable businesses and profits. Rather, the prize invariably goes to the first to *get it right*. Few get it right the first time around. The reasons for failure can range from issues of funding and timing to vision and even positioning.

Consider Motorola's Iridium project: Aiming to provide cellular phones with global roaming capabilities to the mainstream market, Iridium no doubt would have done better with its $5 billion investment if it had instead targeted underserved vertical markets, such as geological surveyors or military personnel stationed in remote locations that lacked readily available substitutes. Or consider the humbling experience of the pure play dotcoms in a wide range of businesses, including banking and retailing. With very few exceptions, traditional assets such as brands, retail store presence, and buying power have proven to be more than enough to counter the initial lead of the startups. In the final analysis, significance may well precede momentum, but for it to matter, profitability must follow close behind.

Of course, that first movers frequently stumble and fall before ever crossing the finish line is the way of the world and not merely an e-business phenomenon. History shows that pioneers often end up with arrows in their backs; it is those who move swiftly and wisely down trails already blazed that generally reap the rich rewards. Examples abound. Quicken, for instance, was far from being the first personal finance software package to be launched in the consumer market. Similarly, Sega's Dreamcast may have been the first to enter the video game console business, but its early refusal to support DVD-ROMs caused it to lose its footing, allowing Sony and Nintendo to race ahead.

As the century drew to a close, the dotcoms were widely hailed as the paragons of speed and agility. To borrow a phrase from Muhammad Ali, they could dance like a butterfly and sting like a bee. Launched by fresh-faced kids out of garages, eToys, Drugstore.com, CDNow, and many others did, in fact, manage to bloody the noses of their bricks-and-mortar heavyweight rivals. Yet in a world where stamina is largely a function of expendable energy, also known as *capital*, many of these same startups, failing to capture value from their activities in the form of operating profits and seeing their funding spigots run dry as a result of this not-so-trivial shortcoming, simply ran out of steam. Meanwhile, from the perspective of the established companies, getting one's nose bloodied tends to have a focusing effect. Major corporations that could only watch in dismay as their businesses failed to be rewarded by the capital markets—which, for a brief period in history, had repealed the rules of business and the laws of economics— have recently begun to pay a certain amount of attention to their fast-footed rivals, to the point of copying some of their moves.

That so many of the dotcoms with disruptive businesses ultimately saw their valuations stumble and fall to the point that they could no longer carry on the attack, at least not as a solo effort, again suggests that at the end of the day the winner is likely to be not the first mover but *the first finisher*. Being the first mover might only prove to the competition that stirring the hornet's nest can cause one to get badly stung, evoking a grateful response of "Oh, thanks for showing that to us."

Increasing returns confer upon a company an advantage along only one dimension of a business—usually, customer acquisition. But what if a company coming from a completely different direction could easily replicate that advantage? Fact is, the customers that the dotcoms spent so much time, money, and effort trying to "acquire" already have relationships with existing brands and companies. These *analog points of presence*—the billions of store visits to Wal-Mart, the billions of hamburgers served by McDonald's, the billions of boxes of Macaroni & Cheese sold by Kraft Foods—may ultimately prove to be far more powerful than the pure play websites that have depended largely on banner ads and desperate TV campaigns to drive traffic. Only now, it seems, are the established companies waking up to the untapped potential of their brands, their customer relationships, and their domain expertise.

Every company wants to "get it right." But in a world where new businesses are constantly emerging and the lines between opportunity arenas rapidly blurring, what does it mean to get it right? Arguably, grand master Garry Kasparov got it right during his fifteen-year reign as world chess champion. Before losing the crown to his former protégé in November 2000, he had been the best at his game—with one minor hiccup. That hiccup came in 1997, when Deep Blue, an IBM RS/6000 computer, took the contest to a whole new level. But however formidable an opponent, Deep Blue nonetheless adhered to the same rules of engagement as Kasparov. Neither opponent was allowed to deviate from the universally accepted parameters by which they could move their chess pieces. In contrast, e-business ushers in not only the possibility of superior opponents playing the *same* game, but ones actually playing a *different* game—for example, Star Trek tri–dimensional chess, in which case the chess pieces can move in myriad new directions. Given that disquieting possibility, long-term success would seem to depend as much on "getting it right" as it does on "*keeping* it right," even as the dimensionality of the game expands.

Today there is no such thing as *sustainable advantage*. This notion has given way to *leverageable advantage*, which means using the position that has been secured on one hill to take the next hill and the next and the next.[2] Using its existing assets as a springboard, Microsoft is an example of a company that has repeatedly jumped—to paraphrase its own tag line—from where it is to "where it wants to go today." In its incessant quest to take new hills, Microsoft has leveraged from operating system to office to networking applications, without ever leaving any of its previous hills undefended (and, in fact, Windows and Office remain its biggest cash cows). Novell, by contrast, failed to take new hills, remaining king of the local-area-network (LAN) market even as the Net steadily chipped away at its core business. The questions every established firm must ask are: In what new directions can we take our business? What are the leverage points? What are the springboards that we can use? What is the next hill that we need to capture?

Getting Oriented

"The beginning of wisdom is the definition of terms," wrote Socrates. Putting a stake in the ground—or, rather, the quicksand—we offer the following definition for e-business: *The use of electronic networks and associated technologies to enable, improve, enhance, transform, or invent a business process or business system to create superior value for current or potential customers.* Important here is the fact that we regard e-business and its tool kit as a *means*, not an *end*. Just as all roads were said to lead to Rome, all e-business initiatives must eventually translate into a concrete value proposition *for current or potential customers.* The customers should be the raison d'être for any e-business initiative. Gary Vanspronsen, Executive Vice President of New Offer Development at office furniture maker Herman Miller, says it well in describing his company's approach: "The only question we keep constant in our e-business initiatives is: How can we create new customer value propositions or dramatically enhance our existing value propositions for customers? We begin with a vision of a better future, by imagining what we want to do for our customers. We don't worry about the means, the technology. We know that if we can dream it, someone has or will soon have the technology to make our vision a reality."

In terms of impact, the outcomes of e-business can range from incremental improvements to an existing business process at one end of the spectrum to the creation of entirely new business systems at the other end. This latter possibility is one that transcends the normally expected outcomes of a typical business initiative—*cheaper, faster, better*—to radically redefine the competitive game within an opportunity arena. Implicit within this expanded definition of e-business is a set of scope issues that extends along four dimensions—*what, who, where,* and *why*. Along each dimension it is possible to think narrowly, think broadly, or think *very* broadly. These four dimensions—*what* is the nature of the connection being made, *who* are the entities being connected, *where* are the e-business applications located, and *why* are the e-business initiatives being conducted in terms of expected outcomes—correspond to the four directions of the e-business scope compass, as shown in Figure 1-1.

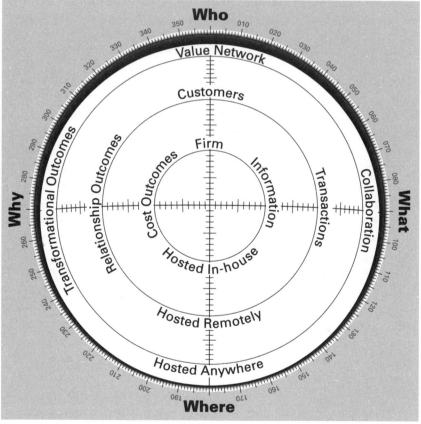

Figure 1-1
The e-business scope compass

What: More than Commerce

Contrary to popular opinion, e-business is *not* synonymous with e-commerce. The latter is focused solely on transacting—buying and selling products and services, using networking technologies to facilitate the transactions. However, e-business—with or without the "e" prefix—entails more than just buying and selling. Therefore, e-commerce, although an important aspect of e-business, fails to paint the whole picture. It only paints that part of the picture that shows money changing hands. E-business is much broader in scope, going beyond transactions to signify the use of the Net, in combination with other network technologies and forms of electronic communication, to enable *any* type of business activity.[3] Therefore, the labels B2C (business-to-consumer) and B2B (business-to-business) e commerce are also limited in their definitions, because they focus only on transactions. A business does more than transact. It communicates. It collaborates. It learns. It makes. It innovates. It plans. It recruits. These are all processes that can be fruitfully impacted by e-business technologies.

Moreover, the power of e-business is such that it actually redefines other words that have traditionally explained the universe of business activity. For example, it changes the meaning of the word *firm*. With the rise of e-business, the boundaries of the firm are blurring to the point that the enterprise has become an entity that transcends the firm to also encompass partners, suppliers, and customers. The concept of outsourcing assumes that there is a rigid boundary between the "inside" and the "outside" of the firm. But when the firm's trading partners are seamlessly connected to the firm, they actually become an extension of an integrated business system. After all, does the brain "outsource" to the arm? It is simply one seamless action, with one central nervous system in control. Likewise, e-business changes the meaning of the term *supply chain*. Supply and value no longer have to live in chains. Unchained, they evolve into dynamic networks in which fulfillment can take place in a nonlinear and adaptive fashion. Just as e-business destroys divisional, functional, and industry silos, not to mention marketing and distribution channels, the word itself transcends the boundaries of definition, existing instead as a fluid, primordial soup from which the business of tomorrow is rapidly emerging.

The definition of a network is easier to pin down. A network consists of entities, which are the nodes of the network, and connections, which are the links that connect the nodes. From the network perspective, e-business enables a broader range of *entities* that are connected, as well as new types of *connections* among the entities. These are the two lenses through which we should view the ever-expanding universe of e-business: *interactions that are enabled*, which illuminate the business processes that are impacted, and *entities that are connected*, which illuminate the types of players that are involved.

Broadening and enriching the links between nodes leads to the creation of a core set of business processes. As a result, enterprise applications, once *function-centric* (e.g., marketing, finance, human resources), are becoming increasingly *entity-centric* (e.g., customer relationship management, supply chain management, partner relationship management). By linking together nodes that previously existed as individual staff functions, e-business makes possible enterprise applications targeted at building and managing relationships with key constituencies. *With* customers. *With* suppliers. *With* employees. *With* partners. E-business reorients a firm's activities from task-specific functions that exist as separate silos managed by individual departments to entity-facing relationships that are seamlessly integrated and managed across the extended enterprise.

Who: More than Customers

A 1960s bumper sticker reads: "The mind is like a parachute; it only functions when it's open." Initially, firms tend to focus their e-business efforts on enabling their internal business processes. Over time, they connect to customers and then to all of the trading partners—leading, ultimately, to the formation of *business webs*.[4] To view e-business as a network that connects only two types of entities—business-to-consumer (B2C) and business-to-business (B2B)—is to wear narrow blinders to a world of rich and seemingly endless possibility. Opening one's mind to the expanded scope of e-business—by cleaning the lens, as well as enlarging the field of view—brings into focus a broad array of entities, which could be *people, things,* and *organizations*. If we were to stick with alphabetic mnemonics, we could go all the way from A to G, as illustrated in Figure 1-2. A can be automated intelligent agents, B a business, C a consumer, D intelligent devices, and so on. By combining different letters of the alphabet, we can create an expanded dimensionality of the entity-centric view to reveal multiple types of exchanges. Many of these exchanges are oriented around interactions

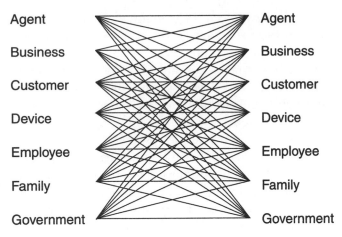

Agent	Agent
Business	Business
Customer	Customer
Device	Device
Employee	Employee
Family	Family
Government	Government

Figure 1-2
An alphabet soup of entity-centric interactions

that go beyond transactions. For instance, businesses may collaborate with one another for the purpose of new product development. Consumers may interact with other consumers in a community, with no monetary transaction resulting from the interaction.

The mnemonic is incomplete, running as it does only through the letter G—e.g., P2P (peer-to-peer) has been widely used to describe decentralized community sites, such as Napster and Gnutella. Also, far from being one-way streets that facilitate only one-to-one and one-to-many exchanges, these interactions are increasingly becoming bidirectional and interactive. In addition, the streets are merging and intersecting with one another, leading to situations that extend beyond simple binary connections. For example, a comparison-shopping engine is the combination of agent, business and consumer nodes (B2C mediated by A). Similarly, the combination of seller bots and buyer bots results in a B2A2B2A exchange, leading to the imminent expression: "I'll have my bot call your bot." The combinations and permutations that can form are constrained only by market forces, desired outcomes, and the human imagination.

Led by startups and established companies alike, each with its own agenda, objectives and motivation factors, most of the network-enabled exchanges presented in the alphabetic mnemonic are already a reality. Consider the letter G, which has been among those arriving late to the party—a small irony, given the government's role in breathing life into the Net in the first place. While G2B (government-to-business) sites provide federal grants and contract opportunities, G2C (government-to-citizen) sites enable customers to pay tickets, participate in government auctions, and submit permit applications. At the same time, B2G (business-to-government) models range from allowing school districts to put procurement into a bidding environment to allowing government agencies to sell surplus property.

Also gathering momentum are the B2E (business-to-employee) models. These range from enabling employees to check benefits data and job postings to delivering enterprisewide sales force automation and knowledge management systems. At a grassroots level, some companies are also initiating employee advantage programs to help close the digital divide within their own workforces. Ford Motor Company, for example, is providing its 350,000 employees with at-home PCs and Net access, for which they pay only $5 a month. Other companies give their employees access to portals that provide a large number of benefits—not all of them work-related. For example, employees at Cummins Engine can purchase entertainment vouchers and travel discounts, while those at Exxon can obtain discounts on a variety of products and services. A growing number of companies are providing ad-hoc demand aggregation services by mediating between employees and various types of service providers.

Variations on the themes of B2B and B2C include C2C (consumer-to-consumer) models, which facilitate horizontal transactions between consumers, and have largely taken the form of online auctions, swaps, and peer-to-peer sharing of music and other files. Here both the buyer and seller are empowered, with the business serving as a facilitator in the transaction process. C2B (consumer-to-business) exchanges facilitate reverse vertical transactions—a buyers club negotiating with GM, for example. The best-known example is the once high-flying Priceline.com, which takes customer offers for products and services and presents them to sellers who can fill as much of that guaranteed demand as they wish at buyer-determined price points.

Of special interest to science fiction buffs may be the types of interactions in which human beings take a back seat to machines. The A2A (agent-to-agent) model involves bots transacting with bots. Already, general-purpose shopping bots are widely used to scan the Web for bargains across a vast range of shopping categories, hunting for the best prices for everything from books and backpacks to computers and airline tickets. Increasingly, as they grow more sophisticated, these so-called shopbots will gather information other than price, such as recommendations and bundling options. As natural aggregators of consumer purchasing behavior, they will also provide customers with various personalization services while giving merchants the ability to target the same customers more deeply and cheaply than ever before. Other types of bots will become indispensable for routine functions such as renewing insurance policies, reordering groceries, making restaurant reservations, and sending birthday cards. In B2B exchanges, some companies are beginning to create bot-driven markets, such as chemicals and financial services, with bots negotiating complex deals between suppliers and buyers for price, delivery, and quality. Bots stand to become particularly sophisticated in the world of online auctions. While auction bidding today is a manual process, with the bidder placing a bid and the auctioneer coordinating all activities, customers can look forward to a day when bots can be used to place bids in multiple auctions, ensuring that they never pay over the odds for an object of desire.

The emerging D2D (device-to-device) arena paints an equally intriguing vision of a technology-enabled future. While Jini, long under development by Sun Microsystems, serves as the most prominent example, other device networking technology efforts include Microsoft's Universal Plug-n-Play, IBM's TSpaces, and Bluetooth, which is being pioneered by a consortium of nine technology firms, including Ericsson, Motorola, and 3Com. Basically a set of specifications that enables network devices to automatically discover and plug into other network devices, device-to-device interactions are most valuable in places without a system administrator, like an airport conference room or a 747 flying over Nebraska. Often described as an intelligent home network with interacting devices and systems such as appliances, alarms, and lighting, D2D could also mean a laptop computer and a printer finding each other on their own and negotiating the appropriate printer driver, or a personal digital assistant (PDA) or cell phone retrieving localized information without any prompting.

While perhaps still ahead of its time (technical, marketing, and licensing problems have recently plagued Sun co-founder Bill Joy's grand vision for Jini, although Bluetooth now appears to be gathering steam), device interoperability conducted through wireless information appliances nonetheless promises to deliver substantial benefit to both customers and businesses. Imagine sending out a request for proposal (RFP) for a meal through a location-based global positioning system (GPS), at which point the nearest qualified restaurant automatically negotiates the terms of that meal. Or while passing a pharmacy, gaining notification that your favorite brand of mouthwash is on sale. Or stepping into a building, at which point the building and PDA automatically negotiate a higher bandwidth. Given such scenarios, it becomes clear that there is more to e-business than first meets the eye, encompassing many different types of "who"s.

Where: Beyond the Firm

With e-business applications cutting across the boundaries that have traditionally defined the firm, process redesign can now take place at the level of the extended enterprise. In fact, the boundaries of the firm have become all but meaningless. For the first time, a whole array of business processes has begun to extend outward from the firm and encompass its various trading partners.

Today, a growing number of companies *outsource* their customer relationship management (CRM) activities. Others hire outside vendors to take care of their enterprise resource, warehouse management, and supply chain management (SCM) needs. Increasingly, companies are even taking to "outsourcing" employees' skills enhancement and learning through Web-based training solutions hosted by third-party courseware providers. Any business process that does not constitute a strategic competency is a candidate for outsourcing. The insight is simple: *Why buy the cow when all you really need is the milk?* A firm can get the milk but not the cow by renting business process applications from third-party service providers. Noncore business processes need not live within the boundaries of the firm. They can reside in any part of the extended enterprise, with any of the trading partners, and within the realm of a growing cottage industry of Application Service Providers (ASPs).

With more and more software vendors reinventing themselves as ASPs, companies are moving away from the purchase-and-install model, until recently the only one that they knew. Instead, they're renting access to software packages, along with related hardware and network infrastructure, on a per-transaction or subscription basis. The ability to buy applications as a service—call it "apps-on-tap" or "software by the drink"—adds up to an infinite amount of gratitude from a world community of CIOs. Why? Because, with ASPs replacing all or part of a company's IT infrastructure, CIOs are free to turn their attention to business issues of greater strategic importance than the tedium of software upgrades and network maintenance. Additionally, ASPs can enable logistics managers to bypass budgetary constraints, to make purchases that would be otherwise prohibitive. The reason: New applications acquired through a monthly "leasing plan," as opposed to an outright purchase program, can be charged against a revenue budget rather than a capital budget.

To understand this shift from software to services, consider the e-services firm Asera. Founder Vinod Khosla, the legendary venture capitalist from Kleiner, Perkins, Caufield and Byers, contends that the model for enterprise software installation, maintenance, and upgrades is seriously flawed, and we tend to agree. Today every enterprise has to deal with a plethora of software vendors and place strategic bets on technology platforms at a time when the winners and losers in e-business software are far from obvious. On top of that, the enterprise has to pay several times the cost of the software to system integrators that stitch together the applications with legacy databases and systems. The system integration process is not only expensive, but also risky and time-consuming. Even after a successful installation, the enterprise remains responsible for operating and maintaining the software and buying costly upgrades. And if a newer, better vendor were to suddenly appear on the scene, *c'est la vie*. The enterprise, entrapped in its previous vendor choice, would have to either suppress the temptation to switch, in which case it would continue to cope with an inferior technology platform, or take a big write-off on a short-lived capital expenditure.

Asera offers an alternative model. Think of it as enterprise software and system integration in a box, delivered over the network as a service. By offering a component-based, pay-as-you-go service, Asera allows enterprises to choose best-of-breed software components, and to adapt and evolve their e-architectures as they grow and their needs change. Asera is one of an emerging breed of Business Service Providers (BSPs), which represent the next level of evolution of ASPs. BSPs manage an end-to-end business process on an outsourced basis by augmenting the application with system integration, consulting services, and support people.

An application, after all, is merely a means to an end. The end is the efficient and effective management of business processes. By making business processes available over the network, vendors become strategic partners. In this context, even the word *outsourcing* is a limited description of the relationship. *Co-sourcing* may better describe a situation in which the application becomes invisible, the boundaries of the firm meaningless, and external vendors merely an extension of a company's core business operations.

The real beauty of Web-hosted applications in the context of e-business is their ability to extend enterprise connectivity, enabling multiple trading partners with disparate systems to access the same real-time views of information. Improved connectivity dramatically reduces the cost of communication and coordination in exchange transactions. It also allows companies to bypass intermediaries that have traditionally facilitated the flow of information and goods between firms and their customers.

Why: More than Costs

By broadening and enriching the links among nodes to create entity-centric enterprise applications, e-business improves fundamentally the efficiency of a company's core business processes. Efficiency is *doing things better*. It is a measure of how well resources are utilized to achieve a particular goal—i.e., streamlining business operations to make a process faster or cheaper. Efficiency often results in cost savings. And indeed, cost reduction is the most often cited objective of investing in e-business initiatives.

While efficiency-driven initiatives are often the most visible and easiest-to-attain outcome of e-business, they are merely the first step on the ladder of e-business evolution. At the next level, e-business can also improve the *effectiveness* of a company's core business processes. Effectiveness is *doing the right things*. It is a measure of the appropriateness of the goals chosen and the degree to which they are achieved—i.e., redefining, or reengineering, a process altogether, resulting in new sources of value creation and revenue generation.

The difference between efficiency and effectiveness echoes the distinction between classic chess and Star Trek tri–dimensional chess; if efficiency means playing the same game better, then effectiveness might mean playing a slightly different game. While reengineering a process doesn't ordinarily change the players or the arena, it *can* change the rules of engagement. And when a firm's redesign transcends a specific business process and affects an interrelated set of business processes, it may have outcomes that go even beyond effectiveness, into the realm of *transformation*. This can mean playing an entirely new game, in which case the arena is turned upside down, different players shuffle in, and new rules are made up. So while the notion of efficiency, and even effectiveness, speaks to a "bottom line" orientation—reducing costs—it is also possible to think about e-business in even broader terms, as a "top line" or game-changing proposition. E-business pioneers like Enron (in energy and bandwidth trading), Progressive Insurance (in Web-based insurance sales), and Charles Schwab (in multichannel integrated financial services) are playing their own games and making their own rules. We present this evolutionary view of e-business in more detail in the next chapter.

Putting Last Things First

"One of the most dangerous forms of human error is forgetting what one is trying to achieve," observed Paul Nitze, the famed foreign policy strategist. Having acquired clarity of vision around what e-business does with respect to efficiency and effectiveness, next comes an examination of the desired outcomes that e-business enables. Building a business case in support of an initiative requires that one think in terms of the specific types of business impact. For example:

- Will it lower my cost of doing business with customers?
- Will it reduce my response time as an organization?
- Will it improve my relationship with my trading partners?
- Will it result in higher customer retention?
- Will it improve relationships with my customers?
- Will it create new ways of getting to market?
- Will it lead to new revenue streams and market expansion?
- Will it reinvent the way that business is done in the industry?

Impact can be defined, and subsequently measured, in many different ways. In the final analysis, however, successful e-business initiatives will *always* result in one or more of four possible sets of outcomes:

1. Cost reduction
2. Revenue expansion
3. Time reduction
4. Relationship enhancement

Of these outcomes, cost reduction ranks as the least strategic. Increasing revenue, saving time, and improving relationships with customers, trading partners, and employees are more strategic, but also a great deal more difficult to achieve. Note that cost reduction and time saving are efficiency plays, impacting the bottom line. On the other hand, relationship improvement and revenue expansion, in particular, are the outcomes of top-line initiatives that can lead to the reinvention of an entire industry, handing out new rules to every last player in the game. It is an accomplishment of which few established companies can boast—although spin-offs, given their relative lack of baggage, have occasionally captured the spirit of the entrepreneurial startup, on rare occasions even acting as a catalyst for industrywide transformation.

What E-Business Is Not

"I don't know who discovered water," Marshall McLuhan, the media critic, once remarked, "but I know it wasn't a fish." That said, if you remove a fish from water, it very quickly gains a deep appreciation for what water is and what water does.

Because fish—and people, too—generally have trouble perceiving the objective details of an environment in which they have become so completely immersed, much can be gained by taking a step back from the incessant noise of "e-business this" and "e-business that" that bombards us each day in the media. Like the fish that lives in water all its life but can appreciate its importance only when it is removed from the water, it pays to pause for a moment to consider what e-business is *not*. Therefore, taking a further cue from McLuhan, who defended his more provocative statements as "probes" that could awaken an audience from its hypnotic trance and jolt them into seeing their environment in a whole new light, the following "probes" are intended to counter some of the misguided assumptions that have inevitably sprung up around e-business transformation.

E-Business Is Not a Bolt-On to Your Business

Because e-business is an integral component of a business, it should be treated in such a way that it becomes centrally integrated and fused with the overall plumbing. The paradox is that the e-business organization should initially be separate from the rest of the organization. It should exist autonomously, incubated at a distance from mainstream operations in order to command a high degree of focus and attention. Longer term, however, to take advantage of the benefits of synergy and learning, and to avoid creating yet another information silo within the organization, there should be a clear integration plan. The e-business organization should be designed so that it becomes assimilated into the parent organization after a period of time and its areas of accountability transitioned into the main body of the corporate structure. One need only imagine a fruit tree that grows on its own in the beginning but which, at a certain point along its development path, gets carefully grafted onto the trunk of the mother tree. Over time, as the tissues fuse, it then *becomes* that tree. The graft needs to be nurtured separately from the tree, but it cannot be kept apart too long, or else it begins to develop its own roots and its own identity.

Remember that e-business is a crutch, not a leg. It is useful to separate it from the lines of business when you are learning to walk, but eventually it needs to become an integral part of the business. This assertion is validated by our conversations with e-business leaders at a host of best-practice firms. The more progress they make in their e-business initiatives, the harder it becomes for them to define what the e-business organization looks like. Why? Because the lines of business take charge of those initiatives, eliminating the need to isolate the initiatives in a separate organization.

E-Business Is Not About Technology

In an age of Net-enabled coffee makers that take brewing orders via a cell phone and bar code readers that scan an empty package's UPC symbol to replenish the supply of coffee beans via an online grocer, practically any new business innovation that can be dreamed up is ultimately doable technology-wise. In fact, technology may be the easiest part of what a firm needs to get done with respect to e-business. Strategy is a more challenging aspect of the transformation process, while the most challenging aspect by far is the *peopleware*: changing attitudes, behaviors, and culture within the organization, as well as within the firm's trading partners.

E-business is fundamentally a change management exercise, as well as a growth management exercise. It is as much about effecting organizational change as it is about strategy and technology. Many elegant B2B initiatives hit a brick wall when they confront a basic human trait: People are loath to change. This explains, in part, why so many procurement exchanges have struggled to acquire new clients—and, ultimately, to keep their lights on. The problem: Employees in purchasing departments are reticent to change their behavior, even if the benefits for doing so would seem to be sufficiently compelling in terms of cost reduction and time savings. Paying an enormous amount of attention to technology but too little to the social dynamics, political intricacies, and other nontechnical considerations between the entities using that technology commonly leads to failure. The lesson is one that many dotcoms have had to learn the hard way. Call it the "Healtheon/WebMD Syndrome," after Jim Clark's deep-pocketed but miscalculated attempt to reinvent the healthcare management industry, by facilitating the interactions between healthcare providers, insurance carriers, diagnostics labs, and other such entities. Despite whatever increased efficiencies its e-business platform promised to deliver, it appears that a critical mass of physicians would simply prefer to manage their relationships the old-fashioned way.

In contrast, newer players like the London-based Global Freight Exchange (GFX), which is creating a platform for airlines and logistics companies worldwide for managing air cargo operations, are investing heavily in change management in their client organizations. According to co-CEO Todd Morgan, every major account that GFX signs up is put through a change management exercise, led by a 15-person team. In his view, the change management skills that he and his colleagues picked up in their previous jobs with McKinsey & Company are coming in handy as they "use machetes to pave the way and clear the path to adoption" within the often archaic IT departments of large established organizations.

That companies neglect to put incentives in place that would encourage employees to change their behavior is hardly a new phenomenon. Consider, for example, that despite the widespread deployment of groupware platforms such as Lotus Notes and Microsoft Exchange to support knowledge sharing, few companies have succeeded in creating the cultural traditions and personal incentives that would motivate internal thought leaders to volunteer their intellectual capital. Clearly, as this oft-experienced example demonstrates, it is not technology alone that drives e-business transformation, but technology embedded within a social context. Human factors intervene and inter-mesh whenever e-business tools are set within the broader context of the social fabric of a company and its environment. For that reason, technology performance depends in no small part on people performance. Technology exists as a *sociotechnical system*, with people a key component of that system. Because even those systems that are completely automated impinge upon human beings at some level of activity, a company that has made a change in its technology must also strive to change the behavior that surrounds it. When redesigning systems, therefore, ample attention must be paid not only to the software and hardware, but also to the peopleware.

Even with the right incentives in place, the rate of technological change is systematically faster than that of organizational change, and over time the gap widens between what technology can accomplish and what organizations can feasibly handle in terms of cultural alignment. Narrowing the gap presents the biggest challenge posed by e-business transformation. The message is simple: Think about the people whom e-business technology will touch. Understand their hopes and fears. Understand what makes them tick and what's in it for them if they change. We devote a whole chapter of this book to the people component of e-business, which, strangely, has not received the attention that it deserves.

E-Business Is Not the CIO's Responsibility

Why not? Because CIOs have traditionally spent their careers managing data centers—and, by the way, those who continue to do so, unable to adapt and evolve, are likely to become extinct alongside their data centers. The more senior of these individuals have played a role in which technology has been used to *support* rather than *enable* decision-making. At the same time, the technology that CIOs used to support is very different from the kinds of strategic business systems that are being created today for such processes as knowledge management, customer relationship management, and supply chain management. To remain relevant, CIOs must acquire a much deeper appreciation for business realities. In large part, becoming more strategic simply means knowing how to ask the right questions and how not to be fooled by an expert. (We discuss this art of *strategic fluency* in Chapter 5.)

Conversely, line managers need to acquire a much deeper appreciation for technology issues. The emerging tools of e-business (e.g., marketing automation, logistics monitoring, and supply chain automation) vary considerably from the traditional function-centric data center applications since they are designed for fighting battles, not for running the back office. And who populates the front lines but the line managers? Today the CIO ought to reemerge as a hybrid between the CTO and the Purchasing Chief, responsible for such day-to-day tasks as vendor selection, technology assessment, contract negotiation, service level agreements, and program management, whereas the line manager needs to wear the Net-enabled hat of a technologist.

E-Business Is Not Tied to a Particular Department or Functional Area

Stories abound of "e-business departments" being created within companies as yet another box that is meant to become a permanent fixture in the functional organization chart. There is no surer way to kill e-business innovation than to box it into a functional silo or to create a huge bureaucracy around the e-business organization. The reason is simple: Functional silos are vertical, while e-business cuts horizontally across the entire enterprise—and beyond. Consider customer relationship management. Touching a customer means touching almost all of the functional departments. Even for function-specific applications, such as purchasing or marketing automation, there is a tight link between the technology and one or more of the functional departments, which means, at the very least, that the technologists and the line managers need to interact. Organizational charts get in the way of architecting e-business applications, which only work when the boxes and arrows have been dissolved to create an organizational structure unconstrained by artificial boundaries.

E-Business Is Not a Middle-Management Initiative

When it comes to e-business, middle managers are stuck between a rock and a hard place. Although indispensable as *change enablers*, they lack the necessary authority to instigate strategic change. Nor are they empowered to carry it out without first achieving buy-in from their superiors. The reason, in large part, is budgets. While organizations tend to function well within divisional or departmental silos, each with its own P&L accountability, e-business cuts across silos, which immediately begs the all-important question, *Who's going to pay for the new initiative?* Because the only individuals who can coordinate across a set of silos are those who hover *above* them, change needs to begin at the top of the corporate hierarchy and work its way down. Not until the agenda is set, the objectives defined, and the turf battles addressed, should top management delegate control to the individuals charged with actual implementation.

Despite frequent criticism that the top of the hierarchy is the very place where the greatest problems reside ("After all," quip the critics, "where is the bottleneck but at the top of the bottle?"), a growing number of CEOs are surprising their detractors by stepping up to the plate to enact large-scale e-business initiatives. For example, Michael Bonsignore, the former CEO of Honeywell, spearheaded the creation of Myplant.com, a B2B exchange geared to workers in plant management and construction. Similarly, Jack Welch, the CEO of GE, Honeywell's new parent, was the driving force behind the company's now famous "Destroy Your Business" initiative, which resolved that the company's twenty-plus business units be willing and eager to cannibalize their own products and services rather than lose marketshare to competitors. And Mike Volkema, the CEO of Herman Miller, is the chief evangelist and cheerleader for e-business in his organization. In an ideal world, the Chief Executive Officer and the Chief E-Business Officer are one and the same, as the initials would suggest.

E-Business Is Not a Fixed Target

Traditionally, companies made most of their money in competitive landscapes that were relatively stable and where the rules of the game were more or less well defined. Now the only real sustainable competitive advantage is the ability to continuously innovate and position your firm to ride the next wave of disruption. Taking part in the current discontinuity—e-business—is quickly becoming a prerequisite to staying in business, with the price of entry increasing all the time as market innovators move on to the next big thing. In the ongoing struggle to keep up with the Joneses (in this case, the Enrons and the GEs!), e-business in some competitive arenas may be best described as the combination of a high stakes poker game and an exclusive country club. Imagine the conversation on the golf course: "What, you don't have an automated supply chain? Everybody else does. What are you waiting for?" At that point, an automated supply chain becomes the ante that a player must put down on the table just to stay in the game—a phenomenon that quickly becomes the Red Queen effect, after her comment to Alice: "It takes all the running you can do to keep in the same place!"

The pressure to keep changing in a never-ending race to simply sustain the current level of competitiveness also conjures up Frederick Hertzberg's classic hygiene-motivation theory. Hertzberg, a psychologist practicing in the 1950s, theorized that there are two sets of factors that explain employee motivation. The first is those whose presence is no big deal but whose absence is highly detrimental—called *hygiene factors* because they are seen to work like preventive medicine, stopping employees from getting sick (i.e., becoming dissatisfied with their jobs) but not really making them better than they were. The second is those that cause people to do their best, called *motivation factors*, by allowing for such things as achievement, responsibility, recognition, advancement, and challenge. Applied to e-business, the class of initiatives that are hygiene factors can be thought of as "stay-in-business" initiatives. Putting a supply chain management solution in place, deploying knowledge management and collaboration tools for employees in-house, and connecting the call center to customers through a Web-enabled CRM system are examples of initiatives that must be undertaken merely to keep pace with the competition, without standing out as a source of differentiation. In other words, "If you've got it, it doesn't help you; but if you don't have it, you're screwed." Stay-in-business initiatives will *not* catapult a company to the next level of valuation. On the other hand, motivation factors applied to e-business tend to be disruptive, leading to the implementation of actual "destroy-your-business" initiatives that *can* open up new revenue growth opportunities while fundamentally changing the mechanisms for value creation. Such initiatives become good candidates to be undertaken outside of the organization, managed by outsiders, and funded externally.

Moreover, the motivation factors of today become the hygiene factors of tomorrow. A decade ago, the implementation of an enterprise resource planning (ERP) system could afford a company a distinct competitive advantage, enabling it to operate at significantly higher levels of efficiency. Today, in contrast, no major company touts ERP deployment, and it's a foregone conclusion that its key competitors also have such systems in place. Likewise, the most cutting-edge e-business innovations are already on their way to becoming as mundane as automobile cup holders—which, as a new product design feature, once had the power to surprise and delight, as did driver-side air bags, power windows, and 60/40 rear split-fold seats. Nowadays the top-selling Chrysler Voyager minivan rolls off the assembly plant with no fewer than seventeen cup holders, and enough air bags to transform it into a blimp.

Keeping up means planning multiple and overlapping generations of e-business initiatives, so that by the time a company has finished implementing one level of changes, it can immediately launch into the next level. Even within the realm of a particular business process, the capabilities are forever advancing. As a result, process-specific initiatives exist not as single checklist items ("We've put in supply chain management, we're done with that") but as moving targets that require continuous enhancement as new applications become available—e.g., upgrading from supply chain *automation* to supply chain *optimization*. Applicable in this context is the "sashimi" process for new product development, or concurrent engineering, in which sequential activities are started before prior steps are finished. Just as sashimi is a way of presenting sliced raw fish where each slice rests partially on the one before it—consider Intel, deep in the throes of designing its next Pentium series microchip even before the release of the current version—subsequent generations of e-business initiatives should be in constant procreation, with the overlaps indicating a transfer of relevant knowledge.[5]

John Chambers, CEO of Cisco Systems, recently observed that his company moves to the next generation of e-business initiatives every six months in terms of level of functionality. The frontier keeps shifting, with the differentiators of today becoming the price of entry tomorrow, and those in the rearview mirror quickly receding into commodities. As a result, besides simply keeping up, companies need to be on the constant lookout for new opportunities to create value. Because business is dynamic, not static, continued market dominance requires continuous business adaptation. Having sat on a throne for a decade, or even a century, bestows no preordained right to continue to reign. Nor does the marketplace offer special privileges based on seniority. Over time, the nature of competition changes—and so, too, do the players, as evidenced by the transitory nature of individual firms that comprise the major stock market indexes. Incumbency grants not an appointment for life but merely a slot on the next election ballot, albeit with campaign infrastructure, partisan support, and other advantages, not the least of which is capital, already in place. Today, more than ever, "built to last" means "built to adapt."

Let the Wild Rumpus Start!

With the stakes so high and the investment payoff not always within view, pulling the trigger on a stay-in-business initiative, let alone a destroy-your-business initiative, often becomes a giant leap of faith. Ensuring that the leap is not taken blindfolded — or not taken at all — is the primary aim of this book. Beginning with Chapter 2, we'll walk through a series of sense-making frameworks that lead the way to Nirvana. And it all begins with a ladder.

2

E-VOLUTION:
CLIMBING THE LADDER

*The reality of the harvesting situation is that most workers
do most of the steps... It is those few that they leave out
that lead to most injuries associated with ladders.*
— Frostproof Growers of Florida

THERE ARE SEVERAL basic guidelines to observe when
using a ladder in a fruit orchard. Set the ladder on a good base of firm,
even ground and against a strong branch. Don't skip steps. When lean-
ing, keep both feet on the rung, and watch out for high winds. Start
picking at the top of the tree with an empty bag and work your way
down. Alternatively, try to fill the first bag with fruit that you can pick
while standing on the ground.

The guidelines are equally applicable when setting out on the
journey toward e-business transformation. First and foremost, anchor
the initiatives to a solid foundation, which, in all cases, should be customer needs. No matter the potential payoffs—top line or bottom line,
time savings or relationship improvement—the underlying value
proposition should be firmly grounded in the only entity that ultimately pays the bills: the end-customer.

In reality, corporate executives have been prone to jump on the e-business bandwagon for reasons that are often far removed from the customer. They have been spurred into action for the same primal reasons that have forever spurred human beings into action: fear and greed. Fear, arising from the need to defend their core businesses against attack from disruptive competitors; and greed, arising from the possibility of juicy capital gains from spin-offs or carve-outs from their core businesses. While such motivators, defensive and offensive, might well factor into the process of deciding where ultimately to place the bets, neither fear nor greed should provide the sole impetus for embarking on the process of e-business transformation.

Instead, the overriding reason to pursue any type of e-business initiative should be to create new and improved value propositions for current or prospective customers. In the stormy seas of change, customer value propositions provide the only safe anchor. In each case, a company should ask itself: Can we clearly define who the customers are for our initiatives? Do we understand their needs? And would e-business allow us to create a value proposition that delivers against those needs? Without a clear line of sight to customer benefits, the initiatives — as evidenced by the countless spin-offs launched for no other purpose than to capture the stratospherically high valuations that the dotcoms were once commanding — can become as meaningless as the dozens of Iridium satellites that now orbit planet Earth.

Incidentally, in this context, we broaden the definition of the word *customer* to include the company's own employees. We would go so far as to call them *internal customers*. Why not? After all, at a macro level, companies regard the two in much the same way: acquire them, retain them, and extract value from their activities. Moreover, companies *should* treat their employees as they would their revenue-generating customers: not as captive worker bees, but as moths at night, free to swarm to whichever company's value proposition happens to shine brightest. Given this view, there are plenty of compelling reasons to invest in internal initiatives such as knowledge management, collaboration, and e-learning that are targeted at employees but which, in fact, ultimately impact external customers as well.

Next, in keeping with the aforementioned guidelines for using a ladder in a fruit orchard, step through the initiatives in a progressive fashion, one level at a time, all the while bearing in mind that the rungs at the top are likely to be obscured by leaves and branches. Why?

Because e-business initiatives grow organically, with serendipity and learning playing a significant role in determining the outcomes. The inability to see the top rungs of the ladder a priori makes it difficult to approach an initiative with a long-term strategic plan. Instead, the goal should be to create clarity about how the initiative would likely impact the firm's value proposition for its customers, and then envision the first steps along the journey. Even with a clear vision, it can be difficult to know exactly how the initiatives would progress over time and what shape they would ultimately take. The rungs that lie ahead become visible only with each additional step. So, only over time does the ladder reveal itself, with the uppermost rungs eventually exposing unforeseen opportunities for value creation.

"Writing is like driving at night in the fog," declared the author E. L. Doctorow. "You can only see as far as your headlights, but you can make the whole trip that way." The same can be said of e-business implementation. Climbing the ladder of e-business initiatives should be deliberate in terms of the destination, yet opportunistic and adaptive in terms of the actual journey. The Spiral Model for Software Development illustrates the point.[1] Used by software designers the world over, the model rests on the premise that, rather than define an entire system in detail right off the bat, it's always better to define just its highest priority features. Implement those features, get feedback from users, and with that knowledge go back to the drawing board to define and implement the next level of features. This iterative approach, firmly anchored in customer needs, provides a semicoherent direction for product development. That the direction is not perfectly coherent is unavoidable, as there's no knowing what the learning outcomes will be in advance of each round of feedback, or what new doors might open up along the way. Such is the Law of Unanticipated Consequences. While an e-business initiative may be launched with a specific mission in mind, the consequences of actions taken along its journey may suggest more promising opportunities to be found elsewhere.

In contrast to the top of the ladder, the lowest rungs are relatively unambiguous, correlating to initiatives that might be generally classified as internal and nondiscretionary. Because trying to achieve too much at the outset may lead to failure, the main objective early on should be to build faith, build credibility, and build a track record in order to increase the level of organizational acceptance and set the stage for later, more ambitious interventions. In short, start small and gain confidence as the incremental successes begin to pile up. Here the motto should be: *Fail fast, fail small, and fail often!*

Another suggestion from the fruit orchard: Resist getting carried away by the winds of e-business hype. How? By remaining forever mindful of where the company gets its bread and butter. If, for example, the power of personal selling has long been the modus operandi for closing large, national accounts, the Net would likely be a poor substitute as the sole channel for reaching those prospects. As such, cutting the sales force's relationship-building budget for the sake of technology-enabled selling would be a fool's game—akin to starving the parent to feed the child. While an excellent channel for conveying information, the Net will never replicate the effectiveness of a human being with a deep, empathetic understanding of a client's needs. Similarly, falling prey to the hype that the Internet is the ultimate disruptive technology might lead corporate executives to believe that they can unlock billions of dollars of market capitalization by carving out underutilized assets and spinning them off with the assistance of venture firms and investment bankers. In reality, however, such spin-offs would likely be nothing more than incremental extensions of the core business, with the Net acting as an enabler, not a disrupter. With very few exceptions, these entities would not represent a viable stand-alone business that deserves to be spun off. Hype and greed can be disorienting when the landscape is unfamiliar and changing by the day.

Finally, decide whether to start at the bottom of the ladder and pick the low-hanging fruit (low cost, low upside potential) or climb to the top of the ladder, where the fruit promises to be a whole lot sweeter (high cost, high upside potential), but where a misstep could result in a painful if not crippling fall. This captures the essence of the dilemma facing most established companies weighing their e-business options: Do we focus on *evolutionary* changes or *revolutionary* changes? Do we pursue initiatives that *improve* the core business or ones that aim to *reinvent* it? Or, given the possibility, do we pursue both types of initiatives at the same time?

The Ladder: The Evolutionary Stages of E-Business

Charles Darwin theorized that it is not the strongest of the species that survive, nor the most intelligent, but the ones that are most responsive to change. The view of the traditional organization as a species that responds to change in a relatively slow-paced, incremental manner would hold that e-business transformation, like any other change initiative, should also be viewed as an evolutionary process. That being the case, the metaphor of a ladder works well to track the stages of that evolution. Each rung of the ladder represents an increasingly broad and complex set of scope issues: the scope of the initiative, the scope of the organization, the scope of the audiences impacted, and the magnitude of the impact. These loosely correspond to *what you do, with whom you do it, whom you do it for,* and *what you accomplish,* as the following questions illustrate.

Who's in Charge?

E business leadership tends to evolve from single-cell organisms in the form of ad hoc committees and decentralized project teams. With the first generation of initiatives emerging from a grassroots level within specific departments, there is little strategic thinking and no formal organization in place. As the initiatives gradually become more strategic, however, sponsorship tends to shift from a department head to a more formal organization headed by a tireless evangelist with the title of Vice President, E-Business, or Chief E-Business Officer. Finally, and somewhat paradoxically, the CEO and the lines of business become the executive sponsors of all things e-business. Having reached this stage along the evolutionary path, it's no longer possible to meaningfully separate e-business activities from the lines of business, because e-business has become an integral part of the company's overall strategy. And here an interesting paradox emerges: The more precise the definition of the e-business organization within a firm, the less evolved the e-business initiatives tend to be within that firm. In firms where e-business initiatives have made only nominal headway, the e-business organization can be neatly drawn as a "box" within the larger organizational hierarchy. In organizations that have evolved well beyond this point, however, it can be difficult for executives to identify where e-business formally sits within the layout of their organization. Why? Because just about everyone at this point participates in the effort, and the executive team that leads the company also leads the e-business initiatives.

Another key trend: In the early stages, firms are apt to view e-business initiatives as information technology initiatives. As a result, the IT staff tends to play a lead role in defining, scoping, and implementing the initiatives. But climbing farther up the ladder, firms begin to view e-business initiatives as *business strategy initiatives* targeted at customers. Consequently, the lines of business and the senior management team tend to play the lead role in bringing the initiatives to fruition. IT contributes, but the leadership role shifts to the people who are closest to customers, as it should. After all, technology is the means to an end, and not an end in itself. Putting technology ahead of customers, and the IT organization ahead of the lines of business, would be like putting the cart before the horse.

Who Pays?

At first, funding for e-business initiatives tends to materialize out of ad hoc budgets scrounged from the marketing or IT department. As initiatives become more formally defined and ambitious in scope, however, capital budgets are set aside as part of the annual budgeting process. At this stage, e-business initiatives require structured business cases, with some clarity around expected outcomes, as well as milestones and metrics for tracking progress and measuring results. At a more advanced stage, the e-business organization may create an internal market for e-business projects, by marketing proposed initiatives to the business units, with a charge-back scheme that pays the bills. In this scenario, business units are free to shop externally or internally for their e-business needs. At the same time, the e-business organization needs to be able to justify its existence as a shared services organization. It may even have its own stand-alone P&L. Finally, there comes a stage when e-business spans the entire enterprise, at which point e-business initiatives are funded as an integral part of the firm's growth and change management activities. Alternatively, advanced initiatives that qualify as spin-off candidates may be funded by external sources of private capital, including venture capital or leveraged buyout firms.

Who's Affected?

In the early stages, e-business initiatives tend to target single, focused audiences that are purely internal or purely external, but without linkages between the two. The locus of activity may begin with customers (customer relationship management), suppliers (supply chain management), employees (knowledge management or human resource management), or partners (partner relationship management). Over time, the scope of the audiences is likely to expand across and beyond the boundaries of the organization, along with the formation of seamless linkages.

While every e-business initiative ultimately cuts across different business processes and functional areas, it is necessary to start by proving out the value of the initiative on a small scale, and for a focused audience, and then gradually extend the linkages. Eventually, the initiative begins to look more like a systemic solution than a point solution, affecting not just a component of the business but all parts of the business. For instance, an internal knowledge management initiative undertaken by a management consulting firm can be leveraged to create a secure extranet site for the firm's customers, who can be offered selected views into the knowledge base of the firm. The extended application really becomes a CRM application, because it deepens the firm's relationships with its customers and enhances customer loyalty. While the initial audience that the initiative was designed to impact is the firm's own employees, the scope of the audience gradually expands to include customers and partners.

What's the Integration Level?

The nature of the information available to customers of an e-business initiative depends on the extent to which the databases and business processes that drive the e-business application are integrated with those that drive the core operations of the firm. By allowing applications to "talk" to each other, and by gluing customer-facing applications into internal legacy applications, customers can gain some level of process visibility. Without complete, end-to-end integration, however, the information contained in the various databases cannot be instantly updated and simultaneously processed. That being the case, customers would be unable to access the information in real time. In addition, it would be impossible to provide process visibility to customers without some sort of human intervention. In the absence of integration, humans must serve as the masking tape that binds together the various shards of information.

At the lowest level of integration, e-business applications lack database connectivity, and customers and partners are left viewing static information-only Web pages. Often these pages serve up marketing collateral, press releases, and gratuitous graphics and gimmicks. But when people try to get actual work done, they invariably hit a roadblock. As a consolation prize, they might be presented with a 1-800 number.

At the next level, database connectivity results in information interaction that is dynamic, but typically managed in batch mode. This means that a customer can submit an inquiry online to check the status of an order, or a supplier can inquire about the inventory level for a specific component. However, these requests need to be processed by a human intermediary, resulting in a delayed response time. The primary limitation at this level is that customers access *people*, not the *process*, because the customer-facing applications are not fully integrated into the internal applications. At this level, while still lacking real-time interactivity, database integration may begin to move from involving a single department or functional silo (e.g., a telephone call center) to involving other parts of the organization, as well as external business partners.

Eventually, at the next level, databases become fully integrated, resulting in real-time responses that cut across departments and pulse throughout the entire enterprise. Figure 2-1 illustrates the different levels of information flows, running from batch to real-time and from narrow departments to the expanded enterprise. The framework can be applied to practically every business process, from customer support to supply chain management.

Real-time interactivity requires end-to-end connectivity across all of the different processes, from the innards of a company's legacy systems to the outer reaches of its suppliers, customers, and partners. Such is the notion of the *real-time corporation*, the ideal to which every e-business should aspire. The real-time corporation behaves like a central nervous system, with every node connected to every other node. Just as a pinprick to the finger triggers an immediate system response in the form of a lurching elbow and an "Ouch!" that emanates from the vocal cords, the true sense-and-respond organization is the notion of a pair of Levi's 501 button-down jeans being purchased at a Sears in a suburban shopping mall and the exact description of the sale rippling from the store, through the warehousing management system, and back to the Levi's factory floor where the product was manufactured.

Consider the real-time, configure-to-order system that IBM has created for its personal systems division. A customer in Europe can configure a personal computer on IBM's website and get real-time availability and order confirmation. Seems simple, doesn't it? But behind the scenes, it takes a team of rocket scientists and a hundred man-years of effort to stitch together the myriad business processes and systems

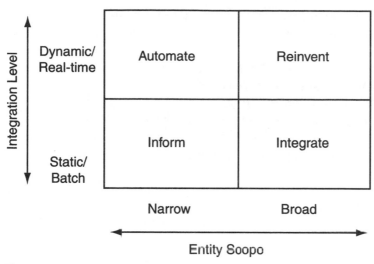

Figure 2-1

The scope dimensions for e-business initiatives

that need to work together to make this simple action possible. Here's what happens when the customer places the order: The order travels to IBM's fulfillment engine located in the United Kingdom; its e-commerce engine located in Boulder, Colorado; its ERP and production management systems located in Raleigh, North Carolina; its sales reporting system located in Southbury, Connecticut; its product database located in Poughkeepsie, New York; and back to the customer's browser in Europe. Every system updates its status and communicates with every other system in real time. And every order placed in Europe zips across the Atlantic an average of four times. In its journey, it touches dozens of geographical units, legacy systems, and databases strewn across the globe.

It is important to understand that the full benefits of e-business cannot be realized until the entire extended enterprise is integrated in a seamless end-to-end central nervous system. If a company is wired but its suppliers or customers are not, then it will never achieve the end-to-end process visibility it needs to deliver a seamless customer experience. A chain is only as strong as its weakest link. And a network is only as strong as its weakest node. To get to the real-time vision, enterprises need to invest in enabling their customers and their partners as an integral part of deploying e-business initiatives. For instance, Eastman

Chemical Company, as part of its "Enable Eastman" set of initiatives, offers subsidized hardware from Dell and subsidized Internet connectivity from UUNet to customers and suppliers so they can get wired faster and communicate electronically with Eastman. Customers and suppliers win by getting financial subsidies and by getting the benefit of Eastman's e-business expertise. Eastman wins by improving its system-wide performance and by securing the enhanced loyalty of its customers and suppliers. And the vendors of hardware and connectivity win by gaining access to a new customer acquisition channel.

Who Implements?

As established companies begin to experiment in e-business, they typically start out with tactically outsourced implementation. A department may hire a consultant or a small Web development outfit to build a website. But as the project grows in scope and complexity, the CIO and IT staff soon typically become injected into the implementation effort, if only for the purpose of managing the strategic outsourcing activities. At a certain point, issues of robustness and scalability come into play, requiring the participation of e-consulting firms capable of building industrial strength, multilocation, highly integrated Web applications. The skills required to build these next-generation applications are rarely available within an internal IT function, and time-to-market considerations typically dictate a "buy" versus "build" approach.

That said, we've noticed an interesting reversal of the outsourcing trend as the e-business organization progresses to the next level of maturity. Firms gradually begin to supplement development efforts with their own internal staff and eventually assemble a dedicated team that combines e-business technology expertise with domain expertise and a deep knowledge of the firm's business. At this point, outsourcing takes on a different flavor: The infrastructure (e.g., application hosting, network operations, and software maintenance) is increasingly outsourced, while strategy and application development as it relates to e-business applications is increasingly brought in-house.

Here's the deal: In the early phases of e-business, companies might be smart to outsource strategy, along with user interface design and back-end technology development. Later, however, as the objectives become clear, companies would be well advised to bring the underlying business logic skills in-house—in short, to *in-source the thinking, outsource the implementation.* Why? Because strategy is the cornerstone of a company's competitive strength, the main engine that drives value creation. Nobody, particularly not hired guns from an outside management consulting firm, should know what the company's strategy *ought to be* better than its own internal leadership team.

In summary, the involvement of the IT department in implementation over time follows a U-shaped curve. Its level of involvement is high at first, owing to the fact that the IT organization presents a logical place to start. However, as the projects become progressively more complex, and the company realizes the need to import skill sets from consultants who can implement and architect industrial-strength systems, its involvement declines. But then it rises again with the rebirth of the IT department as a full-fledged technology organization that is infused with business expertise. The leader of this enlightened organization is a CIO who can bridge the gap between business strategy and technology strategy. The gap between the CIO and the CEO also narrows over time, and the interactions between the IT department, the e-business organization, and the leadership team become deeper and more meaningful.

What's the Outcome?

Jungian psychologists use the metaphor of a pyramid to illustrate the different stages in the development of the human psyche, from immaturity to maturity. Similarly, the hierarchy of e-business outcomes can be viewed as a pyramid that runs from initiatives that have mildly significant outcomes to those that have extremely strategic outcomes. These successive degrees of maturity correlate not only to strategy and technology, but also to organizational readiness. With evolution unfolding in a hierarchical fashion, initiatives tend to move from cost and time reduction outcomes to relationship and new revenue generation outcomes, just as the scope of impact moves from the level of an activity and business process to the level of the enterprise to, eventually, the level of the value network, or business web.

And at the top of the pyramid, behold: a level of business impact that in Maslow's Hierarchy of Needs loosely corresponds to the notion of *self-actualization*. A leading exponent of humanistic psychology, Abraham Maslow developed his theory to describe the mechanism by which an individual progresses from basic needs, such as food consumption, to the highest order of needs, which he called the fulfillment of an individual's greatest human potential. In the context of e-business, such fulfillment, or self-actualization, translates into a dramatically superior value proposition for customers. Just as Maslow viewed the top of his hierarchy in terms of peak experiences, flashes of insight, and a sense of discovery leading to a sea of "Aha!"s, the highest level of e-business outcomes effectively rewires an industry to define an entirely new space, to the point of even reinventing an extended set of related industries. To apply self-actualization to e-business is to imagine, and then actually engineer, offerings completely new to the world. It is to fulfill customer needs that have never before been met. In a way, self-actualization is the ultimate aim of e-business transformation: Even more than serving customers in dramatically better ways, it's the creation of customer experiences previously unheard of, delivered through an offering that until now was simply impossible.

Finding Your Place on the Ladder

"A journey of a thousand miles starts in front of your feet," wrote the Chinese philosopher Lao Tzu. As companies everywhere embark on the journey toward e-business transformation, their first steps differ markedly from one company to another. Some companies may start with a supply chain management initiative — jumping on the business-to-business consortium bandwagon, for example, or deploying a supply chain automation solution. Other companies, even those operating in the same competitive arena, may warm up with a customer relationship management exercise — deploying a sales force automation solution, for example. Yet other companies may tackle several different initiatives all at once.

Because knowing where to start is not always readily apparent, organizations often look externally, to their industry peers, for clues as to how they can best focus their efforts and resources. But like the male Himalayan musk deer, which is said to spend its entire life searching the forest for the source of the ever-pervasive musk scent — which, in fact, is secreted from one of its own glands — the answer lies within. Simply put, you can't look to other people's prescriptions of universal truth. Why not? Because benchmarking and best practices are an "other orientation," not a "self-orientation." While benchmarking comparables may be a useful way to gauge a company's overall progress relative to the best-of-breed, reality is such that every business must ultimately chart its own course.

In this context, Socrates' injunction, "Know thyself," couldn't be more apropos. Only after gaining a deep understanding of its own distinct assets and priorities can a company gaze into the crystal ball and begin to see its digital future. Knowing where an e-business initiative should be headed is simply a matter of knowing where the business itself should be headed. Having formulated a compelling value proposition that delivers against real customer needs, the next step is to determine how the value proposition would translate into specific business processes. The question, then, becomes not, "Which business processes should we start with?" but rather, "What *customer value proposition* should we start with?"

This isn't to suggest that all other factors be ignored. After all, to what extent e-business can be used to fulfill customer needs is, in part, dictated by market conditions, product characteristics, and the suitability of the Net as a channel through which to facilitate various interactions. Competitive pressures also come into play. While the right points of attack should be those that create highest value for customers, a company's "type of business" can suggest which initiatives should receive the most attention. For instance, a company in the hospitality business—a luxury hotel chain, for example—naturally places a premium on providing high-touch, state-of-the-art customer care, and may therefore be inclined to lead with a CRM initiative. Even within the same industry, different companies can be configured in different ways, suggesting different prioritizations of initiatives. For example, some companies operate through a reseller network (suggesting a partnership relationship management solution), while others sell direct (suggesting a sales force automation solution). Or consider the pharmaceutical industry: While Merck may want to focus on e-business solutions that accelerate its new product development efforts, a generic drug company would be more concerned about optimizing its supply chain in order to manufacture more cheaply and flood the market more effectively.

Following are some basic considerations that influence how a company might go about prioritizing its initiatives, or finding its place on the ladder.

Do you use a lot of raw materials and components?   A company, particularly an industrial manufacturer, may want to look at its P&L and ask itself: What are my biggest line items under expenses? If direct materials and operating supplies account for a large percentage of the overall budget, then the raw materials, components, and subassemblies that the company sources may well account for up to 80 percent of total revenues. This is certainly the case in manufacturing industries like steel, chemicals, or automobiles. In this context, any opportunity to reduce these costs, even by a few percentage points, could significantly impact the bottom line. For example, United Technologies purchased $14 billion in direct materials and indirect materials on a revenue base of $24.1 billion in 1999. It expects to save 5 percent on every item purchased by streamlining and centralizing its purchasing with the help of e-procurement technology from IBM and FreeMarkets. In the case of United Technologies, a savings of only 1 percent would add an impressive $140 million to the bottom line.

While direct material purchasing is of greatest concern to firms that manufacture physical products, operating supplies procurement is a significant component of practically every business. But while every firm purchases computers, office supplies, and travel, few firms purchase these things *strategically*. For many companies, e-procurement is the low hanging fruit. This explains why, by developing solutions for automating procurement of operating supplies, startups like Ariba and Commerce One were able to enjoy so much early success. To the extent that a great deal of ad hoc, rogue purchasing happens around operating supplies, concentrated purchasing presents a tremendous opportunity to save money. For example, IBM claims to have saved $270 million in indirect purchasing costs in 1999 as a result of moving $13 billion of its indirect purchasing online. These kinds of savings arise from the fact that the processing cost relative to the product cost is much higher for indirect materials than for direct materials. Similarly, an e-procurement manager at Eastman estimates that the company engages in 30,000 transactions per year for office supplies, at an average of $45 apiece. Yet, each transaction costs $115 to process, and takes 19 days to fulfill! On the other hand, processing a purchase order for 100,000 tons of steel can be negligible relative to the product cost. So the automation of the purchasing process for indirect materials can result in substantial payback in terms of reduced process costs.

What about professional service companies—consulting firms, for instance, or advertising agencies—that don't buy raw materials? Their "raw materials" are smart, motivated people. So, given a desire to improve the inputs side of their business, they may want to launch into an e-recruiting initiative. For these types of companies, thinking about ways to use the Net to better attract and retain talent should become a top priority. In short, one way to prioritize initiatives is to look carefully at the biggest expense items in your P&L and relate the most significant line items to e-business initiatives that could impact these items.

What fraction of your customers is online, and how intense are the interactions? First, a company should ask itself: Do our customers have the systems and processes in place that would allow them to trade or interact over the Net? In some cases, downstream connectivity may be altogether lacking. In Bolivia, for example, what is the probability that the average household has a computer, a modem, and a phone line, can afford the connectivity charges, and has the purchasing power to support online commerce? A consumer marketing company operating in a developing country may be better off to spend its time, at least initially, looking upstream at suppliers, who are likely to have a higher level of connectivity, rather than downstream at end-customers, who may not have the access to connectivity that is essential for conducting e-business.

Next, of the customers who *are* online, how many are likely to take the time and make the effort to interact with the company over the Net? In the case of low-involvement consumer product companies, the cognitive bandwidth that customers allocate to the Net may be very limited, and so, too, may be the company's ability to sell to them. However, while e-commerce may not serve as a leverage point per se, the company may be able to use the Net to build brand equity, by engaging in various online marketing tactics—running temporary promotions, for example.

Another important consideration: How intensive is the interaction with the customer after the sale of the product? In the case of a big-ticket item that involves spares, service, and upgrades (e.g., an elevator, a software application, or financial services), there may be repeated, ongoing interactions with customers. Consider a commercial bank, like Citibank, relative to Procter & Gamble selling toothpaste. The importance of CRM initiatives through the online channel is an imperative for Citibank, while it may not be the case for toothpaste. That is not to say you can't use the Internet to offer information or build relationships with customers. In fact, P&G makes an attempt to do so with several of its product sites. The website for Tide, for example, offers the service of "the stain detective," while the website for Vick's provides "expert advice" for the common cold. Similarly, customers stand to learn a lot about dental hygiene by spending time on the Crest website. But clearly, the benefits of connecting with customers are limited by how much customers *want* to connect. In today's time-starved world, it can be hard to imagine too many people lingering on the Net to learn more about their favorite bathroom cleaner!

Do you have multiple layers of resellers and many different types of channels? If your distribution channels are complex and involve many layers of resellers to reach customers, then the right point of attack for an e-business initiative may be a relationship management solution that streamlines interactions with reseller partners.

Consider the Xerox Corporation. Facing stiff competition in its core business of copiers from the likes of Hewlett-Packard from the printer world, and from low-cost producers like Canon, Xerox faces pressures to improve the efficiency and effectiveness of its interactions with a far-flung network of resellers and distributors. In addition to competition for reseller loyalty, Xerox must contend with shortening product life cycles and an expanding product line that includes printers, copiers, faxes, supplies, and services. The legacy system for interacting with its resellers left a lot to be desired. Xerox resellers and distributors placed orders and inquiries by phone and fax, and in turn responded to customer queries from paper catalogs that were published monthly, and were outdated even before they reached the resellers. This resulted in resellers quoting out-of-date prices and committing to unrealistic delivery schedules. In light of these problems, Xerox embarked on a partner relationship management solution that promised to offer better services and information to its resellers—and, eventually, to its end-customers. The platform, developed using a suite of technologies from Webridge, produces numerous benefits for Xerox and its reseller network. These include the ability to securely deliver customized product, pricing, promotion, and training information to different categories of resellers, based on a set of business rules that define different levels of relationships. The system also allows channel managers to administer day-to-day interactions with resellers, to monitor performance, and to ensure that sales leads generated by the Xerox sales force are followed up on a timely basis.

A vast majority of business-to-business companies use resellers, and will continue to do so, because the channel offers reach, customer knowledge, and services that would be impossible for the firm to replicate by itself. For these firms, using the Net to better manage their reseller relationships may be the most logical place to start.

Do you spend a lot of money on new product development? Consumer products companies spend over $100 billion every year to bring new products to market. The development cost of an average new car or an average prescription drug can be more than $500 million. Firms in the fast-moving consumer electronics, computers, and communications businesses need to contend with very short product life cycles. And while new products are the lifeblood of all firms, they become especially important when the cost of new product development is high, or when time is of the essence in bringing new products to market. For these firms, a logical place to start might be to use the Net for collaborative design and development of new products, by deploying an innovation management system that would improve speed, reduce risk, reduce cost, and increase customer involvement in the new product development process.

Consider the role the Net can play in improving the financial performance of a motion picture studio. The industry relies almost exclusively on new products for its revenues. Major studios spend upward of $50 million to produce and $25 million to market a motion picture, and they do so with very little assurance that the audience will buy the product. Despite the staunch belief that moviemaking is an art, the fact is that the Net can be effectively integrated into a wide range of activities across the life cycle of a movie development project. Before production begins, the studio can survey private panels of moviegoers to read the pulse of the market. When a movie concept or script is created, the Internet can be used to gauge audience response to the concept, the storyline, and the characters. As the production date approaches, alternative positioning and promotion strategies can be tested, along with decision-support systems, to optimize the marketing plan for the movie. Finally, as the movie nears launch, the Net can be used to create "buzz" and word-of-mouth for the movie, as was successfully done by the distributors of *The Blair Witch Project*.

The pharmaceutical industry offers another example of an industry that stands to benefit from e-business initiatives in innovation management. Consider that a major challenge in developing a new drug lies in the recruitment of qualified patients for clinical trials, especially for extremely rare indications that affect only a very small fraction of the population. The Internet can provide an opportunity to tap into communities of patients who share rare illnesses, and to reach out to them with offers to join clinical trials. Pharmaceutical companies can even sponsor or catalyze the creation of online communities focused on specific diseases or ailments, helping them to learn more about patients. Today, pharmaceutical firms spend upward of $12 billion a year on detailing, the time-honored practice of trying to get pharmaceutical sales reps in front of busy physicians to push the merits of the latest drug or medical device. A detailing rep spends an average of 22 minutes in front of a physician in a day, and almost half of sales calls end at the reception desk, without any face-to-face contact with the physician. The Net could flip this expensive and ineffective "push-oriented" process into a "pull-oriented" process, with pharmaceutical companies sending details electronically to carefully targeted physicians, who might request details for any products of interest. Further, the incentives for physicians to accept the detailing pitches can be customized to the level of the individual physician, by matching the profile of the new drug with his or her prescription history. In short, by using e-business technologies, the pharmaceutical industry could interact far more effectively with both physicians and patients during the new product marketing process.

Are you a "knowledge factory"?   For some firms, intellectual capital can be the very basis for competitive advantage. This is certainly true of pure "knowledge factories" like management consulting firms, law firms, and other professional service firms. Of course, even manufacturing firms increasingly rely on their knowledge and accumulated learning as a source of competitive advantage. GE's phenomenal success can be attributed, in part, to its ability to transmit learning gained in one business unit across the organization through knowledge sharing and best practices transfer. On the other hand, firms with far-flung operations in multiple countries and multiple divisions may have perfect amnesia and end up reinventing the wheel many times over without even knowing it.

For knowledge-intensive firms with distributed geographical presences, the logical place to start would be in the knowledge management and collaboration arena. It should come as no surprise, therefore, that every major consulting firm places knowledge management at the highest level of priority in its internal e-business initiatives. Knowledge management allows the distributed capabilities that are dispersed across the globe to be combined as needed on specific projects, and it captures, codifies, and recycles the learning gleaned from every project. Knowledge management also allows consulting firms to gradually "productize" their knowledge, so it can be scaled more effectively. Should knowledge be the key output of a firm's activities, then embarking on e-business initiatives that improve the process of acquiring, disseminating, deploying, and leveraging that knowledge across the entire enterprise would seem to be a wise decision.

Finding your place on the ladder means first knowing yourself: what inputs are most important for your business, and what business processes add the most value to your customers and trading partners. Know the nature of your interactions with customers and partners. Know what capabilities are most important in creating and sustaining your competitive advantage. Your e-business priorities will emerge naturally from this analysis. And as long as this analysis is firmly anchored in customer needs and customer value propositions, your ladder of e-business initiatives will be planted on solid ground and oriented in the right direction.

Climbing the Ladder of E-Business Initiatives

Conceptually, there are four main steps through which a company typically progresses as it advances through the hierarchy of e-business initiatives. These steps can be labeled *Inform*, *Automate*, *Integrate*, and *Reinvent* (see Figure 2-2).

Step 1: Inform

The first rung of the ladder describes a do-it-yourself, grassroots initiative, one typically organized in an ad hoc manner, undertaken within a particular department, and funded out of a discretionary revenue budget. The result is a website that may consist of nothing more than static Web pages displaying marketing collateral, along with the quarterly earnings report and the minutes from the last shareholders' meeting. Perhaps worth boasting about only a few years ago, the novelty of such a website has long since worn off, to the point that posting this type of information has become nothing more than a basic expectation.

While making information available online can result in significant cost savings (as well as tree savings!), the outcome is unlikely to open new markets or revenue streams. Overall, when it comes to Step 1, think McDonald's: fast, cheap, and easy to carry out, with implementation doled out to a freshly minted Web development team.

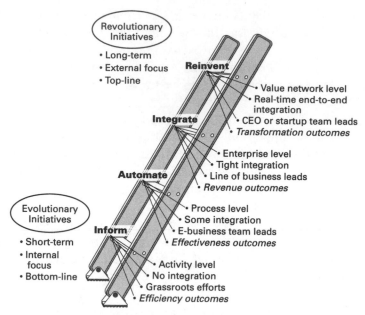

Revolutionary Initiatives
• Long-term
• External focus
• Top-line

Reinvent

• Value network level
• Real-time end-to-end integration
• CEO or startup team leads
• *Transformation outcomes*

Integrate

• Enterprise level
• Tight integration
• Line of business leads
• *Revenue outcomes*

Automate

Evolutionary Initiatives
• Short-term
• Internal focus
• Bottom-line

Inform

• Process level
• Some integration
• E-business team leads
• *Effectiveness outcomes*

• Activity level
• No integration
• Grassroots efforts
• *Efficiency outcomes*

Figure 2-2
The ladder of e-business initiatives

For most companies, these first baby steps coincided with the infancy of the Net itself. While included here for the sake of completeness, a Web presence that consists of nothing but brochureware, without any level of database connectivity, is—or at least *should be*—ancient history. By now, most companies have moved past this first generation of website development to become more strategic in their intent.

Step 2: Automate

Traditionally, having gotten their feet wet and finding the water to be sufficiently inviting, companies advance to the next rung of the ladder. Here they put on their experimentation hats, made possible by a migration from content that is hard-coded and static to content that is dynamically generated from a database. Companies at this level typically commit to some amount of process automation: answering customer queries, for example, or performing online requisitions for office supplies. Such initiatives often revolve around marketing communications and brand building in an effort to reach out to customers.

The business processes tackled at this level can cut across departments. And because the initiatives can consume significant resources, they require "real" budgets, often with the submission of a formal business case to justify the investments. An initiative at this level is considerably more difficult, time-consuming, and costly than at the Inform level. As such, authorization needs to come from a line of business managers, or from the corporate leadership, with implementation handed off to a far more experienced development team, probably an e-services provider.

At this level, initiatives tend to affect not just a single activity but a series of logically related and sequenced activities that accumulate into an entire, end-to-end business process. Consider customer relationship management, which aims to create a unified view of the many types of interactions, or touch points, between an organization and its customers. Here the impact is typically effectiveness-based, with expected outcomes reflected in tomorrow's sales, improved customer retention, or increased customer acquisition, all of which pack a big wallop when compared to efficiency outcomes.

Step 3: Integrate

As companies reach the third rung of the ladder, something powerful begins to happen: the integration of end-to-end business processes that put customers behind the wheel. For the first time, ordinary people can drive the outward-facing business processes of some of the world's most powerful companies. Rather than call a toll-free number to check the status of a flight arrival, an account balance, or a delivery order, only to be put on hold by a "your-call-is-important-to-us" loop for an indeterminable number of minutes, customers can go online to ascertain the information themselves. Examples of self service models that have boosted customer satisfaction while saving tens of millions of dollars in call center costs are numerous: FedEx for tracking package deliveries, United Airlines for tracking flight arrivals, CompUSA for tracking merchandise orders.

Putting the customer in charge is a key benefit of process integration. Behind the scenes, core business processes now transcend the enterprise, going beyond its boundaries to involve partners, suppliers, customers, and other external entities within the business web. Initiatives that deliver process visibility require executive-level direction, and the business case relies less on cost savings and net present value considerations, and more on revenue enhancements and the option value created by the initiatives.

Step 4: Reinvent

The last step corresponds to *Transformation*, a word not to be taken lightly. In nature, a butterfly spreading its wings and taking flight bears little resemblance to its former caterpillar self. In Greek mythology, the river god Peneus transformed his daughter Daphne into a laurel tree. Think literature. Chemistry. Physics. In the new world of business, the types of transformations that companies may undergo can be equally dramatic. Having redefined the basis of its competitive strategy, a company at this level has moved into a whole new playing field — and bursting onto that field comes a whole new set of partners, competitors, and customers. Wherein Step 3 redefines a business, Step 4 redefines an entire industry or opportunity arena.

Such initiatives are invariably CEO-led. Setting a new course for the mother ship, and quite possibly betting the farm in the process, the CEO steps to the podium, takes a deep breath, and before a bank of cameras proudly proclaims that the day marks a radical departure from how the company has previously conducted its business activities. To be the first of its kind to embark on a strategy that knowingly cannibalizes revenues and injects conflict into its channels would seem a bold move. Most famously, it was one that David Pottruck, co-CEO of Charles Schwab, made back in 1995 when he announced the formation of a separate online business unit to compete with Schwab's traditional brokerage divisions. Since then a steady stream of others have followed suit. But then, taking a step back, one has to ask: Are these moves really so bold? In the face of mounting competitive pressures, radical reinvention may be a company's *only* feasible course of action.

Systems Thinking: Putting It All Together

People of a certain age are apt to observe that the more things change, the more they stay the same. Or as the commentator Paul Harvey once remarked: "In times like these, it is helpful to remember that there have always been times like these." Consider the fact that virtually all activities that constitute the core business processes were alive and well long before the advent of the network economy. Most of them predate the Industrial Revolution. For instance, companies have always had the need to source raw materials, communicate with vendors, get products to market, support customers, train employees, and keep tabs on competitor activity. Network technology does not introduce new business processes any more than product innovations create new customer needs. Instead, the Net creates new degrees of efficiency and effectiveness around business processes that have existed since time immemorial.

However, network technology *does* enable companies to shift the emphasis they place on business processes from those that are inward-facing to those that are outward-facing. Certainly, the ability of a company to make connections with external entities, including its customers and trade partners, becomes important when greater amounts of materials and information are being exchanged. In this way, the Net causes value to shift from managing internal processes within the company to coordinating connections with entities outside of the company. As a company becomes less vertically integrated, time, attention, and resources may shift dramatically to managing relationships with a growing network of partners.

Today, companies need to think not only about enabling connections across business processes, but also about the impacts that are systemic in nature. For instance, the first generation of B2B exchanges failed in large part because they were completely focused on facilitating transactions while ignoring all of the activities that came before and after the transactions. In truth, the business process of procurement or supply chain management is a great deal broader than the activity of just buying and selling. It also impacts marketing, sales, and finance. Gradually peeling back the layers, companies are beginning to realize that different business processes are interrelated and intermeshed.

Measuring the impact of a business process can be difficult simply because an investment made in one process may actually be revealed in another. For instance, the investment that Amazon makes in its logistics and warehousing management systems may actually be reflected in increased customer retention and loyalty rates—and, ultimately, in terms of revenues and profits. The fact that Amazon owns its own warehouses means that it has better control over its sourcing, inventory management, and fulfillment processes. This in turn allows Amazon to reduce errors in shipping and handling, reduce the time to deliver products to customers, reduce stock-outs, and increase flexibility by giving customers a wider array of delivery options. These customer benefits—speed, accuracy, and flexibility—in turn translate into a superior customer experience and improved customer retention. So an investment in warehousing and supply chain management, which may not seem like a "customer-facing" process, is inextricably linked to the quality of the customer experience. A company's maniacal focus on its customers may prompt it to make investments that may *seem* far removed from its customers. But, again, anyone who believes that certain parts of a business have nothing to do with the customer is dead wrong. Having uncovered all of the intervening and mediating links, it becomes clear that *every* business process—even inward-facing processes such as knowledge management—ultimately impacts the customer experience at some level. And every e-business initiative needs to be driven with a clear understanding of its probable impact on the customer experience.

To anticipate the possible ramifications, both positive and negative, companies need to think nonlinearly. They need to consider all of the cross-connections between entities. Again, business has always been this way; it's just that the cross-connections were not previously enabled. Traditionally, business was viewed as a set of linear circuits. Today, e-business enables a company to make those connections obvious and salient. Indeed, systems thinking means approaching a business as an interrelated scheme of processes strung together by a cumulative logic and interconnectedness. Just as a butterfly flapping its wings in the air over one part of the globe can affect weather patterns over an area thousands of miles away, or so goes the infamous theory, no activity lives in isolation but is part of a sequence of activities that culminate into a business process. Failure to see the interconnectedness can result in management decisions that are highly myopic.

Such is a shortcoming of business process reengineering (BPR), a popular management theory that assumes the ability to excise a business process from the larger organization, analyze it in isolation, and improve upon it as a stand-alone component. A fallacy of BPR is that you can reengineer a business process without affecting other business processes. To reengineer a business process apart from the rest of the organization is akin to surgically removing the heart, improving its pumping capability, and reinserting it into the chest cavity without considering the possibility that some of the surrounding arteries may need to be unclogged and other organs enhanced to accommodate the increased blood flow. To focus solely on the individual components is to disregard the ecology of the system as a whole. In the context of e-business, there is no such thing as business process reengineering; instead, there is *business system redesign*.

Putting the Ladder to Use: Three Scenarios

Every large-scale business process undergoes its own evolutionary phases as it becomes e-enabled. Consider supply chain management—in particular, the "evolution of customer fulfillment," including both the upstream suppliers and the downstream resellers, as shown in Table 2-1. Here the ends of the continuum are like night and day. With respect to taking customer orders, for example, the evolution runs from manually determined lead times to availability-to-promise scenarios based on internal as well as partner constraints in *real time*. Managing reseller relations runs from a scenario in which product and pricing information are pushed to the channel to one in which new points of presence emerge for delivery and fulfillment. Examples of these new points of presence might include BP using its retail store outlets as e-commerce fulfillment centers, or R.R. Donnelley using its direct mail expertise to create a "logistics management solution" for third parties, with the company taking care of designing, printing, and mailing direct mail catalogs for its customers.

Or consider customer care, where, again, the steps progress from *information access* (static Web pages) to *people access* (batch mode integration) to *process access* (real-time integration). Enamored of the pitches of technology-centric vendors touting their latest customer relationship management solutions, many firms believe that if they put a CRM system into place, with call centers and Web-based customer support, then they are done. Not true. CRM, like every other business process, is a moving target, with the bar constantly being raised. Beyond automation of customer interactions lies integration, where the CRM databases are linked with other internal as well as external databases that have customer-related information. And beyond integration lies *optimization*, where transactional databases are mined in real time as customers interact with the firm, with adaptive offers presented to them based on their personal profiles, their transaction history, and their stated preferences. There is always a next step in the ladder.

But outward-facing business processes are not the only level at which we can study the evolution of e-business initiatives in an organization. The following scenarios illustrate how the evolutionary path may proceed in a department (human resources), around a process (knowledge management and collaboration), and at the level of the industry (insurance).

Table 2-1
The Evolution of Customer Fulfillment

Activity	Level 1: Inform	Level 2: Automate	Level 3: Integrate	Level 4: Reinvent
Taking customer orders	• Product information is available online, but orders are processed manually • Lead times are manually determined	• Standard products are sold online through catalog, with standard pricing • Lead times are based on internal constraints, updated in batch mode	• Customized selling—rules-based configuration, personalization, cross-selling, and up-selling • Real-time availability-to-promise based on enterprise constraints	• Customized ordering for complex products. Cross-selling includes adaptive offerings that combine partners' products and services • Availability-to-promise based on internal as well as partner constraints in real time
Forecasting customer demand	• Multiple conflicting internal forecasts • Manual inputs to forecasts and manual communication of forecasts	• Forecasts are unified at highest levels—division, product, geography • Forecasts are available to partners in batch mode	• Integrated forecasts at all levels of aggregation • Forecasts incorporate partner performance and constraints	• Integrated real-time forecasts throughout value network • Collaborative forecasting with key partners and key customers

continued on next page

Table 2-1
The Evolution of Customer Fulfillment (continued)

Activity	Level 1: Inform	Level 2: Automate	Level 3: Integrate	Level 4: Reinvent
Managing supplier relations	• Product information and specifications are online, but no process visibility for suppliers • Production and inventory status communicated manually or through EDI	• Inventory, demand, and production plans are communicated electronically via the Net • Limited process access for suppliers	• Complete visibility of production, inventory, and forecasts to suppliers. • Integrated collaborative planning with key suppliers	• Multiple integrated channels – private, public, and consortia exchanges; spot and systematic sourcing • Creation of dynamic supplier "webs" assembled in real time for specific customers
Managing reseller relations	• Inventory is pushed to channel without visibility of demand • Product and pricing information are pushed to channel	• Automated information on shipments and inventories • Regional warehouses with links to customers to fulfill regional demand	• Integrated Internet-based partner relationship management system • Complete visibility of inventory and availability-to-promise for channel partners	• Global trading partner collaboration to optimize logistics system • Creation of new points of presence for delivery and fulfillment by leveraging reseller real estate assets

A Department: Human Resource Development

How might the most "high touch, people intensive" of departments—human resources (HR)—journey through the evolutionary path to e-business transformation in the context of e-learning? One possible scenario, beginning with Step 1, is that HR does the obvious, which is to post course descriptions and schedules, along with class registration materials, to an employee intranet. While valuable as "yellow pages" to those seeking skills enhancement opportunities, the functionality of an informational site is severely limited, because it offers nothing more than static Web pages. In reality, the Net can do more than just provide a way to find out about e-learning options. It can actually *deliver* e-learning.

At Step 2, therefore, HR may begin to harness the power of interactivity and personalization to create online learning modules. The topics might range from skills training to employee benefits review, supplemented with live webcasts, simulation exercises, and self-assessment tools. Static information is replaced with dynamic information that is personalized and database-driven.

At Step 3, applying the lessons learned from Step 2, HR may approach external e-learning providers to source content and delivery platforms that are more robust and integrated. It may also outsource the IT infrastructure, by using an ASP model and become a mediator between vendors of e-learning services, as well as the manager of internal e-learning assets. From a shared services organization, it may evolve into a profit center, charging the business units for its services, and even selling e-learning courses to external clients. In fact, HR departments within large companies may even approach universities to co-brand and accredit their e-learning modules as formal degree programs. In this role, HR could become the operator of an internal (and possibly external) marketplace for e-learning, with the lines of business as its customers, and the academics, e-learning vendors, and research sevice firms as its suppliers. In addition, HR could offer line managers other value-added services for a fee, including tools for performance assessment, for career planning, and for creating personalized learning agendas for employees.

Finally, at Step 4, having successfully demonstrated the value of its offering, HR may invest in or co-found a stand-alone e-learning company, especially if it achieves significant scale and has developed unique content. With a differential advantage that stems from its ability to customize learning modules, and working in partnership with a technology firm, the company could be poised to serve a customer base that extends into other companies, and even into other, unrelated industries. This vision, while futuristic, is eminently plausible, as companies like Dupont and Texas Instruments have already begun to join forces with academic institutions like the University of Delaware and the University of Texas to create co-branded MBA programs that are jointly designed and delivered.

A Process: Knowledge Sharing and Collaboration

Here the name of the game is helping people in the company to know what other people in the company *already* know. How can e-business be used to better serve a company's need to leverage its intellectual capital for competitive advantage?

At Step 1, employees might create personal home pages that list their specific areas of expertise and project experiences. Posted to a relational database, the pages could then be made available to any employee in need of identifying others with specialized skills or knowledge for specific projects. Management consulting firms have long relied on human networks to connect to people within the firm who are experts in a specific practice area or who possess deep knowledge of a specific client. But a simple yellow pages application could greatly improve the efficiency and effectiveness of this process and facilitate the creation of internal communities of interest around specific areas of expertise. These communities could cut across functional area boundaries, business unit boundaries, and geographical boundaries. Moreover, the richness of peer-to-peer interaction could be greatly enhanced by allowing people to find "nearest neighbors" in terms of interests or skills, made possible by collaborative filtering technology such as that used by Amazon to recommend books and music CDs.

At Step 2, employees wanting to collaborate on a certain project could use intranet-based groupware technology to create shared information spaces with underlying knowledge repositories. These shared information spaces typically employ robust groupware platforms like Lotus Notes, so that the interactions can go well beyond simply locating people, to collaborating with them. The functionality expands to document sharing, application sharing, and searchable repositories of knowledge. You no longer need a person-to-person connection, because you can access the knowledge of the person that is encoded in the knowledge base. However, at this stage the knowledge repository and collaboration is still limited to employees and does not extend beyond the boundaries of the firm.

At Step 3, the scope of the audience involved in collaboration and knowledge management may expand to the extended enterprise. Customers, key suppliers, and partners may be brought into the community, by offering them selected views of the knowledge repository based on their role and the appropriate level of access. For instance, National Semiconductor has done away with the distinction among intranets, extranets, and the Internet. Instead, the company has created a single repository of product information, collaboration tools, and customer information that is accessible to employees, customers, suppliers, and partners. The only difference is the level of access. But all the audiences see the same information. More important, the different audiences are now able to contribute information and collaborate with the firm's employees. For instance, application engineers from National Semiconductor clients, such as Sony, can use the design tools on National Semiconductor's site as they work on designing circuits for new products. Or suppliers may test new chips using online simulation tools. The information is updated in real time and spans the extended enterprise. What's more, customers, suppliers, and partners can drive the process themselves, without relying on human intervention. Even entities without distinct, preexisting relationships with National Semiconductor can now join in the dialogue. The key advantage at this level is the ability of the company to integrate and aggregate learning across all entities in its business web.

Finally, at Step 4, collaborative enterprises emerge. At this level the idea goes well beyond real-time collaboration among enterprises. It actually extends to the creation of entirely new virtual enterprises that come together on an ad hoc basis to solve a specific problem. Firms like Bowstreet are building software platforms that allow the creation of "dynamic business webs"—collaborating communities of enterprises with complementary capabilities that temporarily coalesce around a project. For example, an enterprise that gets a lead from a customer to create a part may initiate requests for quotes from a materials vendor, an industrial design firm, an outsourced manufacturing facility, a third-party logistics firm, and a financing firm. Once quotes from suitable vendors are accepted, the chosen enterprises can be dynamically assembled for the express purpose of tackling the job at hand. After the job is over, the firms can disband, in much the same way as a movie production team. This is the vision of dynamic collaborative commerce, and it opens up possibilities that go far beyond individual enterprises and far beyond simple collaboration on a process.

An Industry: Insurance

To chart the evolutionary path of an insurance company is to open a window on the potentialities of e-business transformation as it applies to all types of financial services firms, as well as to an even broader array of companies whose lifeblood is information-based services.

Starting out at Level 1, an insurance company could invite customers and the public to visit its website to access general company information, to "shop" for insurance by browsing brochureware that provides static quotes and rate information, and to find agent locations. At this stage the site is completely inward-looking insomuch that it presents information about the company and its products but makes no attempt to personalize the customer experience.

At Level 2 the conversation could start to become two-way, as the website begins to provide agent referrals, lead qualifications, and information for business partners. The site could also connect customers to agents, as well as the company to business partners, such as brokers and distributors. Potential customers could submit an inquiry to request a quote. Based on demographic and geographic information, the website could then return an agent referral by intelligently matching and prioritizing leads. In addition, by plugging customer information into the underwriting engine, the site could return real-time customized quotes.

At Level 3 the website could start to connect customers and partners to *all* business processes in real time. Customers could request instant quotes, access their accounts, submit claims, and have them processed online, and get customer support over the Web, through a call center, or from an agent. Similarly, partners (insurance agents and brokers) could access rate and quote information in real time and could manage their back office operations electronically by connecting to the company's systems over the Net.

At Level 4 the insurance company could create entirely new value propositions using its real-time capabilities. Consider an example from the emerging opportunity arena of "microinsurance," made possible by the Internet. Fueled by companies like eBay, consumer-to-consumer commerce transactions have multiplied. These transactions involve risk, because the buyer has no assurance that the seller is legitimate, has an authentic product, and will deliver the goods on time. On the other hand, the seller has no assurance that the buyer will pay on time. Wherever there is risk, there is a possibility for creating an insurance product to hedge against the risk. An insurance company that has real-time information on the buyer and the seller's credit history, and has real-time connectivity to its underwriting system over the Net, could create a "trusted broker" product by offering a microinsurance policy for a specific transaction. This policy could be offered at the point of purchase or sale to the seller or buyer, and remain in force only for the duration of the transaction. For a few pennies, a seller or a buyer could insure against the risk of nonpayment, nondelivery, misrepresentation, or fraud. Of course, this type of offering turns several conventional assumptions on their head. The fact is that insurance is traditionally seen as a relatively expensive, high-involvement, and long-term commitment, requiring a trusted human broker. However, microinsurance is exactly the opposite: a cheap, low-involvement, and ephemeral product that is sold entirely without human intervention.

The microinsurance concept can be extended to a number of other situations. For instance, some Japanese companies have announced plans to offer "broken-bones insurance," policies that insure elderly people against the risk of falling down and breaking their bones. While the product itself is simply personal accident insurance, what is innovative about it is its delivery channel. The insurance policy will be offered on the wireless i-mode devices that are extremely popular in Japan. With the push of a few buttons, customers will be able to buy the policy from their wireless phones. The "broken bones policy" is to insurance as Bic was to fountain pens and Swatch to the Rolex wristwatch; bought on a whim, disposed of without a second thought, and representing a fundamental change in industry assumptions about consumer behavior and product design. How different is this innovation from the mundane cost-cutting exercises of putting insurance business processes online!

A microinsurance concept is just one example of where the ladder of evolution can take a company: from cost savings to creating new markets, from batch processes to the real-time enterprise, and from firm-specific processes to processes that embrace the entire value network. But it is important to note that you can't get to the top of the ladder without first taking the intermediate steps.

To enable real-time interactions for customers and partners, which are the hallmarks of Steps 3 and 4 on the ladder, the customer-facing system, the underwriting system, the claims processing system, and the partner relationship management system all need to be connected in real time. And all inputs that go into these systems in turn need to be connected in real time. For instance, the underwriting system may take inputs from credit verification agencies like Dun & Bradstreet, or company information from Hoover's, and so on. All these data feeds need to be accessed, aggregated, and analyzed in real time in order to generate a real-time response.

Becoming a real-time enterprise means gluing together all business processes that impact the entire value network. This can be a monumental task. But once you get there as a company, you can achieve self-actualization. At the top of the ladder, the possibilities for innovation and new value creation are limitless.

The Duality of E-Business Initiatives

In its quest to reach the top of the ladder, a company may choose to take the scenic route. It may opt to move forward in a fashion that is systematic, progressive, and pragmatic, but which takes time and lacks a strong sense of urgency. Challengers in your business, however, may be approaching from a very different angle and may, in fact, take a very different route to the top.

To illustrate the point: Think of the process of e-business evolution as a mountain climbing expedition. The first level is base camp, with each subsequent level a camp situated at an increasingly high altitude. Now imagine that you have deployed your best team of Alpine enthusiasts to advance up the side of the mountain—which, naturally, you ultimately intend to claim as your own. Although the journey is fraught with uncertainty, the team makes steady progress, mitigating risk by taking extra precautions with equipment, food, and weather. The climb continues for a long time, until finally, having methodically scaled the mountain, the team reaches the top—only to discover that the summit is already colonized. To the team's surprise and dismay, a challenger has landed there first, using a helicopter to parachute onto the summit and claiming that elusive prize of first mover advantage. This challenger may not be a dotcom but an innovator within your business or an established company in an adjacent business that has made an aggressive move into your business.

The story of the mountain climbers points us to a fundamental dilemma in managing e-business evolution. On the one hand, we recommend that an established company progress gradually through the incremental steps of evolution, starting at the bottom and working its way through the four generations. On the other hand, established companies also need to keep their eyes open for disruptive business innovations, and build a portfolio of innovative options on the future. How can you reconcile the need for deliberation with the need for speed? Should you start your e-business initiatives at the bottom of the ladder and work your way up, or should you go for broke and start at the top? Should companies today be making incremental efforts, or should they be making radical efforts? Clearly, the answer is: *both*.

F. Scott Fitzgerald wrote that the mark of superior intelligence is the ability to hold two conflicting ideas in the mind at the same time and still retain the ability to function. A billboard posted along a highway expressed the same notion: "You are not watching the road." Indeed, there is a need to drive along the road, which is to manage the quarterly numbers and perform the incremental stay-in-business activities that allow payroll to be met. At the same time, however, there is no denying the importance of keeping an eye on left field. Watching left field and nothing else might result in a collision, as was the case with Kodak; by moving too aggressively into digital imaging while leaving its analog film product lines undefended, Kodak allowed Fuji to take a sizable bite out of its century-old core business of selling and processing film. Conversely, keeping both eyes peeled on the road could mean missing out on any fly balls popping out to left field, as was the case with Motorola, which, staying too long in its analog business, almost let Nokia run off with its digital lunch.

The key to overcoming this dilemma is to understand the *duality of e-business initiatives*. As we've already suggested, e-business initiatives can be of two types: evolutionary and revolutionary (see Table 2-2 for a contrast). These initiatives correspond roughly to the bottom and the top of the evolutionary ladder. Evolutionary initiatives allow a company to enable and improve core business processes and protect its market position. They are *hygiene* initiatives; their absence will hurt you, but their presence will not allow you to reinvent your business. They tend to be *bottom-line initiatives*, because they typically create cost sav-

Table 2-2
The Duality of E-Business Initiatives

Characteristic	Evolutionary initiatives	Revolutionary initiatives
Objective	Stay in business	Reinvent your business
Risk-return profile	Low-risk, low-return, short time horizon for payback	High-risk, high-return, long time horizon for payback
Major risk factors	Execution risk, adoption risk	Market risk, technology risk
Outcome metrics	ROI, net present value	Option value, capital appreciation, learning payoffs
Financial impact	Cost impact, bottom-line oriented	Growth impact, top-line oriented
Impact on core business	Enhance and improve the core	Often threaten the core
Capabilities needed	Mostly available internally	Need to be imported
Business processes impacted	Impacts focused processes, can be isolated to a business unit or process level	Systemic impact, typically cuts across business unit and functional boundaries
End state	Integrate into the core business	Spin-off from the core business

ings, as opposed to revenue enhancement. They also tend to be inward-focused rather than outward-focused in terms of the business processes impacted, and narrow in terms of scope and audiences impacted.

On the other hand, firms also need to engage in revolutionary initiatives that seek to exploit e-business tools and technologies to create radical new business architectures. Obviously, these initiatives correspond to the higher levels of the evolutionary ladder. The objective is to leverage the assets of the core business to create new businesses that may end up threatening the core business. They tend to be *top-line initiatives*, because they grow the business by creating new value propositions, customers, offerings, and revenue streams. They create option value for the business, by allowing it to place bets on emerging and innovative opportunity arenas and to defend against the possibility of being blindsided by disruptive competitors.

Evolutionary initiatives and revolutionary initiatives are like oil and water. They are fundamentally incompatible. They require a different culture, a different organizational structure, different capabilities, a different approach to funding, and a different approach to staffing and incentives. And they elicit a very different response from the existing organization and business units. Evolutionary initiatives will typically be viewed favorably by employees of the existing organization, once they overcome their inertia over adopting new technology and new business processes. But revolutionary initiatives will tend to provoke a violent reaction from the business units, because they are seen as foreign, and, in many cases, threatening to the current business or the existing channels.

As the Austro-American economist Joseph Schumpeter observed, innovation involves creative destruction. It involves systematic abandonment of the established, the customary, the familiar, the comfortable — whether products, services, processes, human and social relationships, skills, or organization structures.[2] The organization's natural tendency is to react to radical e-business initiatives much like the body reacts to a virus. Detecting the presence of the virus, the body's immune system produces an army of antibodies that fight it off as a foreign substance. In the same way, a disruptive, discontinuous initiative is unlikely to succeed if housed and staffed within the existing organization.

Dealing with Duality: The Allure of Spin-offs

The difficulty of creating disruptive innovation within the organization has been well documented by academics like Joseph Utterback[3] and more recently by Clayton Christensen, the best-selling author of *The Innovator's Dilemma*.[4] Christensen correctly observed that organizations built around existing sustaining technologies usually fail to exploit the promise of disruptive technologies, because disruptive technologies typically offer a cheaper solution to a small, often unidentified segment of the market that is of little interest to mainstream customers. As a result, large established firms tend to ignore disruptive innovations until the disruptive technology bursts onto the scene, attacking their soft underbelly, often with fatal consequences. The prescription for meeting the challenge of disruptive change, according to

Christensen, is to create a heavyweight team to manage the project and to eventually spin it out as a separate organization.[5] Applying this logic to e-business, the implication is that revolutionary initiatives need to be incubated separately from the mainstream organization and, because they are in fundamental conflict with the mainstream business, eventually spun off as separate organizations.

We agree with the first assertion—that radical e-business initiatives need to be incubated and isolated. But we think that the second assertion—that spin-offs are the logical end-state for radical initiatives that will reinvent the business—is a dangerous generalization. Fueled by the seductive valuations of dotcom spin-offs and the exhortations of strategy gurus that spin-offs are the only logical way to deal with disruptive innovation, a number of established companies jumped on the spin-off bandwagon, with disastrous results. The landscape is littered with failed or wounded spin-offs in industries ranging from toys (KBToys and KBKids.com) to computers (CompUSA and CoZone.com) to new media (NBC and NBCi). The spin-off craze has moved on to the business-to-business arena, with a rash of new B2B consortia being created as "NewCos," with plans to eventually be spun off and taken public.[6]

There are two problems with the simplistic logic of spin-offs. The first is the difficulty of diagnosing whether the spin-off is truly a radical innovation or whether it is a sheep masquerading in wolf's clothing—an incremental extension of the existing business disguised as a disruptive innovation. The second problem is that even if the spin-off is truly premised upon a disruptive innovation, the parent may be losing a valuable learning opportunity by not infusing the radical thinking to energize the core business.

The problem of misdiagnosis is well-illustrated by the ill-fated spin-off venture WingspanBank.com, created by Bank One. The venture was launched in June 1999 with the impressive tag line, "If your bank could start over, this is what it would be." Sounds radical? Far from it. In reality, WingspanBank.com offered essentially the same services to substantially the same set of customers. A year and tens of millions of dollars later, WingspanBank.com had succeeded in landing only 144,000 accounts, compared with 500,000 at Bank One's own website.[7] The irony: Bank One's online customers could use online or offline channels to deal with their bank. But WingspanBank.com's customers could not use Bank One branches to do their banking in person, because Bank One wanted to completely disassociate the new venture from the parent company. WingspanBank.com was not a business. It was merely a *channel*. It was a classic incremental extension of the Bank One business. Spinning off WingspanBank.com as a separate entity was almost as logical as a bank deciding to spin off its ATM network as a separate business. It should have been an internal initiative that became integrated into the mainstream business—which is exactly what Bank One ended up doing; realizing the futility of the spin-off argument, Bank One folded WingspanBank.com into its core business operations.

This story has repeated itself in many other sectors. In spring 1999 the teen-apparel retailer Delia's Inc. spun off its e-commerce operations as a separate business called iTurf. The Net-crazed market rewarded the spin-off handsomely, with the stock rocketing to $60 a share. But a year later the stock was down to $3, and Delia's made the tacit admission that the spin-off had failed by announcing that it would bring the two businesses together again, calling the new company Delia's iTurf, Inc. Delia's management figured that by taking its Internet holdings public, it could raise the capital needed to build a top-notch Web company and, at the same time, create the currency to lure top tech talent. But as the valuations vaporized, this logic started to look deeply flawed, and soon Delia's management faced the difficult task of integrating two very different management teams, cultures, and IT organizations into one cohesive unit. The moral of the story: Creating spin-offs in the pursuit of financial engineering goals is like chasing a mirage. Had Delia's and Bank One allowed customer value propositions to serve as their anchor, they would have realized that e-commerce is incremental and evolutionary, not a radical new business idea.

How does a company know if a venture is disruptive or merely an incremental initiative? The answer is deceptively simple: Does the venture represent a fundamentally different value proposition for *customers*? Is it sufficiently different from what you do for your customers today, or does it merely extend your existing value proposition? So newness and radicalism should never be evaluated with the technology or a channel as a reference point. Again, the reference point should be the customer. Stop the search for disruptive technologies. Start the search for disruptive value propositions. A radical e-business initiative is something that a company would never be able to do without the Internet. Something that utilizes its core assets and capabilities, but leverages them in completely different directions. Something that creates entirely new revenue streams, and doesn't merely cannibalize the current business. Something that a company would never think about doing in its core business.

Consider the launch by Procter & Gamble of Reflect.com, its first consumer-oriented e-commerce effort. Reflect.com starts with a radical value proposition: "Create one-of-a-kind beauty products inspired by your individuality." Think of it as the Dell model of customer-configured computers applied to cosmetics. Clearly, this value proposition simply cannot be realized without the Internet. And it is dramatically different from anything already out there in the world, because it involves customers in the design process. Moreover, delivering on this value proposition requires dramatically different capabilities and processes, ranging from a mass-customized manufacturing process to inventory management and direct shipping. But most important, Reflect.com still utilizes skills that are the hallmarks of P&G: the ability to understand consumer behavior, the ability to build brands, and the ability to design new products that respond to changing customer needs. While the jury is still out on Reflect.com, and P&G fully acknowledges that the venture is an experiment at best, we believe that Reflect.com represents a much better example of a radical initiative from the customer viewpoint.

But Reflect.com may *still* not be a good candidate for a spin-off. Why? Because the potential *learning payoff* of Reflect.com may vastly exceed its *earning payoff* for P&G. Companies should be very clear about what the incubation effort is designed to achieve. If the incubation effort is designed to create a new set of capabilities for serving customers that may have value for the entire enterprise, then the end-goal ought to be to bring it back in. But if it is something that is completely different, then that's a whole different ballgame. When push comes to shove, there is usually far more benefit from taking the new idea and infusing it into the large organization than in taking an equity stake in a company that, if all goes according to plan, may at some point be taken public.

Herman Miller went through this learning process when it launched RED, an initiative that presents customers with a radically new value proposition. Office furniture is traditionally a complex purchase, given the seemingly limitless number of options and configurations. And office furniture is traditionally a very big-ticket purchase, because furniture is bought in bulk for the entire office. And because of the degree of choice and the complexity of the manufacturing process, office furniture typically takes several weeks to deliver. Finally, Herman Miller furniture is sold almost entirely to corporate customers through retail stores. RED aims to overturn these key assumptions. For individual customers who want to buy a few pieces of office furniture, value affordability, need the furniture quickly, and want to shop directly, Herman Miller created a Web storefront and an end-to-end business system that delivers simple, quick, and affordable furniture. The initial thinking was to spin off RED as a separate business. But Herman Miller instead brought RED inside the company. Unlike Delia's and Bank One, it did so not because RED failed, but because it's *successful*, and can share valuable learning experiences to benefit the whole organization. Explains Gary Vanspronson:

> The right way for businesses to do these sorts of initiatives is to have incubation. You can't do it in the core engine because it conflicts with what the core business does. So you start it as a separate business. But then you need to bring the initiatives in to magnify the impact. We said: Look, there's a great idea here, but even if RED continues to grow at a 35 percent compound rate, that won't be as big of an effect as if we can take these leanings and infuse the enterprise with them. Bringing RED in allows us to take advantage of what was created and win on a bigger scale with it.

Thinking Like a Gardener

So we are left with a paradox: A company needs to incubate radical new e-business ideas, but then it also needs to integrate them into the core business. In many cases, spin-offs represent the logic of separation and incubation taken too far. If an innovative initiative can be used to energize the core business, then executives should grow it as a gardener would grow a fruit tree. To grow new kinds of hybrid fruit, gardeners often use the technique of grafting. The purpose of a graft is to infuse new DNA into the fruit tree. But the graft does not thrive in isolation. It is grown by itself and nourished carefully until it becomes a small sapling. Once the sapling has grown to an appropriate size, it is then grafted onto an old tree. You get the best of both worlds. Strong roots and fresh shoots bear tasty fruits. It would take too long to grow the graft into a mature tree, and it would never have roots as strong as the old tree. Conversely, the old tree would never grow as fast or yield tasty fruit without the freshness of the new DNA.

E-business initiatives that seek to reinvent the company are like grafts. You need to incubate them separately and nourish them carefully. You need to prototype and validate your initiatives in an isolated market, or with an isolated set of customers. But then you need to mainstream the initiatives so they can benefit the entire organization once the initiatives have reached an appropriate size and maturity. Just as the hybrid fruit tree combines old roots with new shoots, innovative e-business initiatives can prosper best if fresh thinking and innovation is combined with the bedrock of customers, capabilities, and resources of the established business. And a word of caution: Waiting too long to transplant the graft hinders its ability to take. Grafts begin to deepen their own roots if left alone too long and become difficult to uproot. So the longer the e-business initiative is incubated, the stronger is its sense of identity in terms of the culture, business processes, and incentive systems. In this case, you might have a reverse problem; the graft may reject the mother tree. To achieve the best results, the graft should be transplanted *after* the concept is validated but *before* the business is fully scaled.

Understanding Tether Points

Underlying a new breed of old economy-focused venture funds is the premise that among the large, established companies sits a gold mine of undervalued assets that can serve as the basis for building new businesses. In reality, this logic is somewhat simplistic, given that many such assets may, in fact, be part of a larger system. Again, carving them out can be akin to removing the heart while disregarding its connections to the various other parts of the body. Similarly, the extent to which any asset can be logically decoupled from the parent entity will vary by the nature of the asset. Moreover, assets consist of multiple dimensions, each of which can be decoupled from the parent company to various degrees, ranging from a complete sharing of common resources (e.g., the same customer database) to a complete separation of common resources (e.g., distinct customer databases).

Consider the *brand*, an asset that can be readily transferred from the parent company to a new business. While easily done, brand immediately becomes a strong *tether point*. Like a dog on a leash, able to roam only within a restricted radius, the parent company defines the brand envelope, and thereafter it calls all the shots regarding its values and usage. Moreover, a "namesake business" (e.g., Walmart.com) is destined to operate as an incremental extension of the parent company (e.g., Wal-Mart).

Such businesses should *not* be backed by venture capital investments, which presumes that the new entity will eventually be taken public as a separate company. In contrast to Wal-Mart, Kmart gave its online channel a nonbranded name, BlueLight.com, to allow it the freedom to branch out into SKU categories that the physical Kmart stores would not necessarily have to carry. Had it adopted the name Kmart.com, customers would naturally have expected a high level of consistency and synchronization across the entities. Instead, Kmart chose to create a weak tether on the branding dimension. On a different dimension, however—logistics—Kmart opted to create a strong tether with BlueLight.com. How? By sharing its purchasing and warehousing systems.

The question of whether to create a strong or weak tether when it comes to logistics depends on the consistency of the system with respect to the new business that is being created. Is the new company better off going through the existing distribution center system for serving customers directly? Or is the geographical distribution of the customer base for the direct, online business quite different from the geographical distribution of where the centers and stores are located? Does that difference justify the creation of a new or an incremental set of distribution centers? In some cases the new entity may need to build some additional centers that are better optimized for direct fulfillment. Also, the existing distribution centers may need to be partially redesigned simply because a center that is optimized to fulfill to retail stores is different from the design of one that is meant to fulfill single packages. A distribution center might not be configured to handle individual purchase orders, which requires a great deal of bulk breaking and mixing and matching. To optimize for direct fulfillment of single order lots would likely require the installation of conveyer belts and pick-to-light technology. In the end, a company may end up with a hybrid distribution center design, as well as a hybrid logistics system.

Another tether point to consider is operating processes. What processes are replicated in the new business, and what skill sets can be transferred from the parent company? There are a number of processes in an offline storefront that don't exist in an online storefront—website maintenance and operations, for example, and customer care and support. Buyers may have relevant skill sets that are readily transferable. So, too, might those employees who have promotions, design, logistics, and inventory management expertise. On the other hand, merchandisers may be less relevant in the context of an online environment only because merchandising online is very different from merchandising offline.

In most cases, a weak tether should be used for culture. This applies to governance issues as well. How many members from the board of the parent company should sit on that of the startup? The key is to maximize the transfer of the parent company's expertise while minimizing the transfer of its culture. On the other hand, a strong tether should exist in the reverse direction, given the parent company's need to infuse learning back into the organization. In fact, so strong should be the learning tether that, regardless of any capital gains that may be realized, it may represent the greatest benefit that the parent company could hope to derive from its investment in the new business.

The Revolution Is Dead; Long Live the Evolution

In retrospect, it might be said that the new economy was the best thing to have happened to the old economy. With the high-flying valuations fallen to earth, the lasting legacy of the dotcom revolution may well be the shining examples that hundreds of individual companies set for speed, innovation, and pure adrenaline flow. Unlike anything that came before it, the massive wave of entrepreneurial startups energized Corporate America to change. It galvanized thousands of executives into action, showing them new possibilities for configuring their businesses and fundamentally changing their ways of thinking about the key drivers of competitive advantage, from organizing for innovation and speed to creating value based on partnership capital.

People ask us: "First we had a quality revolution focused on Total Quality Management and the Six Sigma measurements. Now we have a technology revolution focused on e-business transformation. Okay, so what's next?" Our response is: "Wake up! The technology revolution *is* a quality revolution." E-business is about QOE: *quality of experience.* More than anything, it is a set of revolutionary tools that translate into superior customer experiences. In this respect, to call e-business a discontinuity may be a misnomer. To the extent that it takes customer satisfaction to the next level, e-business should instead be viewed as a *continuity—of enhancing the customer experience.*

People also make the mistake of believing that the coast is clear. Indeed, we hear Corporate America breathing a collective sigh of relief that—lo and behold—the dotcoms aren't coming after all. But while there may be no imminent danger of becoming *Amazoned*, in its place comes an equally formidable threat—that of becoming *Enron-ed* or *GE-ized*. By no means should companies be lulled into a false sense of security, for the identity of the attacker now becomes even fuzzier. It may be one of the usual suspects, a player from within the established competitive arena. But the attacker can also come into view tangentially, and quite unpredictably—like Enron, which used its foothold in energy to step into the bandwidth trading business.

Let Aesop's fable of a one-eyed doe serve as a reminder that companies need to pay close attention to anything and everything that may be blipping at the periphery of their radar screens, and to try to anticipate dangers that may not yet be visible. According to the fable, a one-eyed doe always fed on a high cliff near the sea with her good eye looking toward the land. That way, she figured, she could always know when hunters were approaching, leaving her ample time to escape. But one day the hunters learned that she was blind in one eye. Using this information, they hired a boat, rowed under the cliff, and shot her dead from the sea. Companies that take such a myopic view of their competition are likely to fall victim to a similar fate. The question to ask, then, is not whether there is a dotcom nipping at your heels, but, rather, what are the new possibilities, and who is taking the best advantage of these possibilities in creative ways? Remember: The bomb has been invented. It may not be the dotcom guerrilla insurgents that get a hold of it. In fact, it may be a superpower. Either way, nobody wants to be in a battle with bows and arrows when somebody has the bomb.

To be sure, the evolution of the established companies is bound to happen at a slower pace than did the revolution of the dotcoms. Hills will be taken inch by inch, and death will come by a thousand cuts—death in this case being the progressive commoditization of a business because somebody else is being more creative about deploying assets and orchestrating value.

Today, companies need to do e-business for all the right reasons. The wrong reasons are technology reasons and financial reasons, while the right reasons have been staring them in the face all along, even if they had become momentarily distracted. Henceforth, contests will be won not by how quickly a new company can get to an IPO, but by how successfully it can visualize—and then actualize—the next big idea. E-business presents a new set of possibilities, and to think systemically about the possibilities is to think architecturally about strategy.

3

E-STRATEGY: PLAYING WITH LEGOS™

The underlying idea behind LEGO™ play materials is that they are not ready made toys. They are components to be put together and taken apart. This gives children immense freedom to combine, build, alter, dismantle, and play.

—The LEGO Company

A CHILD IS GIVEN a canister of LEGOs™. Pouring the contents onto the floor into a colorful mountain of loose blocks, he immediately goes to work building an airplane. Solidly constructed and aerodynamically designed, the airplane becomes a source of great pride for the child, winning the admiration of his friends and serving him well—until one day his parents surprise him with a second canister of LEGOs. This one is labeled *Deluxe Edition*. And while complementary to the old one in terms of how the pieces fit together, the new blocks turn out to be far superior as airplane building materials.

Taking a moment to assess the situation, the child realizes that by combining the old blocks with the new ones he now has a sufficient number to build a rocket ship. Built from the ground up, the rocket ship would be state-of-the-art; sleeker in appearance than the airplane, and capable of flying many times faster, higher, and farther—at least by the laws of childhood imagination. But then it dawns on him: To assemble a rocket ship that utilizes *all* of the LEGOs would require that he first dismantle his prized airplane. He ponders the situation — but only briefly, for he quickly concludes that he could never take such a risk. After all, he reasons, he doesn't know for sure that he could actually build a rocket ship, having never before done it. And if the effort were to fail, which seems quite possible given its complexity, he suspects that he might not even be able to put his prized airplane back together again. Worst-case scenario: He ends up with no airplane and a rocket ship that doesn't fly. He resolves to play it safe, by using the new blocks to simply enhance the existing configuration of the old airplane. This could include lengthening the fuselage, increasing the wingspan, and installing bigger engines. It will be a better airplane, to be sure, but it will never fly as fast, as high, or as far as a rocket ship.

This metaphorical story contains several important lessons about strategy. First, to think strategically about e-business is to think like an architect, not like an engineer. Consider the role of an architect versus that of an engineer in a construction project. Engineers think about the techniques and skills in *constructing* the building. Architects think about the art and technique of *designing* the building. Engineers think about how they can build better doors and stronger beams. Architects think about how the building will respond functionally and aesthetically to the needs of its inhabitants. Engineers think in terms of *analysis* — the process of solving a problem by breaking it into components. Architects think in terms of *synthesis* — the process of putting components together into a coherent system. Engineers implement and construct. Architects create and configure. You need both to create a building that is solidly built and yet creatively envisioned. But architecture must precede engineering. And as the complexity and scope of the building increases, the task of the architect becomes more important and more difficult.

Architecting an e-business (or, for that matter, a business) is conceptually similar to architecting a product. A company's activities and business processes are like the individual blocks in a LEGO set. But the business is more than the sum of its parts. Like the aircraft that was built using the LEGO set, a business is a system of integrated and interdependent business processes. And architecting a business involves far more than merely reengineering business processes. As we mentioned in the previous chapter, there are two problems with the concept of business process reengineering. First, processes cannot be reengineered in isolation, especially in the context of an e-business, where strategic business systems cut across functional and process boundaries. Process-level thinking is *componential thinking*, while e-business strategy demands *systemic thinking*. Second, strategy is more than reengineering—trying to squeeze greater efficiencies or effectiveness out of current processes. The engineering mindset encourages *incremental thinking*. Instead, e-business strategists should expand their horizons to search for *radical thinking*—new schemes, new configurations, and game-changing business architectures. The strategist must seek to build rocket ships, not merely better planes. Incremental thinking will lead to results that are *cheaper, better, faster*. Radical thinking will lead from propeller planes to jet planes, and from jet planes to the space shuttle. This is the first lesson of e-strategy: Think like an architect, not like an engineer.

The second lesson from the LEGO metaphor is to view e-business as an expanded set of tools for redesigning a business. Like the Deluxe Edition canister of blocks, e-business presents a dizzying array of new choices for architecting a business. The strategy space has greatly expanded on almost every dimension. Consider, for example, how firms go to market. In the insurance business, companies like Allstate and State Farm used to go to market using a single channel: the trusted agent. That was before the Internet. Now these companies have a plethora of distribution and lead generation channels. They can sell and communicate directly with customers over the Net, bypassing agents. Or they can Web-enable their agents and allow them to interact electronically with customers. Or they can work with insurance infomediaries like Quotesmith.com or Quicken.com to generate leads. Or they can affiliate with vertical infomediaries like Edmunds.com (automobiles), Babycenter.com (parenting), or Homestore.com (home ownership) to attract customers at stages in their lives when their insurance needs are changing. Take any business process and the answer is the same. There are many more ways to buy. There are many more ways to make. There are many more ways to sell. There are many more ways to collaborate with trading partners and resellers.

Almost by definition, these new choices mean that your current business architecture is suboptimal. Why? Because it hasn't been designed with the new possibilities in mind. The network economy is the age of choices. It is the age of creativity. But it is also the age of confusion. So, like the child with the LEGOs, don't simply tinker with the aircraft. Instead, make sure you explore all dimensions of the expanded strategy space. In fact, we would go so far as to say that there is no such thing as an e-business strategy. Instead, e-business strategy must be viewed within the broader context as *business strategy* with an expanded set of choices. By seeing e-business strategy as separate from business strategy, you run the risk of putting e-business into a silo. In the context of strategy, the "e" should stand for "enhanced," not "electronic." Electronic networks, Web-enabled processes, and software tools are merely a means to an end. The end is, and has always been, to make smart choices about how to compete. This is the essence of strategy.

The third lesson from the LEGO metaphor speaks to the power of legacy as a constraint for thought and actions in established companies. True, e-business may present a vastly expanded set of possibilities. But like the child who has built a plane and is reluctant to pull it apart, established companies are deeply entrenched in a legacy business. They have already made fundamental choices about their customers, suppliers, and partners—choices that they have long since cemented with an elaborate infrastructure and organization design. For a large, public company to morph its airplane into a rocket ship is a monumental task simply because stakeholders, both internal and external, are naturally reticent to tamper with a business model that seems to work. As a result, the overwhelming tendency is to try to move forward while preserving the existing configuration, by engaging in incremental change rather than radical change. The only problem with incremental change is the likelihood that someone in your business, in an adjacent business, or in a startup company is right now working to reinvent your business, building a rocket ship that will quickly overtake your airplane.

Reinventing a business is hardly a new concept. The CEO has always played the role of an architect, constantly pondering ways to renew or redesign the company. The best are masters of reinvention. In fact, history's greatest CEOs tend to be individuals who have managed through two, three, or even four periods of transition, each time successfully reinventing their companies' business architectures. This CEO Hall of Fame would include people like Andy Grove, who reinvented Intel; Roberto Goizueta, who reinvented Coca-Cola; Jack Welch, who reinvented GE; and Bill Gates, who reinvented Microsoft. That said, each of these CEOs enjoyed the luxury of several years, in some cases half a decade, to plan and implement their next big idea. Given the speed at which change needs to happen in the network economy, new entrants into the hall of fame will have succeeded in reinventing their companies in a matter of months. Change is a constant, but the time constants have changed.

Startups face a different task. For them, it is not about reinvention, but invention. Startups are not hampered by the blueprints of airplanes, nor are they subject to the limitations imposed by airplane design specs. Entrepreneurs start with a clean sheet of paper, their LEGOs still loose in the canister. In building their aircraft, they can fit the pieces together any way they please. Once airborne, an additional potential advantage quickly emerges: Airplanes fly on gasoline, which is operating cash flow, while rocket ships fly on rocket fuel, which is venture capital and private equity.

Indeed, established companies generally face great difficulty in justifying business cases for taking funds out of a business that is measured on earnings and today's profitability, and investing them into a business that is measured along a different set of metrics—e.g., exit value. On the other hand, established businesses have important advantages. They have business models that work, at least for the time being. They have customers. They have brands. They have supplier relationships. They have buying power. And often they have assets and capabilities that are underexploited. The challenge, and the opportunity, is to deploy these assets and capabilities to reinvent the business before the startups can get their unproven rocket ships off the ground.

Thinking like an architect requires some lessons in architecture, for architecture is not only a field of expertise, it is also a way of thinking. And to architect a business requires a blueprint that outlines the process.

Understanding Business Architecture

Stated simply, architecture is the *scheme that maps form to function*. It is the logic that is used to allocate the functions of a product to a set of physical components, as well as the logic that determines how the physical components interact with one another to form a coherent whole. Consider a computer. The set of functions of a computer may include the function of processing data, the function of taking input from the user, the function of displaying output to the user, the function of storage, the function of connecting to a network, and so on. On the other hand, the physical components include the central process-ing unit (CPU), the memory unit, the monitor, the mouse, the modem, and the hard drive. The architecture of the computer is the scheme by which the functions are mapped and allocated across the components. Desktop computers have a different architecture from handheld computers. For instance, the display unit also functions as the user input device in a handheld computer like the Palm VII. But in a personal computer, the monitor acts as the display unit, while the mouse and keyboard take user input. In addition, every computer uses a set of standards and protocols that defines how the components work together. Acronyms like USB, EIA, and PCI are examples of protocols that allow the subsystems of a personal computer to communicate with one another.

The concept of product architecture can be extended to the level of the firm, to understand the concept of business architecture. At the level of the firm, the *function* of a firm is to define, design, and deliv-er a customer value proposition. And the *form* of the business is every-thing it does, knows, and owns in order to bring its value proposition to life. So business architecture is the *scheme that maps the firm's value proposition* (its function) *to its offerings, processes, capabilities, and relationships* (its form). The business architecture encompasses that entire set of choices the firm makes in deciding how to come up with new offerings for customers.

The parallels between designing a product and architecting a business are nicely expressed in the words of Gary Vanspronsen of Herman Miller. As he explains it, Herman Miller competes in the office furniture business

> by elevating product design to the strategic level of business. We are going to compete by how we design business models for customers. My responsibility is to define new value propositions and new offer-ings for customers; and then to build the design, manufacturing, product commercialization, and customer service capabilities that enable us to effectively create and deliver on these value proposi-tions. We begin with a vision, a picture of how we are going to serve customers in the future. Our decisions of where to apply technolo-gy to the enterprise are driven by making real how we're going to serve customers. And so all decisions are driven by a strategic view about what's important to the customer, and what are the key things that are going to make a difference in their experience. We

work backward from this vision to derive the tools that customers need to visualize the product, choose the configurations they want, communicate orders to us, get delivery and installation, and stay informed about new products. The furniture industry has done a great job at designing products, but it has done a lousy job at designing business models. This is how we want to win. Part of our DNA is to design great products. All we have done is to elevate this capability to create great business designs.

If the value proposition is the *why* of strategy—the reason a firm exists, and a statement of the benefits that it seeks to deliver to customers—then the business architecture is the *how* and *what* of strategy—what it makes in terms of product and service offerings, and how it configures its activities, capabilities, and relationships to bring the offerings to life. The business architecture encompasses every business process, skill, asset, and relationship that the firm has in its possession. But it is more than the sum of these parts, because the individual processes operate as a system. The system should have a cumulative logic that transcends specific business processes. With e-business initiatives cutting across business processes and functions, it becomes important to think about e-business strategy in the context of the entire business system.

To understand the systemic nature of business architecture, consider the experience of Sears, Roebuck & Company. Sears began its forays into e-business with Sears Online. According to Alice Peterson, the ex-General Manager of Sears Online, the e-commerce site had a simple objective, which was to create an online channel for selling Sears products. Get as many product categories online as possible, so that customers can buy online. This is selling and online merchandising, plain and simple. But this is also componential thinking. As the Sears Online team quickly discovered, e-commerce is only the tip of the iceberg. To work effectively, Sears Online needed to connect to several other business units. For instance, customers who buy appliances online naturally expect that the website should also allow them to get their appliances serviced. After all, Sears Home Services is part of Sears, and getting appliances serviced is a natural extension of the appliance ownership experience. But unless the Sears Online systems are seamlessly integrated with the Sears Home Services systems, there is no way that customers can schedule repairs, check the status of their warranties, or order spares for their appliances. The website merely points them to a 1-800 number they can call. Similarly, a customer buying an appliance may wish to have the Sears credit card division finance the purchase, and perhaps the division should offer different customers different financing terms depending on how much they typically spend using their Sears credit cards. But without real-time integration between the credit card customer database and the online store customer database, it is impossible to use information about the customer that sits in one part of the firm to make better decisions in another part of the firm.

So while it may seem that e-business initiatives should be addressed only at the business process level, the truth is that they end up touching many, if not all, business processes. Thinking about e-business as e-commerce is a manifestation of component-level thinking. To think like an architect, Sears Online should have started with a different premise. It should have asked: How do we use the Internet and its associated technologies to create a superior experience for our customers? Certainly, the customer experience goes well beyond buying an appliance through an online store. It spans the end-to-end ownership experience for an appliance. It includes learning about appliances, evaluating different brands of appliances, thinking through financing and warranty options, buying the appliance, maintaining the appliance, monitoring its performance, and getting it repaired. This customer experience in turn touches many different parts of the Sears organization—the merchandising function, the sales function, the buying function, the financial services division, the home services division, and many more. Without all these connections e-enabled, the customer experience remains incomplete. To think like an architect, Sears Online would need to begin with the customer and the new customer experience. E-business is not about selling appliances online. Rather, it is about happy customers.

Benefits of Architectural Thinking

An ancient Indian fable tells of a frog that lived in a well. Thinking his world to be limited to the well, he fancied himself master of the universe—until one day when a man lowered a bucket of water into the well and accidentally pulled the frog out along with the water. Seeing the frog in the bucket, the man picked up the frog and placed him on the ground. The frog looked around, and was astounded to see a vast rolling plain covered with grass, trees, and animals. Looking upward, he saw an expansive blue sky filled with clouds, birds, and the sun. The frog was deeply humbled, as he now came to realize the true vastness of the universe.

Just as the frog was severely limited in his view of the universe, to think of innovation only in terms of *products* or *technologies* is to take an equally narrow view. Instead, thinking in terms of architecture allows you to climb out of the well and discover a whole new world of possibilities for business innovation—around new choices, combinations, connections, and configurations.

Most successful companies have been built not on the basis of product or technology innovation, but on the basis of business innovation—innovations in business architecture.[1] In fact, firms that have developed innovative technologies have rarely been the same ones to capitalize on their innovations. Xerox's vaunted Palo Alto Research Center (PARC), the Mecca of innovation, bears eloquent testimony to this fact; the parent company struggles for dear life in the marketplace while countless others have profited from PARC's innovations. Bell Labs, the famed technology innovation engine behind Lucent Technologies, has also been of little help as Lucent stumbles in the optical networking market despite its vast store of intellectual property. The graveyards of business are littered with technological breakthroughs like the AT&T Picturephone, the GM EV_1 electric car, and the NeXT computer—all of them technological marvels that made little or no business sense.

On the other hand, history is replete with companies that created innovative business architectures, often by capitalizing on a single customer insight. Home Depot innovated on the customer target (do-it-yourselfers, not building contractors), Starbucks innovated on the need served (little indulgences, not coffee), and USAA innovated on customer relationship management for a specific customer segment (military personnel in globally dispersed locations).

Often, companies fail to recognize that radically new products are part of a larger system. As such, they require supporting services and infrastructure. Without a complete system in place, the prospects for success are bound to dim quickly. Consider electric cars. Even if automobile manufacturers were to introduce an electric car that traveled as far and as fast as a conventional car powered by gasoline, and at more or less the same cost, the new car would never leave the dealership on Main Street, USA, unless the company also introduced an entire set of services and infrastructure to sell, refuel, repair, and resell the electric cars. Without established suppliers, established channels of distribution, and a widespread network of outlets for recharging batteries and repairing electric motors, electric cars are doomed to failure.

Technological innovations create discontinuities across the enterprise and across the supplier and partner base. Thinking in terms of business architecture sensitizes you to the interrelated and interdependent nature of business processes involved in coming up with a business innovation. By becoming aware of this interdependence, companies have a better chance of making the business system work.

Dimensions of Business Architecture

While it is difficult to write a user's manual for business architecture that applies to all businesses and all situations, we can certainly identify a generalized set of elements and a generalized process for configuring a business. The elements are the interrelated components that define the architecture of a business. They are the specifics of how the *functions* of a firm (to create value for a carefully selected set of customers) are mapped to the *form* of the firm (what it makes, does, owns, and knows). In addition to the elements of the business architecture, there is a set of *engines* that determines the potential of the business architecture to create sustained profits and growth. These elements and engines are shown in Figure 3-1.

The value proposition   The starting point for any business (and for any e-business initiative) is the selection of customers and the definition of the customer value proposition. Every business, and every e-business initiative, must begin with a definition of the customer segments that will be served, based on a deep and imaginative understanding of customer needs. While we do not discuss the techniques that can be used to arrive at customer understanding, we do emphasize that they should rely on "thick" observation of customers in their native surroundings, in order to discover their unarticulated and latent needs.[2] Unmet and underserved needs are the foundation for any new business initiative.

Having made the selection of customers, the firm needs to define what it will do for them by articulating a value proposition for each customer segment. This proposition is a concise statement of what value the firm seeks to create for customers, stated from the customers' frame

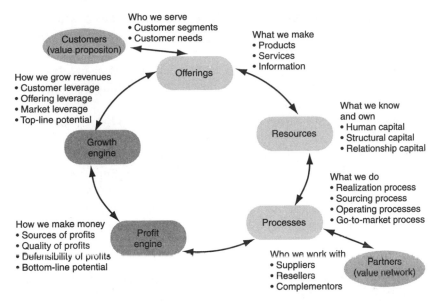

Figure 3-1
Dimensions of the business architecture

of reference. What problems does it solve for customers? Why are the existing alternatives not satisfactory solutions for these problems? Why is the firm the first choice for its customers? What is different or distinctive about the firm's value proposition relative to alternatives in the marketplace? These are essential questions that every business needs to answer in coming up with its value proposition and in redefining its value proposition in the context of e-business.

The value proposition is the "big idea" or key insight upon which the business is founded. It is the raison d'être for a business, or for any e-business initiative. A big idea ought to anchor every business. For instance, Federal Express was founded on the premise that packages expedited overnight would produce a breakthrough in business communications. Dell was based on the big idea of allowing customers to buy computers customized to their preferences directly from the firm. Starbucks was founded on the insight that cafés are less about coffee and more about the entire consumption experience. General Motors was founded on the premise of delivering a car for every purse and every purpose. The Domino's empire was built on the key insight that time-definite and time-sensitive delivery would create a whole new market for pizza. In movie industry parlance, the value proposition is the "pitch": a clear, concise, 30-second statement of what the company does for its customers. A clearly articulated "big idea" creates a singularity of focus that energizes the firm to confront much stronger but less focused competitors.

An Aesop's fable illustrates the point: One day a hound, out hunting by himself, flushed a hare from a thicket and gave chase. The frightened hare gave the dog a long run and escaped. As the disappointed hound turned back toward home, a passing shepherd said jeeringly, "You're supposed to be such a fine hunter! Aren't you ashamed to let a little hare one-tenth your size get the better of you?"

"You forget," replied the hound, "that I was only running for my supper, but the hare was running for his life."

In our conversations with e-business leaders, we have found that enlightened firms always begin their e-business strategy with a customer value proposition, instead of starting with a three-letter acronym like CRM, SCM, or ORM. In fact, technology doesn't enter the discussion until much later. For instance, Edward Liddy, the CEO of Allstate Insurance, in discussing the company's Good Hands Network initiative, told us that the vision was "to serve our customers in a consistent and seamless fashion whenever and however they want to reach us, by integrating all forms of customer interactions into one platform." Similarly, Hemant Dandekar, the Digital Ventures Manager at Eastman, explained how the company began its initiatives around supply chain management:

> We first went to our customers and asked them, "How would you find it easier to do business with us? What would make you do *more* business with us? How can we become your favorite, and ideally, your one-stop-shop supplier?" Some customers told us that they wanted to buy directly from us over the Internet. So we created Eastman.com. Others told us that they might prefer to buy commodity chemicals from Eastman through an e-marketplace like ChemConnect or e-Chemicals. So we are offering our products through multiple chemicals e-marketplaces. Yet others told us that they would prefer to deal with distributors. So we are investing in e-enabling our resellers. The guiding principle remains the same. We are no longer talking about the quality of the product. That's a given. We are talking about the quality of the relationship with our customers.

Even if your e-business initiative doesn't seem to directly touch your end-customers, you should nonetheless think about the initiative's value proposition in terms of your customers. As previously discussed, customers may be internal—for example, business units may be customers for the e-business group. Or employees themselves can be customers for a knowledge management initiative. And customers can also be suppliers, channel members, or partners. Treating suppliers as customers might sound odd at first. But to persuade them to cooperate and invest in your initiatives, it becomes necessary to articulate for them a clear value proposition. So we use the concepts of the customer and the value proposition more broadly than simply end-customers. However, we do caution that the initiatives *ultimately* must add value to end-customers, and the linkages between the value proposition for the immediate customers of the initiative and the end-customers of the firm need to be considered in advance. Otherwise, firms can end up with value propositions that are channel-centric or supplier-centric, without a clear understanding of how the initiative will eventually add value to the firm's end-customers. As the Allstate and Eastman examples suggest, even supply chain initiatives, which don't seem to directly touch customers, should in fact be developed and implemented with the end-customers in mind. In this sense, there are no customer-facing and supplier-facing e-business initiatives. All initiatives must simply begin and end with customers.

The offerings   If the value proposition is the promise a firm makes to its customers, then the offerings represent its *physical manifestation*. Value propositions are the statements of benefits. Offerings are the embodiment of the benefits in the form of products and services the firm creates. We define offerings as *seamless bundles of products, services, and information that a firm creates along with its trading partners to solve a customer problem, and to create an end-to-end customer experience*. An offering is not a product or a service. It is a combination of products and services. In fact, there is no such thing as a pure product or a pure service. This is a false dichotomy. Products have always been augmented by services, and the Net greatly expands the avenues for associating services and information with products. Similarly, services have often included products as part of the offering. So why is it more important than ever to think in terms of offerings?

A by-product of the network economy is the dramatic increase in the importance of partnerships and alliances in how a firm sources its inputs, and how it realizes, augments, and goes to market with its offerings. Firms are doing less and less in-house, and relying more and more on partners to bring their offerings to life and to market. A consequence of the increased number of handoffs to partners is the number of ways that the firm's ability to deliver on its value proposition can be stymied by the nonperformance of partners. So if the firm thinks only in terms of its narrow slice of the offering, its customers will inevitably suffer from a lack of integration and a lack of seamlessness. The firm's product or service may be excellent, but the customer experience may still be poor.

As an example of an offering that has become ineffective due to the number of handoffs and disconnects, consider the market for residential high-speed Internet access over phone lines using DSL (Digital Subscriber Lines), currently offered by a number of nationwide service providers like Covad, Telocity, and NorthPoint. These service providers do not control the actual provisioning of the DSL service because they do not have access to local telephone lines. They have to rely on local phone companies (e.g., SBC, Bell Atlantic, and PacTel) to install the DSL modems and maintain the DSL service. This handoff creates serious problems for DSL customers, who are bounced around like shuttlecocks between the DSL provider and the local telephone company when things go wrong, with each party pointing fingers at the other. To make matters worse, local telephone companies are also DSL providers in their own right, so they have very little incentive other than regulatory pressures to cooperate with the DSL providers with whom they compete. In this case, the offering is the DSL modem, the phone line, the provisioning, the maintenance, the billing, and the customer support. For their part, customers don't care about who is responsible for what. They simply want to get on the Net, fast.

Similarly, many Web-based businesses rely heavily on referring business to affiliates or partners based on a pay-for-performance scheme. For instance, Edmunds.com, an automotive website that aims to provide unbiased buying advice to auto buyers, sends leads to auto manufacturers like GM, which pay Edmunds based on the number of customers who fill out a request for a quote from a GM dealer. If the GM site is not well designed, or if the form for initiating a quote request is too long or difficult to understand, the conversion rates for the Edmunds leads will be lower, even though Edmunds "did its job" by sending high-quality leads. But Edmunds has to think about the end-to-end customer experience, and it has to take responsibility for the actions and the quality of service of all its partners. Thinking in terms of offerings sensitizes managers to the fact that they are not in the business of designing products. Rather, they are in the business of designing superior end-to-end customer experiences.

Kodak's forays into digital imaging offers a good illustration of the difference between thinking in terms of products versus thinking in terms of offerings. In the 1980s Kodak became serious about digital imaging when it realized that it was in the imaging business and not the silver halide film business. As imaging went digital, Kodak needed to change with the times. Kodak developed a range of digital cameras in the early 1990s that were state-of-the-art—the Rolls-Royces of digital cameras. The problem. These early digital cameras cost several thousand dollars and required skills that were well beyond the reach of mere mortals. Moreover, they required equipment like high-quality color printers and software that consumers did not own and could not even find at their nearby Kinkos or photo-finishing labs. What good is a digital photograph if you can't process it or print it? Kodak ended up creating a digital product that was an *incomplete offering*, because it did not solve a complete problem and did not create an end-to-end experience. As a result, Kodak's early efforts in digital imaging fell far short of expectations and it resulted in Kodak losing valuable ground to Fuji in the bread-and-butter film business.

To think in terms of offerings, Kodak should have begun with a value proposition, not a technology. And it should have created a complete offering, not a stand-alone product. After all, consumers could care less if their cameras are analog or digital. They don't think about cameras or film or imaging. They want happy memories. They want to take better pictures, and they want to do more with their pictures. They want to capture memories. They want to share memories with their loved ones. They want to relive memories. Despite its advertising tag line, Kodak is not in the business of "taking pictures further." Instead, the company is in the business of helping customers "cherish memories forever." This is the lens through which Kodak ought to have seen its business and the "big idea" that could serve as the foundation for creating a new digital offering.

It turns out that analog film is a great way to capture memories but a lousy way to cherish memories. Analog pictures are difficult to archive. They are a hassle to store. They degrade over time, and negatives tend to get lost or misplaced. A fire in the home can destroy all valuable memories. Analog pictures are difficult to edit, enlarge, or reprint. And they cannot be easily shared. As a result, valuable memories often end up locked up in shoe boxes in a closet, gathering dust.

But the Net changes all this. In its second act, Kodak is harnessing the power of the Net to create a digital offering that, paradoxically, has some very traditional analog components. In 1998, Kodak took a majority stake in a software company called PictureVision, which it used to create a Web-based business called Kodak PhotoNet online. The service makes it possible for customers to post their photos on a password-protected space on the Kodak site. Customers simply place a check mark in a box when they drop off their film, and their pictures go online for 30 days. PhotoNet could evolve into a family's online digital asset management site—a permanent image archive, indexed and organized by event or by year, stored securely, and accessible forever.

Unlike digital cameras, PhotoNet is an offering, and not merely a new product. It begins with a clear customer value proposition: "Cherish memories forever." It minimizes the behavioral change expected from consumers. It relies on conventional cameras and conventional film. Consumers don't need to invest in new equipment or learn about digital image processing. It works with existing distribution channels, as traditional photo-finishing outlets are still the starting point for creating the digital images. It uses the Net to leverage existing assets, and existing customer relationships to create new service revenue streams at little incremental cost. But most important, PhotoNet interweaves several business processes and entities to create an end-to-end customer experience that spans image capture, storage, retrieval, editing, sharing, and repurposing.

While it's too early to say whether PhotoNet will prove successful, the lesson is clear: A digital offering is very different from a digital product. The product is only one component of the offering, and it needs to be augmented with services, information, and complementary products in order for it to be embraced by mainstream consumers. So the second question to ask when embarking on an e-business strategy is: How does our value proposition translate into an offering that will solve a complete problem for our customers, and will result in a seamless customer experience?

The resources Returning to our LEGO metaphor, if the firm's offering is like the aircraft and the associated services, then the firm's resources are the tools and know-how that the firm uses to actually build the aircraft. Before we describe what these resources are, some clarity on labels is essential. Strategy theorists are not known for achieving consensus on labels and vocabulary, especially when it comes to defining the nature of resources that create competitive advantage for a firm.[3] Some call them *competencies*. Others call them *capabilities*. Still others add adjectives like *core*, *distinctive*, *enabling*, and *supplemental*. So are resources interchangeable with capabilities, skills, competencies, or assets?

We define resources as the *assets and capabilities the firm deploys to create competitive advantage* in its core business, or in new businesses that leverage the core business. To be considered strategic, resources must meet two essential tests. First, they must be valuable to customers, or enable the creation of value to customers. Second, they must not be easily imitable by competitors. And resources can be of three broad categories: resources that reside in people (human capital), resources that exist in physical form (structural capital), and resources that take the form of relationships and knowledge of customers, partners, and suppliers (relationship capital).[4] Human capital is the sum total of all the knowledge, experience, and skills represented within the minds of a firm's employees and management. Human capital resources are the basis for creating the other types of resources, because it is human skills that result in the creation of products, technologies, systems, processes, and relationships. Human capital resources are intangible and tacit in nature. They cannot be captured on paper or in the artifacts that humans create.

The artifacts, systems, policies, procedures, and technologies created by human capital represent the structural capital of the firm. This includes patents, trademarks, physical assets, technologies, and anything else that takes physical shape or form or can be expressed on paper. Structural capital outlives humans. Unlike human resource capital, it is explicit, and it is tangible.

Finally, the relationship capital of the firm is the wealth-creating potential that resides in all the relationships that it establishes and maintains with external entities. The customer base, the supplier base, and the partner base all represent resources that can be effectively deployed or leveraged to create value.

To make these ideas more concrete, consider a consumer products company like Kraft Foods. The company employs tens of thousands of people with a deep understanding of consumer research, packaging, logistics, chemistry, brand building, advertising, direct marketing, merchandising, promotions, strategic marketing, manufacturing operations, sales, and several other areas. This expertise and know-how has been accumulated over the long history of the company, and it has been transmitted through generations of Kraft employees. These human skills and know-how in turn have, over the years, resulted in Kraft's most valuable asset: its portfolio of brands. It has also resulted in well-documented processes, including manufacturing, new product commercialization, distribution management, and R&D, as well as a wealth of technologies and intellectual property. And finally, Kraft possesses a unique set of relationship assets not only with consumers, but with retailers like Wal-Mart and Safeway, with packaging companies, advertising and market research firms, raw material suppliers, the media, and many other external entities.

Why is it so important to understand the concept of resources, and to document the firm's resources, in the context of strategy? For a very simple reason: Any of the strategic assets that a firm possesses can serve as a platform for growth and reinvention of the business. Like a diver launching from a springboard, firms can use their existing resource base to launch new growth initiatives. Resources can be "Rembrandts in the attic," hidden assets whose value can be unlocked in dramatic new ways in the network economy. Whether it is a brand that can be extended into new businesses or a customer base that can be used to sell new products, intellectual property that can be licensed to new players, or managerial know-how that can be redeployed, the firm's resource base is the basis for leverage. In fact, resources are no longer the basis for sustainable competitive advantage, because competitive advantage is rarely enduring in a hypercompetitive world. But resources can be the source of *leverageable* advantage, the stepping-stones to a better tomorrow. Of course, to know where to jump you first need to know on which stones you are standing.

The processes   If resources are the tools for building the LEGO aircraft, then processes are the activities that are performed with the tools. Resources determine the capacity of a firm to act. Processes are the resources in action. Resources are like potential energy. Processes are like kinetic energy. We define a process as *a logical sequence of activities spanning multiple entities that employ resources to produce a defined set of outcomes for an identified set of customers.* A few aspects

of this definition deserve mention. Consistent with our thematic assertion of the importance of customers (most definitions of processes
don't address *who* is the ultimate beneficiary), we emphasize that every
process needs to have an identified set of customers before it can be
designed. Otherwise, processes can become the ends in themselves,
rather than the means to an end. We also assert that business processes are not confined within the boundaries of a firm, or even within the
supply chain. Value in the networked world does not live in chains,
and processes are not linear in nature or bounded in scope. In fact, the
essence of e-business in some ways is to design a new category of
"metaprocesses" that span an entire network of interrelated entities.
There are numerous examples of firms that are creating innovative
business processes that transcend the firm itself, and that connect webs
of interdependent entities in creative ways.[5]

Consider how the startup firm eTrak is rewiring the information
chain for the towing of illegally parked vehicles. Traditionally, the towing process involves a complex sequence of interactions among the
police officer at the towing site, the dispatcher in the police station, the
towing company, the towing company's drivers, and, potentially, with
insurance companies in the case of an accident. The police officer
radios the dispatcher in the police station, who then contacts various
tow companies by phone. The tow companies in turn radio their drivers
to locate a suitable truck in the area. Once a truck is located, confirmation is passed from the towing company to the dispatcher and back
to the officer. This complex and inefficient process takes a lot of time,
during which the officer is forced to remain near the vehicle.

The eTrak information network connects law enforcement agencies to towing companies. Police officers arrive on the scene and initiate a tow request through a radio link or a mobile display terminal
connected to a computer. The tow information is sent to the eTrak system, which uses a database to automatically select the best towing
company based on availability and proximity. The company receives
the tow information through an eTrak terminal in its office, and it
communicates with the driver via radio, computer, or pager. The
eTrak system has allowed law enforcement agencies to cut response
times from 30 minutes to 10 minutes, enabling them to handle twice
as many tows without increasing staff. What eTrak has designed is a
process, but it is not a linear process, and it is not a process confined
to a firm interacting with its suppliers or customers.

The core processes that a firm employs may differ from firm to firm, but every firm has some form of the following core processes:

- New offering realization process—how it defines, designs, and brings new offerings to market
- Customer relationship management process—how it creates and builds relationships with its customers, and how it interacts with its customers
- Fulfillment management process—how it sources its inputs and goes to market with its products and services
- Human relations management process—how it attracts, grooms, and retains talent in the organization
- Market sensing process—how it gathers intelligence from the market, disseminates this intelligence within the organization, and acts upon this information
- Operations management process—how it transforms its inputs into outputs
- Business development process—how it renews its business and finds opportunities for growth
- Strategy development process—how it defines its end-goals, and the means for achieving the goals
- Partner management process—how it identifies, selects, coordinates with, and manages relationships with key partners and complementors
- Financial management process—how it deploys its financial resources and allocates capital within the business

These processes are not independent of each other. They operate as a system. To form a coherent business architecture, the processes must be consistent and appropriately interfaced with each other. The art of configuring individual processes in unique and advantage-creating ways is far more difficult than the science of defining an efficient and effective process. A process may be optimized perfectly, but the system that it is a part of may fail miserably if the processes are not designed and optimized jointly.

Consider the experience of a bricks-and-mortar retailer that decided to launch an e-commerce store. It began with a website and technology platform designed to handle a modest amount of order volume and site traffic. Things went well until the marketing department initiated a customer acquisition campaign that was extremely successful. The campaign produced massive spikes in traffic, which practically brought the site to its knees. Frustrated customers could not access the site to place orders. The marketing campaign was quickly scaled back, to allow the technology team to enhance server capacity and to upgrade the technology platform. When the campaign resumed, the new site worked beautifully. But this time the logistics and fulfillment system choked. The third-party firm handling the inventory and the fulfillment for the retailer had a manual picking and packing system that simply could not keep pace with the increased volume of orders. The logistics system had not been pushed to the maximum extent earlier, because customers had given up before they could place orders. But now that the orders were flooding through, the fulfillment system could not keep up. It was back to the drawing board again, this time to search for a new logistics vendor with a bigger warehouse capacity, a better warehouse management software system, and a more highly automated picking and packing system. As this story suggests, poor coordination among the marketing process, the technology operations process, and the logistics management process will ensure that the system as a whole will fail to perform, even though individual processes may be working perfectly well. Design and optimization of processes needs to be done at the system level, not the process level.

The partners In the network economy, "no company is an island," to paraphrase the seventeenth-century poet John Donne. Rather, to deliver against its value proposition, a company exists as a member of a network of firms with which it collaborates—the value network, or business web.[6] One of the key decisions in architecting a firm is the decision on the scope of the firm's activities. What processes and activities should be handled within the boundaries of the firm, and what ones through partners that are outside the boundaries of the firm? If a firm were to possess all of the resources required to create and deliver its offerings, and if it was the best in the world at all the processes to deliver on its value proposition, then there would be no need for partners. Obviously, this can never be the case. Despite the often-heard expression, "If you want something done right, you've got to do it yourself," no organization, and no individual, can be the best at doing everything. Increasingly, firms are focusing on what they do best, and are outsourcing the rest to partners. The Net has greatly accelerated this partnering trend by sharply reducing interaction costs. Effective partnering is the secret to flexibility, focus, and leverage in the network economy.

To manage partnerships effectively, a company must think systemically about its partnerships. Partnerships must have a cumulative logic, just as the business architecture must have a cumulative logic. The business web presents a systems view of partnerships. We use the *business web* to mean *the system of partnerships that a firm creates to source, deliver, and augment its offerings*. It consists of a *vertical* dimension and a *horizontal* dimension.

The vertical dimension includes all the partners that help the firm source its inputs (the suppliers) and deliver its outputs (the resellers and channel partners). Traditionally, these have been called the firm's supply chain and demand chain, respectively. But the chain metaphor is too limiting, too linear, and too static. It also assumes that supply is somehow delinked from demand, a vestige of functional thinking from the industrial economy. In the connected economy, you need to think in terms of dynamic networks, not static chains. Therefore, we see the vertical dimension of the business web as the sourcing and fulfillment network that the firm creates. It includes long-term relationships as well as ad hoc, dynamic relationships with suppliers and resellers. And it should be designed by working backward from the offerings and service outputs desired by customers.

The horizontal dimension of the business web consists of the partners that augment and enhance the firm's offerings and customer relationships. The vertical dimension leverages the firm's assets, while the horizontal dimension leverages the firm's offerings and relationships. Unlike the partners in the vertical dimension, the partners in the horizontal dimension do not get involved with the direct inputs or direct outputs of the firm. Quite like the tag line from the industrial conglomerate BASF—"We don't make plastics; we make plastics better"—the partners on the horizontal dimension include *complementors*—partners that make the firm's offerings richer by providing complementary offerings. And they include *affiliates*—partners that make the firm's customer base richer by providing complementary customers.

Consider the business web of Palm, Inc., the leading manufacturer of handheld devices. The vertical dimension consists of a number of component suppliers and assemblers that produce or assemble semiconductor components, plastic cases, LCD displays, and accessories. It also includes a diverse set of reseller channels, including computer retailers, value-added resellers like IBM, and online retailers. These resellers allow Palm to go to market through a variety of channels.

The horizontal dimension of Palm's business web is the dimension that creates its greatest competitive advantage. This dimension consists of some 45,000 complementors—independent software vendors that have created over 5,000 applications for the Palm operating system. These applications augment the Palm offering and allow the company to defend itself effectively against competitors like Microsoft, which is promoting the rival Windows-based handheld devices. Palm's business web—what the company calls the "'Palm Economy' to refer to the economical implications, in terms of total revenue and job creation, generated by the efforts of this active community"—also includes firms like Handspring and Sony, which have licensed the Palm operating system and will compete with Palm in the device market. These licensees are complementors and competitors at the same time.

As Palm enters the era of wireless networks, it is dramatically redefining its value proposition and its business architecture. There was a time when PCs were actually used as computers. Now they are primarily used as Internet access devices. The same trend is impacting the world of handheld devices. Palm devices originally served as personal organizers—your schedule and your contacts in the palm of your hand. They were not connected to the Internet, and they functioned as stand-alone devices. But the Palm VII changed all that. Now, as a handheld Internet access and communications device, the value proposition has become: services and information, anytime, anyplace, in the palm of your hand. This new value proposition has dramatic implications for the Palm business web. Joining it are new suppliers that source the wireless modems that connect the Palm device to the Internet. Also joining the network is a whole new class of resellers like OmniSky, which offers a wireless data service based on the Palm device, and Fidelity Investments, which provides its customers with special Palm VIIs that allow them to trade stocks while on the move. Palm now has to develop relationships with a whole new set of content and commerce providers like ESPN, CNBC, C|Net, and Amazon, who will customize their Web-based content and commerce sites to the handheld platform. And it has to come up with innovative revenue-sharing arrangements with these new partners, because revenues for Palm will increasingly come from services, not the device itself.

This example illustrates the integral link between the value proposition and the business web that it creates. A new value proposition demands a new business architecture, which in turn demands a new value network.

The Two Little Engines that Could

Having built the metaphorical aircraft, how do you know if it is any good? An aircraft can be evaluated on a few simple measures: How far and fast does it fly, how safe is it, how fuel-efficient is it, and how comfortable is it for passengers? And what are the comparable measures for evaluating a "good" architecture? Stated simply, the purpose of a business is to generate sustained growth and profits. A business should be built to grow and to make money over time. These are the two engines that drive the business: the profit engine and the growth engine. Together, these engines paint a clear picture of the ability of the business architecture to drive a business profitably into the future.

The Profit Engine

For a brief period in the heyday of the dotcom frenzy, entrepreneurs forgot that the purpose of a business is to make money— not from venture capitalists and capital markets, but from actual operations. The profit engine is the answer to a simple question: How do we make money in our business? It is the mechanism that a company uses to recapture value from its offerings. The profit engine allows it to evaluate the bottom-line potential of a business architecture.

How companies make money is not always obvious—not even to their own employees. Blockbuster's profit engine is overdue charges on video rentals. Sears may seem to be a retail merchant, but it makes most of its money from financial services, with its stores merely serving as a vehicle for acquiring customers for its credit card operations. Similarly, GE makes nearly half of its money through GE Capital, not by bringing good things to life. Business schools make money from executive education, not tuitions. Authors make money from speaking tours, not book royalties. Movie studios make money from ancillary markets, not from showing movies in theaters. Newspapers make money from classified advertising. Towing companies make money from parking charges for vehicles not claimed in time.

John Seely Brown, for many years the Chief Scientist at Xerox, and director of its PARC, tells the story of a copierlike device that his team developed. Using an optical character recognition engine and artificial intelligence, the device does more than copy a document. It actually analyzes the document to identify the key concepts, and it generates a summary document with only the key concepts in the original document. You can feed in a 30-page document and the copier will spit out a one-page summary document. Unveiling the breakthrough at a board meeting, Brown expected to receive thundering applause. But he was met only with stony silence. Finally, one of the board members cleared his throat. "John," he asked, "how do we make money around here?" The answer was revealed in a single word: *toner*. The new product would strike at the very heart of the Xerox profit engine.

Value creation is a necessary condition for value recapture, but it is not a sufficient condition. To capture value it becomes necessary to first create value. But creating value does not always result in a profit engine. In 1997, Kevin Kelly proposed twelve principles for the new economy.[7] One of them was "Follow the Free," which put forth the then-radical idea that giving stuff away garners human attention, or *mind share*, which invariably leads to market share. "Give it away, and get rich," chanted the masses of early Internet entrepreneurs who took this two-step process to heart. Unfortunately, most of them only managed to implement the first half. In a mad race for eyeballs, they gave away information, content, e-mail, Internet access, and even PCs. Hotmail created value by offering location-independent and ISP-independent e-mail. MP3.com created value by giving away music. Bob Young, the founder of Red Hat Software, a provider of the free Linux operating system, once commented, "Software companies make money selling software, and give away T-shirts. We make money selling T-shirts, and give away software." Success was measured in terms of exotic new metrics like page views, hits, unique visitors, and impressions. Internet analysts, pressured by the need to justify sky-high valuations for companies with negligible revenues and no profits, argued that these metrics would presage profitability, as the business found a way to "monetize the eyeballs." However, as it turned out, there is a long way from a customer's eyeballs to her wallet. A business without a clear profit engine is really no business at all.

Where do profit engines live in a business? There may be many drivers of profits, and each source may serve as a profit engine. A company's profit engine may be rooted in customer loyalty and lock-in, as is the case for airlines and their frequent flier accounts. Or it may be based on increasing returns, as is the case for Microsoft and Yahoo! Or it may derive from the ability to sell follow-on supplies and upgrades, as is the case for Red Hat software and Xerox copiers. Or it may be embedded in a suite of network-based services that produce annuity revenue streams, as is the case with the Blackberry wireless e-mail device. Or it may be based on revenues generated from customer referrals, as is the case with C|Net, which refers leads to computer manufacturers.

Because profit engines tend to wind down over time and individual recapture mechanisms may be subject to volatility and fluctuations, a good business architecture should have *multiple* profit engines. With multiple ways to make money, a company can insulate itself against the erosion of a specific profit stream, as well as uncertainty in the marketplace. For instance, while the profit engine in AT&T's core long distance telephone business sputters, its wireless business continues to generate healthy profits, without which the company would be in far worse shape. A good business architecture should also have *sustainable* profit engines. The sustainability of a profit engine is the length of time the engine can produce profits reliably. Sustainability may derive from ownership of proprietary knowledge or proprietary intellectual property. Sustainability may derive from relationships with customers, suppliers, and partners. Sustainability may derive from increasing returns to scale on the demand side in businesses where variable costs are low, because profits increase dramatically as the size of the customer base grows.

In summary, profit engines speak to the ability of the business architecture to generate profit streams that can be defended over time.

The Growth Engine

The profit engine determines how the company makes money in the current business. But profits today are no guarantee of profits tomorrow. If a business is going to continue to make money, it needs to renew itself and grow. A profitable business may be a cash cow today, but it may also be a mature business with very little growth potential. The ability of a business architecture to deliver revenue growth is determined by its growth engine. The growth engine is the set of mechanisms that a business uses to grow revenues. The growth engine determines the top-line potential for a business.

Where does growth come from? Like the profit engine, the growth engine can have many different sources. However, the springboard for growth almost always comes from a key asset or a key relationship. Growth vectors may be along the customer axis (who), the offering axis (what), or the geography axis (where). The customer base can be a powerful vector for growth, if the business can create new offerings for its existing customer base. Adjacencies in customer needs can be used to increase the revenues from each customer account. For instance, Intuit has used the large base of users of its personal financial software package, Quicken, to expand into online banking, online bill payment, mortgage origination, and credit card businesses. In evaluating the existing customer base as a growth engine, the questions to ask are: What needs do we serve for our current customers? What needs are adjacent or complementary to these needs? How can we exploit these adjacencies to expand our offerings for current customers? What related products and services can we create for our customers? The richness of adjacent needs determines the extent to which customers can serve as the growth engine.

The actual offerings can also serve as an engine for growth. For example, a company can exploit a different adjacency by leveraging current offerings to new sets of customers. In this case, adjacent customer bases—not adjacent offerings—serve as the vector for growth. Again, consider the growth strategy that Intuit has followed from its origins in the consumer financial software business. Intuit's personal financial management software was initially targeted at consumers. But market research revealed that a significant number of Quicken users were actually using the software to manage the finances for their small home based businesses. Capitalizing on this finding, Intuit adapted its offerings and created a suite of products for small businesses. Today, Quicken's small business offerings account for 35 percent of its revenues, while its original consumer finance business accounts for less than 20 percent of its revenues.

The Internet opens up new avenues for growth by allowing a firm to leverage its customer base in new ways. Again, consider Intuit, which realized that its customer base of over 5 million small businesses is a powerful asset that could be leveraged through partnerships with providers of online services for small businesses. In January 2000, Intuit launched a new suite of online e-services called the QuickBooks Internet Gateway as part of its QuickBooks 2000 offering. The QuickBooks Internet Gateway gives QuickBooks 2000 customers direct access to over a dozen services from third-party vendors that address the specific needs of small businesses. These services include the QuickBooks Merchant Account Service, which enables small businesses to accept credit card payments from their customers; the QuickBooks Postage Service, which allows customers to purchase postage electronically; and the QuickBooks Shopping Source, which enables customers to find, compare, and purchase office supplies and other small business products and services. Intuit generates revenues from slotting fees as well as a share of the transactions that it generates for vendors that offer these services. Intuit has also created a new offering called Quicken Payroll Services, to enable small businesses to manage their payrolls. The service produces recurring revenues from Intuit's existing base of small business customers that would not have been possible without the Internet.

In summary, the growth engine reflects the *option value* that is embedded in the customer base the firm serves, the offerings it creates, and the markets in which it participates. This option value arises from the fact that firms can exploit adjacencies in customer needs and adjacencies in offerings to find new avenues for growth. So the quality of the growth engine for a business is a function of the variety of options the firm has to leverage its customers and its offerings. Like the soldiers landing on the beaches of Normandy, the current base of customers and offerings can be a beachhead for conquering new markets and creating new offerings. Landing in Normandy is far more valuable than landing in the Virgin Islands, because Normandy is a beachhead for a continent, while the Virgin Islands are simply an isolated set of islands, with limited possibilities for growth and territorial expansion.

Breaking Free from Legacy

"The thinking that we have has brought us to where we have already been," Albert Einstein once remarked. "In order to go somewhere else, we must think in a different way." To think in a different way, and to fully unleash the power of the imagination, we need to break free of the constraints and assumptions that shackle our thinking. As we discussed in Chapter 1, we are all prisoners of what we know. Our mental models—theories of how the world operates—can become deeply ingrained in our thinking and limit our capacity to imagine new possibilities. At the level of the firm, the tyranny of the known becomes even more dangerous. The older the organization, the greater likelihood that it has accumulated a deeply ingrained set of practices, rituals, and assumptions. The problem, however, is that assumptions are not facts. And the facts in the world of business have changed so significantly that many assumptions that once were valid are no longer tenable. As we pointed out earlier in this chapter, most large businesses were not designed with the possibilities of e-business in mind. Their business architectures have not taken into account the myriad new ways to configure their businesses. So we must start anew. But how can we break free from the shackles of legacy?

The late Senator Everett Dirksen of Illinois was fond of saying, "When I feel the heat, I see the light." Fear may be a good way station on the road to opportunity identification, as people tend to respond more quickly to fear than they do to opportunity. Certainly, they think more creatively when scared into imagining how a competitor could destroy their business than when asked how they could improve their business in the context of business as usual. This was brought home to us in an executive education course on e-business. At the end of the course, we gave participants an exercise to come up with an innovative business idea to improve their business, using the e-business concepts and tools we had introduced. The ideas that resulted turned out to be quite incremental. Participants tended to begin with their legacy business as the starting point, and they fell prey to all the constraints that legacy imposed upon them. In the next seminar, we altered the exercise, telling the executives to imagine the "worst nightmare competitor" for their business. We asked them to imagine how a potential competitor could completely undermine the profit and growth engines of their current business. The results from this exercise were stunningly different. This time, participants came up with innovative business architectures that would destroy their businesses quite effectively. Freed from their legacy, they were able to think far more creatively. Next, we asked the executives to consider why their business could not preemptively become its own worst nightmare competitor. While a number of difficult issues arose, ranging from channel conflict to management inertia, participants began to realize that their ideas for radical business architectures were not as unfeasible as they had originally thought.

This two-step process of fear followed by opportunity identification was pioneered by firms like GE.[8] In January 1999, Jack Welch created a cross-functional "Destroy Your Business" team within every business unit of GE. Each DYB team analyzed current and potential competitors along dimensions that included their business processes, their offerings, and the economics of ordering through the Web versus ordering through the sales force and call centers. The goal was to present GE's top executives with a hypothetical Internet-based business that a competitor could use to erode GE's current business. In the second phase of this exercise, the same teams were asked to propose how they would change their existing business architecture to respond to this threat. This latter part of the exercise came to be known as GYB— Grow Your Business—because its objective was to find fresh ways to reach new customers and better serve existing ones.

Fear and Opportunity: Reinventing R.R. Donnelley

To illustrate the process of reinventing the business architecture through the "fear and opportunity process," consider the challenges faced by R.R. Donnelley & Sons, a 136-year-old company in the commercial printing, communications services, and logistics business. With 34,000 employees and $5.4 billion in sales, R.R. Donnelley has traditionally been in the business of "putting ink on paper."[9] The company offers its services in a variety of markets, including magazine publishing, book publishing, direct mail catalogs, advertising inserts, financial services, and directories. Its resources include its expertise in content management (the company processes 40 million pages of content *every day*), its expertise in printing plant operations, its relationships with major publishers and corporate customers, its trusted brand name, and its reputation for quality, service, and reliability. The company's key processes include customer acquisition, content creation, content repurposing, print/bind production, distribution and logistics management, and customer contact management. Its business web includes suppliers of paper and printing supplies, content management software, hardware, and printing machinery. The business web also includes book and catalog publishers, the U.S. Postal Service and UPS, as well as retailers and direct marketing firms. Its profit engine is the printing and binding business, while its growth engine relies on its ability to sell printing and binding services to more customers in more markets. Clearly, R.R. Donnelley is saddled with a traditional business architecture designed for the analog age, with profit and growth engines that are fast running out of steam. Its core printing and binding business is steadily becoming commoditized, putting pressure on the profit engine. And its core business is being eroded by digital distribution channels, putting pressure on the growth engine. As a result, its stock trades at a price-to-earnings multiple below 10.

It is not hard to imagine a number of threatening scenarios that could cripple R.R. Donnelley's existing business architecture. After all, the productivity of the printing business is appalling. Direct mail catalogs take 40 days to print, and 97 to 98 percent of catalogs are wasted. Bestseller books take 53 days to print, and 30 to 40 percent are returned to the publisher and destroyed. Newsstand magazines take 45 days to print, and 60 percent are destroyed. Telephone directories take 25 days to print, and only 7 percent of the headings are ever looked up. The printing and publishing business is entirely "push" oriented— "print it, and they will come." And here's the really scary thought: If direct mail catalogs were targeted more accurately to customers so that they produced response rates of 20 to 30 percent, then R.R. Donnelley's customers would only have to print one-tenth of their existing print runs. So, in a sense, R.R. Donnelley's current profit engine benefits from the inefficiency of its customers! The worse the customers are at forecasting the demand for books or in targeting direct mail, the larger the print runs for catalogs. Clearly, this is a profit engine destined to go off a cliff. As R.R. Donnelley's customers start taking advantage of the Net to improve the efficiency and effectiveness of their marketing communications and the accuracy of their demand forecasting, the company's core business will be threatened. Here are some ways in which this might happen:

- Books move to a print-on-demand model that relies on customer pull, not publisher push. Books become digital, going from authors to publishers to retailers to end-customers, or even directly from authors to end-customers, bypassing commercial printers. Bits that are created digitally remain bits, either in the form of e-books or in the form of digital files transmitted to computers. And if they do become ink on paper, they do so at the consumer's printer or copier, without ever taking shape as a book. Already, authors like Stephen King are beginning to experiment with direct-to-customer publishing, bypassing the publisher as well as the printer, as was the case with his book *The Plant*. It is a horror story that should strike fear in the heart of a company like R.R. Donnelley.

- Books are disaggregated into chapters that can be purchased individually. Customers can create "custom books" by mixing and matching chapters from multiple books based on their individual preferences, just as a custom music CD can be created by aggregating singles from a number of different CDs. Already, startups like MeansBusiness.com provide book summaries and allow customers to buy books by the chapter, for a few dollars each. Book print runs plummet.

- Directories and yellow pages become digital, as do financial services documents like SEC filings, a lucrative business for R.R. Donnelley. Direct mail catalogs become electronic. Coupons become digital. Companies like CoolSavings.com allow customers to download coupons to their computers or handheld devices, without ever going through a commercial printer. The number of coupons and direct mail catalogs printed on paper plummet.

We could go on, but the trend is clear. The future of "putting ink on paper" in the age of the Internet seems as bright as the very tools that were once used to produce the printed word: the quill pen, which was replaced by hand-set wooden type, which was replaced by lead type. Now, the question is, how can R.R. Donnelley turn these aforementioned trends into an advantage, to push its business in new directions?

As a first step, R.R. Donnelley would need to redefine its value proposition (which it no doubt is already in the process of doing), in which case it becomes obvious that "ink on paper" is a product orientation, not a customer-oriented value proposition. What do its customers *really want*? Just as Kodak's customers don't care about cameras or film, R.R. Donnelley's customers don't care about paper or ink. Authors care about getting their ideas out to their audiences as quickly, cheaply, and effectively as possible. Companies care about communicating their marketing messages or information to their customers. From this perspective, R.R. Donnelley's real value proposition should be not to help commercial printing customers to put ink on paper most efficiently and effectively, but *to be the most efficient, effective, speedy, and flexible platform for communicating ideas and information between creators and consumers*. Ideas and information should be conveyed:

- Through multiple channels (print, Internet, wireless)
- To multiple user interfaces (a book, an e-book, a desktop computer, a personal digital assistant)
- In multiple formats (text, audio, video, animation)
- At multiple levels of aggregation (books, chapters, objects, elements)
- In real time (defined by the customer, rather than at a fixed point in time)
- With personalization (ability of customers to choose formats and form factors)

For instance, if an author publishes a book that is printed by R.R. Donnelley, the "book" actually becomes a digital asset stored on the company's computers before being shipped off to its printing presses. The content is used only once, and it produces revenues for the author as well as for the company only once. Instead, R.R. Donnelley could allow each author to take control of their digital assets, by allowing them to reprint, reformat, reaggregate, syndicate, license, and repurpose their book or parts of their book content. Authors and their audiences could combine the author's work with that of other authors to create custom versions of the content, which could be analog (printed as "custom books") or digital (in the form of "custom collections"). Each time the content is processed or repurposed, R.R. Donnelley could extract a small fee for the transaction. So R.R. Donnelley could transform itself into a provider of Digital Asset Management platforms, a new-breed ASP that would mediate between creators and consumers of content. The platform would allow the company to monetize its massive store of "digitize once, use once" content in multiple ways, at multiple points in time, and with very little incremental cost. With some additional work on publishing standards like XML, the company could also provide a syndication service to originators of content, whereby they could market and distribute their content at will.

This new business architecture would leverage many of the existing resources R.R. Donnelley already possesses, such as content creation, archival and content repurposing. It would require the creation of additional assets and capabilities, mostly around document transport protocols and around the infrastructure it would need for hosting and syndicating content. New processes to be put into place would include customized printing, Web hosting, content syndication, and payment processing for microtransactions. The growth engine would be rooted in asset leverage, by virtue of the fact that digital assets become a source of multiple incremental revenue streams. While several aspects of the new business architecture obviously need to be defined in much greater detail, and while a number of hurdles and problems would undoubtedly need to be overcome in implementation, this example shows how to rethink the business architecture by following the two-step process of challenging existing assumptions and then building a new business architecture that is free of the constraints of legacy.

Brain Candy for the E-Strategist

As the R.R. Donnelley example suggests, the Internet can enhance a business along a number of different dimensions, to the point that it can be difficult to know where to start. In this respect, the strategist is like a kid in a candy store, overwhelmed by the number of choices—but of course it always helps when the goodies are sorted and organized into clearly labeled containers. Following are some conceptual containers that can be used to organize the strategist's thinking around e-business innovation.

Net-enhanced yield management   Does your business use a large base of fixed assets or human resources to create its productive capacity? Are you faced with a situation where your capacity is quite inflexible in the short run, but the demand for your offerings is highly variable or seasonal? Is your customer base very diverse in its sensitivity to price versus the nonprice attributes of your offerings? Does productive capacity in your business perish as soon as it is created? And are your operations running well below their capacity on any average day?

If your business meets these criteria, then you can dramatically increase the revenues and yield from your operations by using the Net to design and deliver a vast array of offerings that accurately match supply with demand in real time. Industries that can benefit from Net-enhanced yield management include the travel business (airlines, hotels, rental cars, cruise operators), the cargo transportation business (air freight, ocean shipping, land transport, container shipping), the telecommunications business, the professional service business (management consulting, software consulting), and the contract manufacturing business. Even Pepsi and Kmart can benefit from yield management. In fact, every business can benefit by being able to adapt its offerings to moment-to-moment variations in supply or demand.

Yield management is the art and science of extracting the highest possible revenues from every customer based on their willingness to pay, based on a dynamic matching of supply with demand. Yield management typically involves the creation of "buckets" of capacity with differing levels of flexibility, convenience, and price to customers, and allowing different customer segments to self-select the offerings that best match their needs and their buying situations. Airlines are the pioneers in yield management. They use complex algorithms in conjunction with automated customer reservation systems to price every seat on every flight by matching available buckets of capacity against customer preferences for flexibility versus price.

Despite the sophistication of yield management in the airline business, over 500,000 airline seats go empty every day in the United States. If half of these tickets could be sold for an average of $100 each, airlines could increase their revenues by almost $10 billion every year! For yield management to be most effective, airlines need to be able to communicate their offers to customers in real time, because the supply and demand situation changes on a moment-by-moment basis. The Net greatly expands the channels through which airlines can present their offers to customers. Consider American Airlines. Until a few years ago, travel agents and telemarketing were the only channels available to American Airlines for presenting customers with differentiated offers. With the Internet, however, American Airlines is able to make far more fine-grained trade-offs between the flexibility and prices that it offers to its customers. In particular, it now offers, or will soon offer, the following sets of purchase options:

- Valuable full-fare tickets to business travelers through travel agents, through its own website, as well as through online channels like Travelocity and Expedia. Customers buying through this channel have full control over what airline they fly, what day they fly, what time of day they fly, how many connections they make, and what seats they choose.
- Full-fare business as well as leisure travel tickets through Orbitz, an Internet venture founded by American Airlines and five other U.S. airlines.

- Last-minute discounted fares (called AA Saver fares) through a direct e-mail that it sends out to millions of customers every week. Customers give up choice of the date of travel, but they do know the prices and the identity of the airline before they book a flight.
- Deep discount leisure fares, called Hotwire, through a collaborative venture with five other major airlines. Hotwire pits multiple airlines against each other to provide deals that are consistently lower than published prices and make travel more affordable. Customers know the price and the day of travel, but not the identity of the airline, the time of day, or the seat assignment. And customers are not eligible for frequent flier miles. This bucket of capacity is even lower in price, because it demands more flexibility on the part of customers.
- Distressed inventory through the "name your own price" service offered by Priceline.com. These seats represent the lowest price, are the least flexible, and are the most inconvenient bucket of capacity.

The same principle can be applied to improve the yield from manufacturing capacity for a contract manufacturer by creating a capacity brokering service. Motion picture distributors and exhibitors leave money on the table by pricing their tickets too low in the opening week and too high in later weeks. Why does the price of a movie ticket need to be the same, regardless of demand? One could imagine a website that would auction movie tickets on a theater-by-theater and show-by-show basis, for every movie. *Terminator 3* could cost $50 for the first show in Manhattan, but might be available for $1 in the suburbs in the tenth week. Even Pepsi could benefit from yield management, by pricing each soda bottle in a vending machine based on the location, the inventory, and the ambient temperature. And why not have a dynamic brokering service for utilities like electricity and natural gas, where customers may be offered an opportunity to reduce their utility bills by running their washing machines and dishwashers in the middle of the night? In all of these cases, the Net can be used to automate the creation and the presentation of dynamic offers, greatly expanding the possibilities for yield management.

Net-enhanced life cycle value management   In many businesses, what seems to be the dog is actually the tail, and what seems to be the tail is actually a very large dog. The initial product purchase of almost any big-ticket product usually represents only a small part of the lifetime ownership experience for that product. And this life cycle typically involves a diverse set of services that can produce very profitable annuity revenues. In fact, the product may only be the Trojan horse that allows a company to sell a range of follow-on services to customers. The average aircraft engine sold by General Electric consumes $5 in supplies and service for every dollar the airline pays to buy the engine. The average homeowner generates $20 worth of home services over the lifetime of ownership of a home for every dollar generated in the initial home-buying transaction for a real estate broker. The initial price of a cellular phone or a Palm VII pales in comparison with the service and subscription revenues generated from the devices over their lifetime. In the networked world, value is systematically migrating from products to services and from onetime transactions to ongoing services that are sold to customers over their entire lifetime. If you do not exploit the power of customer life cycle value management, you may be presiding over massive leakage of value from your core business, without even knowing it.

Customer life cycle value management has been used successfully by business marketers like GE and by consumer marketing companies like GM but the Internet allows life cycle value thinking to be extended to a much broader set of industries and firms. Consider the real estate business. The real estate broker is the first person a new homeowner touches. Then there's the move to a new location, which triggers the purchase of a slew of services—a plumber, electrician, maid, landscaper, Internet Service Provider, day care facility, elementary school, tax preparation agency, and so on. And the home itself becomes the basis for a broad range of repair, remodeling, and maintenance services. The real estate broker, through real estate companies like Century 21 and ReMax, and Internet-based firms like Homestore.com and HomeAdvisor.com, could position herself as the logical source for advice and referrals to a broad range of services that are triggered by the purchase of the home. Each of these services could produce referral revenue streams for the Realtor and be used to subsidize the fees she collects from the initial transaction. A real estate agent who thinks in life cycle terms and develops these follow-on revenue streams may be able to price brokerage services dramatically lower than can her competitors.

To further illustrate the power of life cycle value management, consider recruiting season at any major business school. It's a time when MBA students urgently upgrade their sartorial standards—ditching worn jeans and T-shirts for snappy suits from Hickey-Freeman (a brand owned by Hart Schaffner & Marx), which has pioneered the concept of "catch 'em young." The company hires students as temporary salespeople and dispatches them to campuses where they demonstrate various fabrics and styles, take measurements, and place orders for a commission. While many suits are sold, no lifetime relationships are built. What a missed opportunity! Instead, Hickey-Freeman could combine "bricks" and "clicks" to create greater customer lifetime value, by asking students who buy suits on campus detailed questions about their fabric and color preferences as they react to different samples. Customers could be queried about their existing inventory of suits and business casual clothing and their preferences on dress style. They could also be asked about their future employer (to be sure, an investment banker on Wall Street is likely to have very different needs for formal clothes than an executive in a startup firm). Having ascertained all this information, Hickey-Freeman could then broaden its identity from being a seller of suits to being a "lifetime wardrobe manager" for students as they progress through their professional careers. Every six months or so, they could be presented with customized e-mail messages announcing preselected sets of new offerings based on their color, fabric, style, and price preferences. They could be updated on new fashion trends and presented with other brands from Hart Schaffner & Marx. They could even receive recommendations on third-party providers of accessories such as shoes, ties, and outerwear.

The insight that Net-enhanced life cycle management offers is simple: See your product not as a transaction but as an opportunity to create a long-term relationship with customers that can be enhanced by the Internet. To guide your thinking, ask yourself what products and services your customers buy over their lifetimes to support, maintain, enhance, repair, renew, protect, finance, or augment the products that you sell to them. Ask yourself if you know the full extent of the lifetime spending associated with your products and services and the fraction in which you are currently participating. Then analyze the margins in these complementary products and services and see if they're higher than the margins in the products you sell today. If you find attractive missed opportunities, ask yourself how you could use the Net to create a comprehensive life cycle management offering. This offering could leverage your knowledge of customers and your existing customer relationships to generate new revenue streams from complementary offerings or through referral revenues from third-party partners and affiliates.

Net-enhanced asset leverage   Leverage is a powerful principle in physics, expressed most eloquently by the ancient Greek scientist Archimedes, who said, "Give me a place to stand on, and I shall move the Earth." A lever creates mechanical advantage, allowing you to lift loads far beyond your natural capacity. The principle is equally powerful when applied to the realm of strategy. Think of the Internet as a lever that creates strategic advantage, by allowing you to utilize your assets in ways that far exceed your normal returns from these assets. In fact, the secret to creating higher returns on assets (ROA) is to amplify the numerator—that is, the revenues you can produce from your assets. But to get there you first have to expand your thinking and see your assets in a whole new light. What are these strategic assets? They may be customer access. They may be databases. They may be patents and intellectual property. They may be physical assets. They may be production processes. They may be brands. They may be distribution channels. The Net can amplify the power of these assets in ways that were simply not possible in the analog world.

Consider the quintessential fast food icon, McDonald's Corporation. Through its 27,000 restaurants in 119 countries the company serves nearly 43 million customers *every day*. In comparison, the world's most popular website, America Online, claimed in late 2000 to have 60 million unique users a month. McDonald's sees many more times the number of customers than the biggest digital economy. And unlike AOL, McDonald's doesn't see only eyeballs. It sees feet. It sees mouths. It sees wallets. But what does it do with these customers? Serves them a burger, fries, and a drink and sends them on their merry way. It doesn't know the individual consumer. It doesn't know how often they buy from McDonald's. It doesn't know what they like and what they don't. And unlike AOL, which manages to pull in billions of dollars in advertising by renting its customer base, McDonald's actually pays movie distributors millions of dollars to run the next big promotional tie-in.

Now McDonald's is waking up to the power of the Internet to leverage its tremendous customer base in creative ways. An initiative called "Big Deal" that was recently piloted in Sweden might very well be the shape of things to come. Customers in selected restaurants there are presented with a choice of several promotional offers from McDonald's partners, listed on a set of cards placed prominently at the checkout counters. For instance, Volkswagen offers 100 free liters of petrol to customers who buy a new car through the promotional offer. Customers go to a website and fill out a personal profile, and McDonald's gets paid for the leads it generates for its partners. And as a tasty by-product, the company is able, for the first time, to gather information about individual customers and their purchase behavior. In this way, the entire McDonald's storefront acts as a banner advertisement for its partners. Except this banner advertisement makes customers "click through" from bricks to clicks by using the store-based promotion to go to a website. Any referral revenues generated by McDonald's are almost purely profit, because the incremental costs of offering the promotions are minimal. This is leverage, pure and simple. And this is something every consumer packaged goods company can potentially do: *get into the customer leverage business.*

Other examples of asset leverage abound. Travelocity realized that it was the only online reservation site to know exactly where a traveler is going, and when. The company now uses this information, and its relationship with customers, to create a complementary business called Virtually There, in which it serves up a set of offers for hotels, restaurants, and tourist attractions. Similarly, CCC Information Services, a leader in the auto claims processing business, realized that its key asset was its relationships with over 350 insurance companies and over 3,500 auto repair shops. It is now using this database and these relationships to create an Internet-based venture called DriveLogic, which will provide end-to-end accident management services for auto consumers. DriveLogic will encompass the entire information chain, from claim reporting to claim investigation to claim settlement. It will connect auto parts providers, insurance companies, consumers, and auto repair shops and extract service fees from the multiple transactions flowing from an auto accident.

Net-enhanced service   Remember the last time you got your driver's license renewed or your vehicle registered? You probably had to take time off from work, travel to a remote location, and wait in a long line to get to a teller. And then hope that the teller wasn't having a bad day. Teller-based customer support plagues service quality in a number of government departments and in a number of service businesses like banks, airlines, and grocery stores. But perhaps not for long. Look no further than the Arizona Motor Vehicle Department for a lesson on how the Net can be used to transform the service experience, by creating a self-service model that puts customers in control. The Arizona MVD's Web-based service, called ServiceArizona, offers a quick and easy way to renew vehicle registrations. In a simple five-step process, auto owners can enter their vehicle information, pay their fees, and collect written proof of registration. The online process costs the state $1.60 per request, as compared to $6.60 for the teller-based alternative, creating an annual savings of about $1.2 million. And customers love the new system. In its first year of operation, it was used by 5 percent of the state's residents, who gave it a 99 percent approval rating. So, customer service cost declines, while customer satisfaction actually improves.

Net-enhanced service can provide companies with other benefits, too, even in the absence of the self-service model. For example, customer service reps no longer need to be scattered all over the country. Instead, they can be located centrally, in places that may be more cost-efficient. Customer care infrastructure can be centralized, too, to achieve the obvious benefits of scale. Customer care centers need not even be in the same country as the customers themselves. They can be located in countries where labor is cheap and where there is an abundant supply of English-speaking workers. India, the Philippines, and Ireland are just a few of the countries that can provide attractive locations for customer care centers.

Ask yourself if you currently offer a self-service model to your customers. If you don't, then you need to. Customers sometimes prefer self-service, because they don't always want to take the time to explain the problem to another human being. And the calls that do get escalated to customer care reps should be those that are of higher quality and which require specialized attention.

Building the Rocket Ship

Beginning with the story of the child playing with LEGOs, our key message in this chapter has been to think like an architect about strategy. Thinking like an architect will open your mind to new possibilities for business innovation. It will help uncover new connections, combinations, and configurations and help you to think holistically and systemically about your business. By understanding business architecture, you will be armed with a powerful tool to analyze your business and have a starting point to reinvent your business.

But the biggest challenge on this journey is to find a way to blend the old with the new, in order to get the best of both worlds. You need to confront cannibalization and channel conflict. You need to think beyond disintermediation, by integrating the Net into all aspects of your channels and your business. You need to find a way to synchronize the new channels with the existing channels. This is the challenge we turn to in the next chapter.

4

E-SYNCHRONIZATION: BREAKING THE BOUNDARIES

For he that is freed from the pairs, is easily freed from conflict.

—The Bhagavad Gita

Step in the arena and break the wall down;
Step in the arena and break the wall down.

—Kid Rock

AN INDIAN FABLE tells of a debate over the true language of God. One man argues that when God gave Moses the Ten Commandments on Mount Sinai, He spoke in Hebrew, and so Hebrew is the language of God. Another man declares that when Allah spoke to Muhammad, He spoke in Arabic, and so Arabic is the language of God. Yet another man argues that because the Bhagavad Gita was written in Sanskrit, which predates both Hebrew and Arabic, then it only stands to reason that Sanskrit is the language of God. Finally, a wise man adds his voice: "If I were hungry and you were to give me an empty vessel of gold, would it fill my stomach?" "No," reply the others. He continues: "And if you were to give me an earthen pot filled with food, would that make me happier than an empty vessel of gold?" With that, the others came to realize the truth: Language is a vessel, and what matters is not the words but the meaning.

Similarly, imagine a conversation in which multiple languages are fluently spoken and used interchangeably for greatest effect. With the colloquialisms of one language flowing into the idiomatic expressions of another, the conversation takes on a contextual richness that could never be achieved were only a single language being spoken. Communication that combines multiple languages, allowing each to do what it does best, echoes a vision for how e-business can help an enterprise to synchronize its activities across different *channels* (offline versus online), across different *stages of the experience* (presales, sales, and postsales), across different *offerings* (product and service lines), and across different *business units*. It also brings home the insight that the role of the Internet is not to introduce yet another language into the conversations between firms and their customers and between different parts of the firm. Rather, its role is akin to a simultaneous translator, allowing different channels and different silos within the firm to complement each other and to act in unison toward the common goal of creating superior customer experiences.

The challenge of synchronization—a word derived from the Greek *sync*, meaning "same" and *chronos*, meaning "time"—involves breaking boundaries on two fronts. On the *external* front, synchronization means presenting a seamless face to customers, regardless of what they buy, where they buy, and how they choose to interact with the firm. External synchronization requires breaking outward-facing boundaries that separate the different channels the enterprise uses to connect with customers, and to go to market. On the *internal* front, synchronization involves creating a unified knowledge repository that stores everything the firm knows about its customers and its offerings, without regard to business units, geographies, or functional departments. Internal synchronization requires breaking inward-facing boundaries that divide functional departments, product divisions, business units, and geographical units across the enterprise.

External synchronization facilitates seamless customer experiences by allowing customers to cut across channel silos in dealing with the firm. Internal synchronization facilitates seamless learning by allowing customer knowledge to be stored and accessed across organizational silos. External synchronization and internal synchronization go hand in hand—you cannot interact seamlessly with customers without learning seamlessly about them. The benefits of synchronization go well beyond seamless customer experiences. Synchronization can lead to new views of customers and of markets in which the firm participates. These new views in turn lead to new possibilities for creating new offerings and serving new customer segments.

External Synchronization:
Presenting One Face to Customers

Established companies, in a show of devotion to customer service, commonly invite their customers to contact them in any way they please—*fax us, e-mail us, call us, visit us in person, chat with us online, send us an old-fashioned letter via the U.S. mail.* Yet despite the placards in their windows that read, "We speak *every* language," relatively few companies can, in fact, carry on a conversation that changes from one language to another—moving from a service rep at a website call center, for example, to one at a telephone call center. Consequently, a customer who tries to cross channels—in this case, resuming by phone a conversation that began with an e-mail exchange—may be disappointed to find that the company that seemed to understand her situation so well when she was typing at her keyboard, and which at the time had promised to immediately resolve the issue at hand, seems now to have erased all memory of those interactions (including the promises). Why the amnesia? It's merely a symptom. The real malady is the fragmentation of databases and systems, a consequence of a long pattern of different customer touch points funneling data into separate silos that fail to "talk" to each other. As a result, organizational memory is often channel-specific. Customers are forced to stay with the channel with which they originated, as if they were driving along a divided highway where vehicles are prohibited from changing lanes. The remedy? Break down the divider walls of the silos and allow the data that was captured through one channel, or customer touch point, to instantly become available to all other channels and touch points.

Easier said than done. In reality, database integration, essential for propagating a current, consistent, and comprehensive view of the customer relationship to the farthest reaches of the organization, can present an enormous challenge.[1] And when all *is* said and done, it can also present an enormous invoice, line-itemized by the system integration and software development firms that painstakingly carried out the implementation work. Integration can become particularly challenging when the client happens to be a conglomerate whose growth was fueled largely through acquisitions. After all, a bunch of businesses cobbled together can only mean stockpiles of data sitting across multiple pieces of the company. On the positive side, synchronization usually does *not* require that all of the pieces be hauled away and replaced with one giant, unified system—or, for that matter, that the pieces even be physically connected. Instead, following the example of the United Nations Security Council, the best course of action may be to hire a simultaneous translator that can make all of the pieces "talk" to one another. Today many companies are doing precisely that, deploying middleware solutions that extract data from their legacy databases, regardless of where and in what format the data is stored. In effect, these solutions pull customer interaction data from isolated and incompatible legacy databases into a common pool that speaks a common language. This is the concept of *virtual seamlessness*—achieved by blending the old with the new. Established companies have so much invested in legacy systems that they cannot, and should not, throw legacy away. Again, the good news is that databases need not be physically co-located, as long as the data can be tracked in one place. Provided that all interactions can be mapped to a central repository to create a single view of the customer relationship, a company can have its cake (silos) and eat it, too (synchronization).

That said, when creating new channels of connecting with customers, resist the temptation to set up additional data silos—or be prepared to pay the price. Consider the new silos that have emerged in the world of retailing. In their early forays into online merchandising, many bricks-and-mortar retailers opted for state-of-the-art e-commerce platforms that allowed them to get to market quickly. The e-commerce platform, and in many cases the entire e-commerce organization, was decoupled from the legacy systems and the core organization. Furthermore, retailers were forced to create new channels for supporting customers, including e-mail and live help on the Net. These customer care systems were also not integrated with the legacy call centers that the retailers employed in their core businesses, and new data silos were created to store e-mail, fax, and chat-based customer conversations. As a result, a host of leading retailers, from Sears and Wal-Mart to Barnes & Noble and Bloomingdale's, soon found themselves confronting a difficult synchronization challenge. If all of a retailer's channels, both online and offline, carry the same brand identity, then customers will naturally expect to be presented with one face. They will expect a seamless customer experience, which means interacting not only in multiple ways but also in internally consistent ways. They will expect synchronization of *prices*, synchronization of *inventory*, synchronization of *return policies*, and synchronization of *customer service*.

But reality can have a way of disappointing expectations. An executive at a consumer products manufacturer told us about the synchronization challenges that his company faced in managing customer promotions. Visitors to the manufacturer's website would learn of a promotion that the company was running in collaboration with retailers. Offered a retail store locator, they would drive to the nearest store, only to find that not only would it refuse to honor the promotion, but that the desired item was not even in stock. Conversely, a customer might see a promotional offer in a newspaper advertisement and decide to take advantage by visiting the retailer's website, only to find that the online prices failed to reflect the in-store sale. The problem often persists past the purchase, as customers may not be able to return merchandise that they had bought on the website to a store location. And even if retailers allow store returns for items bought on their websites, the stores may still have to manually ship the products back to the e-commerce operation's warehouses due to a lack of integration with the inventory management systems.

The need for synchronization further reinforces our argument that e-commerce spin-offs should be handled with caution, because they can create new synchronization problems. Although separation of the e-commerce operation from the parent company leads to fresh thinking and fast execution, it may also proliferate unwelcome silos. In the final analysis, synchronization may be more important than speed. Generally, it is better to be a few months late with a synchronized offering than to create new silos that may prove to be very difficult to break in the future. Ironically, in the rush to create new ways of serving customers, retailers might actually be doing their customers a disservice by funneling customer information and customer interactions into new silos. To lose the customer in the process of creating new channels is a cardinal sin. It means losing some of the most important benefits of a multichannel strategy.

While the amount of time, money, and effort spent on synchronizing touch points can vary significantly from one company to another, what remains consistent across all companies is a fundamental and irrefutable fact about customers: They don't come in online and offline versions. All are simply customers—people who expect to be treated in a consistent manner, no matter how they choose to do business with the firm. "There is no such thing as an Internet customer," agrees Rakesh Kaul, CEO of Hanover Direct, a direct marketer of specialty goods. "Customers want to be able to access their conveniences of life on a 24/7 basis through the Internet, through the telephone, through retail stores, and through catalogs."

So, while the market research firms regularly publish well-documented reports detailing their latest projections for "online versus offline sales," it becomes obvious that, no matter the results, the studies are grounded in a flawed premise. Distinguishing between "online sales" and "offline sales" is meaningless when one considers that the average customer will no doubt touch the Net at some point during the presales process, especially in the context of a major purchase or high-involvement decision. The Net and the physical channels often reinforce each other even for relatively low-involvement products. On this point, Rakesh Kaul tells of an experiment that Hanover Direct conducted with customers who had made purchases on the company's website. The customers were divided into two matched groups. One group received the regular frequency of print catalogs, while the second group received no print catalogs whatsoever. The results? "The customers with whom we communicated both through the Net and through our print catalogs turned out to be *four times* more valuable to us in terms of their order frequency than those with whom we communicated only over the Net."

The reasons that print and Web channels work so well together can be traced to how people naturally learn and process information. Studies by cognitive researchers suggest that people differ in the way that they take in and process information—some people are verbal processors while others are visual processors; some respond more strongly to images, others more to text.[2] This research strongly favors a multichannel strategy. Here the implication is that seeing a product in a print catalog, reading about it on a website, seeing the product on a store shelf, and talking about it with a sales rep all become reinforcing components of the learning experience that eventually culminates in a purchase. Consequently, for any multichannel firm, all channels, including the Net, can play an instrumental role in the customer's buying experience. How and where the actual transaction takes place would seem to be of no greater importance than whether the customer pays by check or by credit card. Yet companies continue to treat the Net as something that exists separate from their business. Take, for example, the oft-used expression "branding on the Net." There is no such thing! Branding does not happen on the Net any more than it happens on television. In truth, branding happens in the minds of customers. Like the vessel in the Indian fable, the medium is the messenger, not the message. After all, people who glance up at a billboard while cruising down the highway do not become "billboard customers" any more than do people who use automated teller machines become "ATM customers."

As capabilities around e-business evolve at a breakneck speed, so too do customer expectations from e-business. Synchronization can afford customers unprecedented degrees of convenience and flexibility. Call it "the freedom to hop around." Sometimes customers want to speak to a support rep, other times they want to go the self-service route. Sometimes they want to buy online, other times in-store. Sometimes they want to return merchandise through UPS, other times at the shopping mall. As competition intensifies and customers become more demanding, firms need to be everywhere that customers want them to be—marketing in all the ways that customers want to be reached, selling in all the ways that customers want to buy, and providing support in all the ways that customers want to interact.

Consider insurance customers. In discussing the rationale for an integrated, multichannel customer care network, Edward Liddy, the CEO of Allstate, explained that if at two o'clock in the morning a policyholder should be seized with the desire to check the deductible on his homeowner's insurance, there ought to be a place on the Net where he can go to access that information. If, however, that same customer should want to modify the terms of the policy or initiate a new policy, he might want to seek the advice of a knowledgeable agent, which would naturally mean a phone call or an in-person visit. Because customers use different channels for different purposes and in different situations, firms need to maximize the number of ways that customers can interact with them.

Within the realm of insurance and other types of financial services, an additional dimension of synchronization emerges. It stems from the simple insight that a person is not the same person over the course of his entire life. Over time, both his product needs and his channel preferences will tend to change. Consider that most young, single professionals have relatively simple insurance needs. Because a bare-bones automobile policy might be their only need at this stage in their lives, they may be drawn to single-product financial services firms that offer only automobile insurance, offer it only through a direct marketing channel, and compete only on price.[3] But as these young, single professionals grow older, start their own families, and begin to accumulate material assets, their insurance and investing needs become more complex, triggering the need for such products as home-owner's insurance, umbrella insurance, long-term disability insurance, supplemental term insurance, whole and variable life insurance, and estate planning. Their lifestyle changes also shift their channel prefer-ences, because the neighborhood insurance agent may now be better equipped than a direct marketing channel to help them with their complex needs. Therefore, insurance firms that offer a wider range of products through a wider range of touch points are better positioned to serve customers over a longer duration, allowing them to maintain their relationships with customers even as their needs change.

And how does an insurance firm attract these young, single pro-fessionals in the first place? The most obvious tactic is to use low-price products and low-touch channels, with the objective of gradually cross-selling other products and serving them through a variety of channels. In an effort to achieve early "lock-in," a company might even subsidize the cost of an introductory offer—again, in anticipation of the cus-tomer moving over the years from few insurance needs to multiple insurance needs. Sales reps, as well as independent agents, should always think in terms of the lifetime value of their customers, even to the point of pricing a bare-bones insurance policy as a loss leader.

The logic for synchronization, then, stems from the recognition that customers want to interact and transact with companies based on who they are, what they seek to accomplish in a specific situation, and where they are in their life cycle. To respond to this diversity of needs and situations, firms need to create multiple points of presence, fully integrated in order to deliver a seamless customer experience. They need to treat every customer as a unique individual, regardless of the channel that they selected to interact with the firm, instead of treating all customers alike and discriminating between them based on their channel preference.[4] Indeed, in a quiet moment of introspection a firm might ask itself: What is the object of my devotion? Am I devoted to my channel or to my customer? At times, it seems, marketers are beholden to their channels but agnostic when it comes to their customers. Clearly, the opposite should be the case—that is, a company should be *channel-agnostic* and *customer-dedicated*. A channel is merely a means to an end. In the case of customer care, the end is the resolution of a problem or the fulfillment of a request. What matters is not the channel through which the customer communicates that request, but, rather, the ability of the company to capture, store, and track all interactions with that customer across all possible touch points to create a seamless conversation.

The Case for Selective Synchronization

Although generally viewed as the ideal to which every company should aspire, complete synchronization may in fact *not* be desirable in all situations. In some cases a company may deliberately refrain from fully synchronizing its brand name with its product and service offerings, even while working hard to fully synchronize its inventory management and procurement systems. Call it *selective synchronization*. The result is greater flexibility and looser "tethers" between the parent company and its e-commerce venture.

Consider the contrasting strategies of two titans of discount retailing: Wal-Mart and Kmart. Wal-Mart opted to name its online venture Walmart.com, while Kmart chose a separate but synergistic brand name, calling its online venture BlueLight.com, after the famous "blue light specials" with which its shoppers are so familiar. Wal-Mart, by choosing a unified name, has committed to a deep level of synchronization and tighter tethers to the mother ship. Of course, tight synchronization can have its advantages. For instance, the common brand name confers instant recognition to Walmart.com, thereby obviating the need to invest tens of millions of dollars to build a new brand identity. The online channel can be effectively promoted in Wal-Mart stores, and vice versa. But this strategy has its drawbacks, too. Walmart.com faces constraints in what it can do online, as enforced by "the branding police," as everything on the website impacts the customer perception of the unified entity. The customer experience has to closely mirror the retail store experience in terms of prices, inventory, variety, credit policies, and return policies. Because the online venture cannot stray too far from its roots without the risk of diluting the parent brand, Walmart.com will always be seen as just another channel for the parent firm, limited in its ability to strike out in new directions.

Kmart took a different approach. Here the goal was to leverage the brand equity of Kmart, which has a loyal and expansive customer base of middle-class Americans, with 85 percent of them living within fifteen minutes of one of Kmart's 2,164 store locations. With BlueLight.com, Kmart also aimed to reach a more upscale customer segment, and also extend into new categories and new offerings. By avoiding the direct use of the Kmart name, BlueLight.com would be able to enjoy greater flexibility in merchandising—and, in fact, about 20 percent of BlueLight.com's products are unavailable in Kmart stores. That said, the stores offer BlueLight.com kiosks and accept BlueLight.com returns. Eventually, the point-of-sale systems in the stores will become integrated with the online e-commerce system, as will the affiliate rewards programs. So, BlueLight.com is synchronized in some respects, while remaining separate in other respects.

While time will tell whether Kmart's selective synchronization or Wal-Mart's deeper synchronization will prove superior, it's clear that the Kmart strategy will act as a centrifugal force, gradually driving BlueLight.com in a different direction, while the Wal-Mart strategy will act as a centripetal force, gradually creating tighter integration between the online and the offline operations. To the extent that both ventures involve venture capital firms that intend to take them public as independent entities, the centrifugal force may be more in line with this objective.

Internal Synchronization:
Creating New Views of the Company

On January 13, 1999, Michael Jordan announced his retirement from the Chicago Bulls. The very next day, eBay announced the opening of a brand new storefront on its website. Entirely devoted to Michael Jordan memorabilia, its products ranged from Jordan's 1986 Fleer rookie card to autographed game jerseys to Upper Deck's "Last Shot," a photo showing Jordan in a familiar situation—sinking the final shot in a Bulls victory. "Now looks like the right time to capture one or more of his epic performances in the form of a Jordan collectible," wrote a contributing editor to the world's fastest-growing auction website.

How was it possible that in such a short amount of time—literally, overnight—eBay was able to aggregate dozens of different products from hundreds of individual sellers to create a one-stop shop devoted to Michael Jordan memorabilia? The answer, of course, has everything to do with the use of a single relational database for all product information. A virtual storefront that revolves around a certain theme, such as Michael Jordan, simply becomes a view into the unified database of products offered for sale by eBay sellers. Gil Penchina, an executive at eBay, calls this "adaptive categorization." Because the storefronts are merely ways of slicing the database, new ones can be created on the fly, based on new categories that emerge over time or in response to specific events.

Look inside any traditional multidivisional company and you will find impermeable silos that reflect the traditional definition of its business. Product lines, business units, and geographies are separated by walls of tradition. Different parts of the company can end up selling to the same customers, and even competing for the same business, without even knowing it. And the more decentralized the business, the greater the silo problems and the more the missed opportunities to sell across silos.

Consider the 3M Corporation, a 98-year-old paragon of decentralization and innovation.[5] The company is a study in product diversity. Brands that begin with the letter A alone include everything from wallpaper remover and antacid tablets to fiberoptic cable and firefighting foam. The $15 billion company sells more than 50,000 products in 200 counties through over 40 divisions. These divisions function as separate companies, with their own processes, products, and systems. Until recently, sales reps from each division called on customers independently, and each business unit collected its own sales and product information which it would then store in its own data silo. As a result, the left hand never quite knew what the right hand was doing, and it was impossible to answer a simple question: How much business does 3M do with a specific customer? Without knowing this answer, it was impossible for 3M to uncover cross-selling opportunities, or to even assess how important each customer was to the company as a whole.

Indeed, a customer who makes purchases from several different business units, all within the same company, is likely to be viewed as several different customers. Consider an AT&T customer who has five different relationships with the company: long distance, wireless, cable TV, cable modem, and credit card services. Today, that customer is likely to be tracked in five different databases as five different customers. Similarly, as most customer databases are currently configured, phone customers are phone customers and Web customers are Web customers, and never the twain shall meet. Simply put, when it comes to managing customer data across the entire organization, many established companies bump up against divider walls. One divider wall is the channel through which customers come into the company, another is the business unit, or product division, from which they make their purchases.

In the case of 3M, each business unit had to keep its customer database separately updated, a mammoth task that was duplicative and error-prone, to the extent that 40 percent of the records in its customer database had invalid addresses. Decentralized and poorly coordinated, the 3M websites mirrored the structure of the company itself, where customers had to visit several different websites to get information on products that cut across 3M divisions and departments. For instance, a healthcare professional might buy products and services from the Pharmaceutical Division, the Skin Health Division, the Medical-Surgical Division, the Medical Specialties Department, and the Office Supplies Division. To get information about these products, the professional would have to register separately with each of these division's websites, with a different password and user ID. And if a customer transacted with one business unit, no record of that transaction would be available to any other business unit. To make matters worse, the websites all had different design layouts, navigation schemes, and registration procedures. In short, 3M offered many different faces to its customers, all of them organized around its internal silos.

In 1997 the company decided to fix the problem by implementing a $20 million initiative to create a global enterprise data warehouse to store customer, product, sales, inventory, and financial data across all product divisions and geographies. The integrated database tracks 250,000 customer relationships and 500,000 product configurations. The site itself features a single registration and password, a single search engine, a consistent look and feel, and a proactive product recommendation engine. The product database displays all prices, availability, and specifications across all geographies and all product divisions. All of 3M's employees and partners can query the database directly from their desktops, using a Web browser. Individual records can be summarized to give a global picture of each customer account. Customer profitability, product profitability, and partner performance can be analyzed to improve resource allocation. Internal synchronization allows 3M to present a unified face to its customers, as well as to its employees and partners.

Moreover, internal synchronization allows 3M to present *new faces* to its customers. With customer relationships and product configurations now stored in a unified database, the company can turn on a dime to redesign, reaggregate, and reconfigure new views of its customer base in a fashion that resembles eBay's "adaptive categorization" capability. Although 3M remains organized by product divisions, its offerings are now free to coalesce around new points of aggregation that are customer-centric, not product-centric. For instance, the company has created a new set of "views" through ten "customer centers" organized around various customer segments and vertical markets. These customer centers, each of which pulls together all of the relevant products and services from across the entire 3M organization, include Health Care, Home & Leisure, Graphic Arts, Architecture & Construction, and Office. These are the new faces of 3M, organized around customers, not around products. No longer do the company's wares need to be presented silo by silo — even though the silos themselves continue to exist for a good reason, which is to drive new product innovation.

Unification of product and customer databases breaks down the walls between silos, even though the silos themselves don't go away. In particular, unification of the product database allows the company to look *across products*, while unification of the customer database allows the company to look *across customers*. Why do the two databases need to interact? Because the same customer may be interested in products and services from more than one product division. The goal should be twofold: create one view of the customer relationship, and create one place for storing the product information. By combining these two repositories into one, a company can then slice it and dice it to create *targeted bundles of products and services*, in combinations perhaps never before offered, much less imagined.

The notion of bundling can be expressed in multiple ways, above and beyond just stapling invoices together and sending them in a single envelope (and integrating invoices doesn't just mean printing one out after another!). First, bundling presupposes a deep understanding of a customer's purchasing behavior. Second, as we suggested, it recognizes the amount of value the customer brings. Without unified customer databases, a company can never know how much a customer spends and would therefore have no basis for projecting the lifetime value of that relationship. Furthermore, it would never know what products and services to cross-sell and up-sell. To push ancillary products and services, the company would have to adopt a sledgehammer approach. Given unification of databases, the company could instead cross-sell and up-sell in ways that are finely tuned to a customer's individual buying patterns.

An interesting paradox: The more unified the internal customer relationship repository, the more diverse and flexible the external faces the firm can present to its customers. This brings us to a deeper and more general insight about synchronization. It stems from a fundamental fact about customers: They don't think in terms of products. Instead, they think in terms of the activities they perform and the benefits they seek. Products are a means to performing these activities and satisfying their needs. Customers think about markets very differently from the way sellers think about markets.[6] Sellers organize themselves around *products*, while customers tend to think in terms of related *activities* and *needs*. The disconnect between how customers think and how firms sell commonly results in inefficiencies and missed opportunities. Activities that would seem to be logically related in people's minds may, in reality, be spread across diverse product divisions.

The automobile industry provides an excellent example of the difference between product-centric markets and activity-centric markets. For instance, a person may own a Ford Taurus, rent from Hertz, have an account with Ford's Credit Department, get his car serviced at a Ford maintenance and repair center, and want to sell a used car to a Ford dealership. Customers think about these activities as logically related, because they constitute elements of the end-to-end Ford ownership experience. But, conversely, the Ford Motor Company has no single memory of the customer. Its knowledge of the customer is pigeon-holed in the various Ford business units. To repair this disconnect, Ford has created a joint venture, called Percepta, which is creating unified customer relationship management centers across the entire company. These centers will compile a cumulative memory of the customer relationship with the entire Ford Motor Company, a relationship that may cut across the boundaries that separate brands, business units, and geographies.

When you break boundaries through internal synchronization, you can realign your markets and your offerings to see new connections. The new boundaries of markets can be drawn around how customers actually think, buy, and behave. Internal synchronization allows firms to remove artificial distinctions of product lines, business units, and geography. With an integrated customer and product database, companies can start to see not only *one* view of their customers, but also *new* views of their customers. For instance, advertisers have always used geography as an important basis for segmentation, not because doing so makes the most sense, but because they've had little other choice. In reality, certain customer segments—the global teen market, for example—transcend national boundaries. Called *echo boomers*, the *baby boomlet*, and *Generation Y* in the United States, their wants, needs, and spending power are hardly unique to this country. Until now, however, advertisers have never had the means by which to reach the global teen market en masse. They were ham strung to run ad campaigns on a country-by-country basis using conventional media—newspapers, magazines, radio, and TV. But now companies can mine a global database and target customers based on criteria unlimited by geographical boundaries.

In making the transition from being a product-driven organization to one that is customer-oriented, the start and end point should be: How do customers buy? How do they think? What makes them tick? By removing such artificial distinctions as geography and product lines, a company may be in for a big surprise: It may learn from its own customers that its business actually looks very different from how it is currently structured and organized.

Knowledge Synchronization: Learning Across Boundaries

Step inside the corporate headquarters of Palm, Inc., in Santa Clara, California, and the first thing you're likely to notice is a poster-size image of the defining feature of its handheld computer products: the HotSync button. As millions of Palm users know, dropping the handheld into its docking cradle and pressing the HotSync button allows it to effortlessly and seamlessly synchronize its data with the desktop. In one fell swoop the boundaries between the two data silos disappear. The poster speaks volumes about one of Palm Inc.'s key innovations and biggest selling points, and it also speaks volumes about the promise of e-business in general. Ask yourself: Does *my* company have a HotSync button?

The question is especially applicable in the context of knowledge transfer. Ask yourself: Does my company learn across the boundaries that divide its operations, or does it have knowledge silos that prevent it from learning in a seamless manner? Knowledge synchronization is the vision of every new insight and every new piece of knowledge becoming instantly available to every employee across the organization. To illustrate the power of knowledge synchronization, consider a scenario that takes place in Malaysia: A brand manager working for a multinational consumer goods company wants to create a local advertising campaign for a new brand of deodorant. As a first order of business, she hires a local ad agency, which immediately puts its creative juices to work to create a positioning statement. Weeks later, having racked up considerable fees, the agency unveils its plan of attack as it prepares to move forward with the creative execution. At that point the brand manager and ad agency can only cross their fingers and hope for the desired results. In the process of creating this advertising campaign, the brand manager, sitting at her desk in Malaysia, probably reinvented the wheel. Somewhere, sometime, someone in the company probably knew something about advertising campaigns for deodorants that might have saved her a lot of time and effort, and given her better odds at success. But this company was suffering from a common disease: corporate amnesia caused by ineffective knowledge synchronization.

Now imagine a contrasting scenario. This time the same brand manager, rather than picking up the phone to call the ad agency, logs onto her computer and connects with an enterprisewide knowledge base. There, she inputs basic information about the product category, the market conditions, the competitive context, and the demographic profile of the target audience. She answers questions about market share, the depth of distribution, and the primary sales channels—in this case, department stores, specialty boutiques, and drugstores. Finally, she enters information about the specifics of the advertising campaign. What's the budget? Is the media print, TV, or radio? Will the approach be "celebrity endorsement," "man on the street," or "the product as hero"? Based on these and other inputs, the program conducts a search on every advertisement that the company has ever run, returning the results that most closely match the current context. In this case it turns out that the "nearest neighbor" is an advertisement that ran two years ago in Brazil for another personal hygiene product and produced favorable results in terms of brand awareness and trial.

The results include the video clip of the actual advertisement, the awareness and sales numbers that were produced as a result of the campaign, as well as dynamically generated notes that explain some of the contextual differences between the Brazilian campaign and the one currently under development for Malaysia. While the knowledge base cannot create an advertising campaign by itself, it certainly can give the brand manager a significant head start in strategy formulation by supplementing managerial creativity with the objective knowledge that the company has gathered over time.

Without a unified knowledge management system, this scenario could never become a reality—which in fact it is. In 1994, P&G pioneered a standardized worldwide ad-testing system. Loaded into the system were all of the ads that P&G had ever produced (at the time, the company was market testing over 2,000 ads per year). The indexing scheme supported unconventional search queries. For example, a user could search by benefit: "Show me all advertisements that we have done on 'cream' or 'shine.'" The results might be a hand lotion or a furniture polish. And the system could produce some unconventional insights and patterns. For instance, a brand manager struggling for a creative way to communicate the benefit of "skin as fresh as a baby" for a face cream may find inspiration from an advertising campaign for diapers that was effective at communicating the benefit of "clean bottoms for babies."[7] Like neurons in the brain that connect in unforeseeable ways to create new insights, the elements of knowledge in a rich knowledge base can connect and combine in serendipitous ways.

A company needs to know what it knows. It needs to collect the world's knowledge and put it all in one place. But whereas all the managers once had to come to that place—a climate-controlled room featuring a mainframe computer—now, what if everything the company knows could be brought to the desktop of every manager across the entire organization? The power of a conglomerate shines when it is able to transmit learning across all of its silos—its geographic silos, its lines-of-business silos, and its brand silos.

Now, let's take a broader view of capturing and sharing information. Imagine that every time any operating unit were to submit a request—be it in reference to acquiring a technology, hiring a consultant, hiring a vendor, or developing software code—the request would get logged into a database. Then, any other business unit with a request could rummage around in this "pizza bin" to see whether others have already had that request fulfilled. So while the e-business organization would not subsidize any of the costs, it could serve as a matchmaker between external vendors and internal customers for the desired technologies or services, in which case it could *share* the costs. By aggregating demand across business units to create an internal marketplace, the e-business organization could help the company better realize economies of scale in purchasing. It becomes the hub, with the vendors as the sellers and the business units as the customers. By screening vendors and making introductions between vendors and business units, the e-business organization could facilitate interactions across the business units, ensuring that learning about e-business experiments conducted by one business unit is rapidly and instantaneously made available to all other business units in the company.

For instance, the e-business organization might have helped one business unit to develop a Web-based wireless application for its field sales representatives. This application would involve teaming with a software application provider, a hardware vendor, a connectivity provider, and a system integrator. If the application and set of partners work well, then the e-business organization immediately has a new "offering" that it can then market to other business units. The pitch: "We know that this application works, and we know that these partners will deliver. Here are the results, and here's the internal team you can use as a reference." As additional business units buy into the application, the e-business organization can then turn around and ask for a discount for additional implementation. Imagine the power of being able to learn from every single e-business experiment in any business unit. Not only does a company avoid reinventing the wheel, but the wheels actually end up costing less.

The power of knowledge synchronization grows exponentially with the size and diversity of the business. Industry giants like GE, 3M, and Unilever have far more to learn across their business units, product divisions, and geographical locations than do single-product companies with operations in only a small number of markets. In fact, a key factor in GE's success has been the company's ability to transfer learning and best practices across all of its business units in a highly effective manner. The Net can take knowledge sharing and cross-leveling to new heights. And the cumulative learning is far greater than the sum of its parts, given the new insights that can emerge from having connected knowledge across very different knowledge domains.

In summary, let's take a simplistic notion of what a company does. It buys. It makes. It sells. In terms of buying, synchronization with suppliers creates economies of scale. In terms of making, synchronization enables learning, collaboration, and better coordination across business units. And in terms of selling, synchronization creates unified views of customers and products that permit new points of aggregation, new views into the marketplace, and new cross-selling and up-selling opportunities. A combination of external synchronization and internal synchronization leads to the vision of the seamless company, with no boundaries inside or outside (see Figure 4-1).

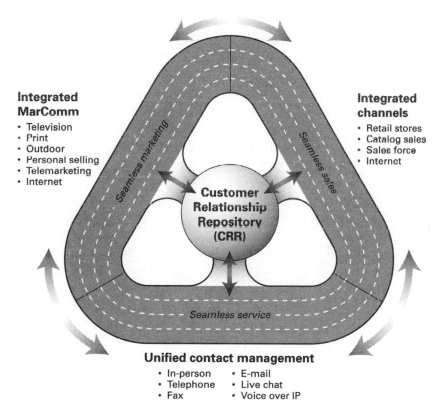

Figure 4-1
The seamless company

Barriers to Synchronization:
The Problem of "Plus One" Thinking

"Several years have now passed since I first realized how numerous were the false opinions that in my youth I had taken to be true, and thus how doubtful were all those that I had subsequently built upon them," wrote the seventeenth-century philosopher René Descartes. "And thus I realized that once in my life I had to raze everything to the ground and begin from the original foundations."

Questioning underlying assumptions, and feeling the need to justify the underpinnings of every undertaking anew, describes the notion of *zero-based budgeting*. If Descartes were a modern day project manager working in Corporate America, he would surely insist upon starting each new project with a clean slate in terms of budget allocations. Starting from scratch, he would then assess all of the line items that make up the budget, as opposed to merely adding or subtracting on an incremental basis with respect to a preexisting budget—e.g., a request for a 10 percent increase over FY 2000.

In creating a vision for synchronization, executives need to think like Descartes. Which is to say that they should eliminate the all-too-common perception of the Net as a *plus-one* solution. Many people still have a tendency to view the Net as an additional channel to the n number of channels already in use. In fact, the Net is *not* a plus-one solution. It is not a new channel that can be simply plugged into the well-worn scheme of existing channels—e.g., TV, radio, and print for marketing communications; phone, fax, and mail for customer support; and catalogs and retail stores for actual sales—with the expectation that it will then perform a discrete set of functionalities for a discrete set of customers. It is a mistake to view the Net as a channel that operates autonomously, distinct and separate from the other channels. This plus-one thinking leads to the mistaken idea that the Net is a substitute for existing channels, and the myopic notion that it will disintermediate the channel partners with which the firm does business. Plus-one thinking is the antithesis of what e-business is about. E-business is the *destroyer* of boundaries that separate functions, geographies, and enterprises. Seeing the Internet channel as a bolt-on to your business involves *creating* new boundaries, and new boundaries always lead to conflict, because they encroach upon turf that people already occupy. We believe that plus-one thinking leads to a myth of substitution, and this in turn is the cause of much of the channel conflict that paralyzes businesses as they embark upon their e-commerce initiatives.

This substitution mentality also underlies the flawed concept of the pure play e-retailing firms that viewed themselves as perfect substitutes for bricks-and-mortar incumbents. In reality, as we discuss later in this chapter, the Internet should be viewed as an *enabler* of all existing channels, rather than a substitute for existing channels, or a disintermediator of existing channel partners. To understand why this plus-one and "either/or" thinking is so pervasive, we need only look back at how people have always tended to respond to new ideas and new technologies. This look back will allow us to look forward in creative ways, by finding the "and" where there seems to be "either/or," and by finding the complements where there seems to be only substitutes.

Inside "Either/Or" Thinking: The Myth of Substitution

In 1982, John Naisbitt wrote about "megatrends."[8] With respect to everyday consumer goods, he observed that until the 1950s or 1960s customers often had only two basic options from which to choose. They could choose from chocolate or vanilla ice cream (with strawberry occasionally thrown in for Neapolitan). They could choose a Chevy or a Ford. Only relatively recently did Baskin-Robbins 31 Flavors appear, along with an assortment of imported cars from Japan and Europe. Gradually, we became transformed from an "either/or" to a "multiple option" society. And yet our thinking continues to be grounded in the "either/or," as we struggle to expand beyond binary thinking to greater intellectual diversity.

At the same time *Megatrends* was climbing the charts on its way to becoming an international bestseller, the videocassette recorder was beginning to make inroads into people's homes. When it came to this particular trend, movie studios were up in arms. Why? Because they were certain that people would no longer go to the movies, but simply stay home and watch them on VCRs. But while the fear that videocassette rentals would cannibalize ticket sales in movie theaters prompted intense resistance within the industry, theaters did not go the way of the buggy whip. Quite to the contrary, U.S. box office receipts grew 55 percent in the 1990s, reaching an all-time high of $7.5 billion in 1999. The number of movie theaters has more than doubled in the past two decades, from 17,590 screens in 1980, when the VCR was just beginning to emerge, to 37,185 screens in 1999. Meanwhile, by 1998 renting and selling videocassettes and DVDs had grown into a $17 billion business, with sales estimated to reach $22 billion in 2002.[9] Therefore, not only did the VCR *not* kill off movie theaters, it was quite possibly the best thing that could have happened to the motion picture industry, because it created a market that complemented the business of showing movies in movie theaters. It did so by creating alternative viewing occasions for customers who otherwise would not have gone to movie theaters, like parents with small children, kids who watch the same movies over and over again, or people who simply prefer to watch movies in the comfort of their own home. In fact, the reason the motion picture industry exists in any profitable form today may be credited to the invention of the VCR. The two channels turned out to be complements, not substitutes. However, the industry establishment failed to appreciate this possibility, simply because its view of the world was based on historical moviegoer demographic trends. Movie makers were prisoners of their own knowledge and experience.

Television serves as another example of the myth of substitution. With the rise of television, many predicted the demise of radio. Like their later movie theater counterparts, these naysayers were victims of a view based on an incomplete understanding of the new technology's benefits. Today radio is alive and well. However, it has moved out of the living room and into our automobiles. Radio now serves a different need in a different situation—streaming news, weather, traffic, talk shows, and music to commuters who spend billions of hours commuting to and from work. The morning radio talk show has become as integral a part of people's lives as the evening news bulletins on radio fifty years ago.

The entertainment industry has seen many substitution myths in addition to the TV and VCR. For example, electric keyboards and guitars did not replace their acoustic counterparts; instead, they spawned new musical genres. In a similar vein, digital audio recording technology has reached such an advanced state that a "perfect" performance is now feasible. But people still happily fork out $50 or more to see an imperfect concert. Why? For the same reason people still go to the movie theater: The consumption experience is fundamentally different.

Analog watches did not disappear with the introduction of digital watches. Rather, they moved to serve a different customer segment, for a different purpose: analog watches for those seeking a fashion accessory, digital for the practical-minded. Similarly, the microwave was originally positioned as a substitute for stovetop cooking. Yet today it is hard to imagine getting by with only one or the other. The common theme: Rather than serving as a perfect substitute for an old technology, new technologies often end up complementing the old technology. However, in doing so, the old technology often ends up satisfying a different need, serving a different customer segment, or being utilized for a different end-use situation. The new and the old end up co-existing in a hybrid world where the roles of both technologies are different from what was originally envisaged.

The myth of substitution arises from our tendency to think in terms of opposites and substitutes. It arises from our tendency to create artificial boundaries that divide the old and the new into mutually exclusive "black" and "white" categories. However, the truth is rarely black and white. It is somewhere in between. Thinking in terms of substitutes drives us toward channel conflict and the creation of new boundaries. Thinking in terms of complements drives us toward channel synchronization and allows us to break boundaries. To break boundaries, we must get past thinking in terms of opposites.

The Tyranny of Opposites and the Wisdom of Grayness

At first glance life always seems to come in opposites. Up versus down, in versus out, us versus them, north versus south, Internet versus intranet, bricks versus clicks, new economy versus old economy, and so on. So commonplace are these dichotomies that we hardly give them any notice. But when you do think about opposites, you begin to realize that opposites are often an illusion and are often two sides of the same coin. In the words of Nicholas of Cusa, reality is *coincidentia oppositorum*—the coincidence of opposites.[10] The boundaries that we draw between opposites are rooted in *duality*, a concept with deep roots in philosophy and religion. In theology, duality is the doctrine that there are two eternal and opposing principles—one good and the other evil. In philosophy, duality is the idea that there are two fundamental substances or principles—the mind and the spirit.

Duality fosters boundaries by emphasizing the black and the white end points of a continuum of gray. In focusing on the black and white, we often lose sight of the fact that the end points are dual but the underlying continuum is unified. Indeed, black and white illuminate the nature of grayness. This is the paradox of opposites. At a deeper level, as we've said, opposites are often two sides of the same coin. Where we see apparent opposites or duality, there is often a deeper principle that unifies the opposites into a broader construct. Eastern religions observe that duality is an illusion. To overcome the illusion, we need to search for the unifying principle.

Interestingly, the principle that knowledge advances through the unification of apparent dualities also characterizes advancements in modern physics. Indeed, the twentieth century saw the resolution of three major conflicts in physics, all of them resolved with a unification principle. In 1905, Albert Einstein resolved a fundamental conflict between Newton's laws of motion and Maxwell's theory of electromagnetism. Newton's theory stated that if we caught up with a beam of light by traveling at light speed, light would appear stationary. But Maxwell's theory contends that light never slows down. Einstein's Special Theory of Relativity resolved this paradox by arguing that space and time are not absolute and separate. Rather, they are interwoven and unified in a four-dimensional space-time. Einstein also showed that matter and energy are not dual and separate. They are unified and inconvertible.

Moreover, Newton's theory suggests that gravitation involves influences that are transmitted instantaneously across space. But this conflicts with the assertion of Einstein's Special Theory of Relativity, which states that nothing can travel faster than the speed of light. Again, Einstein made a breakthrough by unifying gravity with space and time in his General Theory of Relativity. He showed that space and time actually warp and curve in response to the presence of matter and energy. Indeed, gravity *is* the curvature of space and time. Einstein allowed us to see space, time, matter, energy, and gravity as a unified whole.

Yet the General Theory of Relativity, which seeks to explain the behavior of matter at the largest of scales, created another conflict, this time with Quantum Mechanics, a theory that seeks to explain the behavior of matter at the smallest of scales. These two theories produce views of the world that are so contradictory, it would seem that only one of them could be right. But recent developments suggest that String Theory may be the Holy Grail of unification.[11] String Theory may finally unify all known forces in nature. The pattern that emerges across these three conflicts and their subsequent resolution is clear: As science advances, duality blurs and yields a powerful unification principle.

At a more mundane level, we can apply the wisdom of grayness by observing that duality between polar opposites is often an illusion fostered by boundary-focused thinking. In understanding a dual concept, we tend to focus on the boundaries that define the end points, causing the pendulum of our understanding to swing violently between the extremes of black and white. Upon deeper reflection, the pendulum usually settles in the middle, with the emergence of a unifying principle that merges the opposites. Figure 4-2 illustrates this idea within the domains of business and technology. For instance, the boundary between e-business and business is blurring as the Net becomes an integral tool for doing business. Similarly, the pendulum that swung in favor of pure play B2B exchanges later swung back to the other extreme, with the announcement of the industry-led B2B consortia. Given the general pattern, one can see the emergence of hybrid exchanges that will combine the liquidity and assets of the established bricks-and-mortar companies with the speed and neutrality of the independent exchanges.

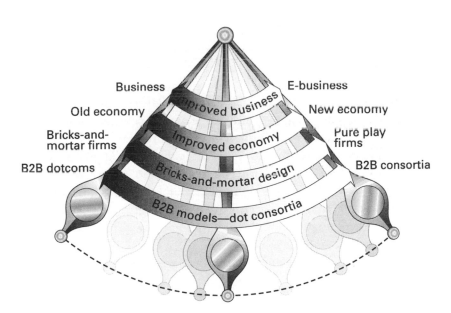

Figure 4-2
The pendulum swings, but then settles

The wisdom of grayness leads to a simple, yet profound, insight about the role of the Internet in channels. It allows us to shift our thinking from channel conflict to channel *enablement*.

Transcending Channel Conflict

The biggest hurdle in channel synchronization is the conflict that arises from the fear that the Internet will allow firms to connect directly with their customers and will end up substituting for existing channels. Open the business section of any newspaper and there is bound to be some version of the online *versus* offline story. But online versus offline is a myth; in reality, online *complements* offline.

Drawing inspiration from the myth of substitution and the tyranny of opposites, it becomes clear that the concept of channel disintermediation is deeply flawed, for a simple reason. A fundamental premise in channel design is that different channels are good at providing different service outputs to customers.[12] So substituting one vertically integrated channel (say, a retail salesperson) with another vertically integrated channel (say, the Net) is an "either/or" approach, where the assumption is that one channel will be used to perform all channel functions and provide customers with all of the service outputs. In reality, this is too extreme a course of action, because it is a *corner solution*—a channel design where one channel ends up doing nothing, and is therefore eliminated, while another channel performs all the functions.[13]

Suppose that a customer at a salad bar wants to make a fruit salad composed of apples, oranges, and bananas. The corner solution dictates that the customer use only apples or only oranges. The *hybrid solution* allows the customer to mix and match the fruit and make the salad to his or her taste. Very rarely will firms find corner solutions to be optimal. In most cases the optimal channel design will be a hybrid solution, where channel functions are reallocated across different channels and all channels work in tandem to provide the best configuration of service outputs to customers.

Corner solutions are the black and white extremes that give rise to channel conflict. Hybrid solutions are the grays in between, which allow us to move away from conflict and toward synchronization.

The myth of substitution also teaches us that in the hybrid world where the old and the new co-exist, both get transformed. And in some cases the old technology gets relegated to a niche role, while the new technology comes to dominate the market. The same is true of the role that the Net will play across specific industries as a sales and customer interaction channel. In some industries the Net will become a primary channel for sales and customer interaction, while in other industries conventional channels will remain the primary point for conducting transactions and demonstrating products, with the Net playing a supportive role in providing information to customers.

Understanding the Net Effect on Channels

Until somebody figures out a way to digitize gasoline, drivers stand little chance of one day being able to download it to their fuel tanks over an Internet connection. Equally unlikely, though not altogether impossible, is a scenario in which they would have gasoline brought to the home via a delivery truck. While practically every commodity under the sun can now be ordered online and shipped to consumers within a few days of ordering, drivers in need of refueling will have to continue to pump gasoline the old-fashioned way: at brick-and-mortar service stations.[14] Indeed, when it comes to their traditional sales and distribution channels, executives at Mobil, Exxon, and Shell need not lose sleep over the prospect of an unseen competitor one day using the Net to render obsolete their existing channel design. However, the same can't be said for executives at companies whose products are far less dependent than twenty-gallon units of gasoline on a physical point of presence for sales and distribution—and are instead far more amenable to being sold over the Net.

Several structural factors related to the product, the channel, and the industry dictate the extent to which the Net can assume the functions of traditional channel intermediaries and emerge as a stand-alone direct channel. The first factor is the *complexity of the exchange*, which refers to the amount of information exchanged between the customer and the firm throughout the entire presales, sales, and postsales process. If the buying and ownership experience demands intense interaction with a significant amount of back-and-forth communication, and if the customer requires a large amount of advice and consultation during the purchase decision process, it is unlikely the Net could serve as the *sole* channel for conveying that information. In this case, disintermediation of the salesperson is not feasible, because consultative selling and customer advising add significant value in the sales and support process. On the other hand, in situations where customers demand only a minimal exchange of standardized information, say in buying a book or a domestic airline ticket, the Internet may well emerge as the primary sales and support channel, while in-person selling gets gradually pushed to the sidelines.

A second factor is *asset specialization*. Two key questions to ask: Is the channel using specialized fulfillment, warehousing, and logistics such that these assets would need to be replicated if the company were to go around the traditional channel? Would the company have to create its own direct fulfillment systems, or could the logistics be easily outsourced to a third-party distributor? For instance, in the chemicals manufacturing industry, specialty chemicals and reagents can generally be shipped through third-party logistics providers like UPS, whereas bulk chemicals may require 6,000-gallon low-pressure tank trucks, which chemicals distributors may have, but UPS certainly does not. Similarly, crates of apples and oranges can be shipped via FedEx, but bulk grain requires specialized transportation, such as rail cars. In general, the more specialized the assets needed in fulfillment and logistics, the less the probability that the channel intermediaries can be replaced with a direct marketing and an outsourced direct fulfillment mechanism. Business-to-business e-commerce startups are quickly discovering that they cannot afford to ignore the events that happen before a transaction (e.g., vendor search, vendor qualification, negotiation, and specification of designs), or the events that occur after the transaction (e.g., credit approval, financing, transportation, settlement, and service). Merely facilitating transactions is not enough; a "low-touch" solution is a low value-added solution. The low-touch model may work just fine for eBay, which sells Beanie Babies and proudly proclaims that it is merely a venue for millions of other products, but it does not work well for steel, chemicals, and agricultural equipment. In these settings, the domain expertise and the specialized assets the channel partners bring to the party are valuable and dictate that the channel remains an essential participant in the Net-enabled world.

A third factor that affects the extent to which manufacturers can go direct is the level of *fragmentation* on both the supply and demand sides. The balance of power between manufacturers and resellers dictates whether manufacturers can create a direct sales channel. Companies with substantial market share and a highly fragmented constellation of resellers are typically better positioned to sell directly to end-customers than are those that would need to go around a strong and concentrated reseller like Home Depot or Wal-Mart. Where channel power is concentrated in the retail channel, distributors may use their clout to resist the attempts of manufacturers to set up their own direct commerce operations. For example, in May 1999, Home Depot issued a letter to several of its manufacturer partners, including Black & Decker and Rubbermaid, warning them to think twice before selling their products directly to customers via their own websites. The letter read, in part:

> It is important for you to be aware of Home Depot's current position on its vendors competing with the company via e-commerce direct to consumer distribution. We think it is shortsighted for vendors to ignore the added value that our retail stores contribute to the sales of their products. We recognize that a vendor has the right to sell through whatever distribution channels it desires. However, we too have the right to be selective in regard to the vendors we select, and we trust that you can understand that a company may be hesitant to do business with its competitors.[15]

On the other hand, Herman Miller has been able to initiate a direct selling program with the cooperation of its retail partners because it maintains a leading market share position and sells mostly through dedicated Herman Miller retailers. The company has succeeded by being able to convince its retail channel partners that, at the end of the day, their interests are closely aligned. Approximately 90 percent of Herman Miller's sales go through the retail distribution channel, and the retailers in turn rely almost exclusively on the company for their sales. This reciprocal dependence creates a more cooperative atmosphere for incorporating direct sales into the channel mix.

Beyond complexity, specialization, and fragmentation, a firm needs to ask itself: How well do we know our end-customers and their needs? In many cases, channel partners have intimate knowledge of end-customers because they are at the front lines, interacting with them on a daily basis. Firms that go to market through multiple layers of resellers may know very little about who uses their products, where they get used, and how they get used. In the words of an Intel executive, all that some high tech firms know about their end-customers is that "they have two legs and own a computer." If channel partners possess deep customer knowledge, either the firm has to continue to work with them for service-related and relationship-oriented functions, or it needs to replicate this knowledge in some other fashion.

The factors that drive the Net effect on channels can be summarized along two dimensions of interaction: the richness of *physical interactions* and the richness of *informational interactions*. Physical interactions refers to the interaction of customers with products, with their environment, and with other people during the buying and ownership experience. Informational interactions refer to the amount of information customers require in the entire search, evaluation, purchase, and postsales experience, and the extent to which this information can be effectively delivered over the Net.

The first aspect of physical interactions is the richness of the interaction between customers and the physical product. Some product categories are experiential in nature; they engage multiple senses, including sight, sound, taste, smell, and feel. Customers have the need to kick the tires, feel the fabric, smell the coffee, bounce on a mattress, and stroll around a new home before they feel comfortable buying in these categories. Since the Net is primarily a "sight and sound" medium, it does not permit a high fidelity of experiential interactions between customers and products. The more experiential the product category, the less likely it is that the Net would act as an effective substitute for physical channels.

Another aspect of physical interactions is between customers and the buying environment. Customers who start each morning with a rich cup of coffee at Starbucks experience an equally rich interaction with the retail environment. In some cases, as with certain chains of theme restaurants, the retail environment may actually become the primary draw. Certainly, the "atmospherics" are an important basis for differentiating department store shopping experiences. Think about the last time you entered a Nordstrom store. A man in a tuxedo is playing a grand piano. The lighting and colors are muted. An enticing aroma fills the air. The sales personnel are friendly and helpful. You inspect a rack of suits. You pull one out to match the color and feel the weight of the fabric. Sitting in front of a screen on the Nordstrom website is not quite the same experience.

Then there's the aspect of physical interaction between customer and salesperson. Consider a customer making a decision on buying an enterprise software application or a multimillion-dollar office furniture system. These big-ticket offerings are complex and customized, and customers generally require an intense level of personal handholding by salespeople during the sales process. Such selling situations are consultative in nature, where customers value the advice and empathy a salesperson can provide. They call for rich interactions between the salesperson and the customer, through a personal selling channel. Even after the sale, customers need to interact personally with the firm for installation, maintenance, repair, upgrades, and customer support. In these cases, the Net cannot function as a stand-alone channel.

Turning to informational interactions—obviously, a customer may need a significant amount of information before making the decision to buy an automobile, a house, or capital equipment for a chemical plant. In other cases, even when the offering itself may be information-rich or even pure information personal financial services, software, and airline tickets, for example—customers may actually require less information leading up to the purchase decision. Most convenience products, and some shopping goods such as books and music, also fall into this category.

These two dimensions can be crossed to create a simple framework for divining the effect that the Net will have on existing channels and the role it is likely to play in a hybrid channel world. This framework is illustrated in Figure 4-3. The four very different channel outcomes are: *channel augmentation*, *brand augmentation*, *channel proliferation*, and *channel deconstruction*.

Channel Augmentation

In high-involvement and highly experiential buying situations, customers generally need all the information and physical interaction that they can get. Most business-to-business selling situations and big-ticket consumer products fall into this category. In these situations, all possible channels need to come together to create a joint set of service outputs that satisfies the customer need. No channel is good enough by itself; all are required at some point or other. In these cases, the effect the Net has on channels is one of channel augmentation—becoming an essential ingredient in the channel mix, but not a stand-alone recipe.

Contrary to popular belief, the so-called "direct selling" that companies like Dell and Cisco tout does not just "happen" over the Net, which merely serves as the transactional channel and the channel for

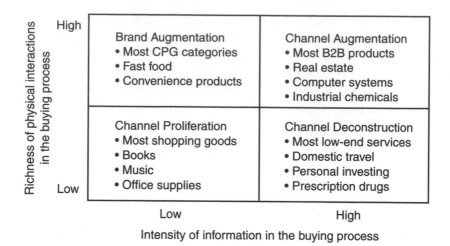

Figure 4-3
The Net effect on channels

first-line customer support. Behind the scenes, an army of salespeople is pounding the pavement and pressing the flesh. The mere fact that the Net serves as the transactional channel does not foretell the death of the salesman. Rather, the Net can be used to strengthen the sales force's reach and effectiveness with a variety of Web-based tools that can offload a large amount of routine work. Then, once a salesperson has successfully secured a new client account, the Net can take over as an effective channel for placing orders and receiving support. So even as Dell actively promotes itself as a paragon for disintermediation, the company actually uses its sales force and the Net in tandem, to keep sales humming.

"I know who I was when I got up this morning," muses Alice, in *Alice in Wonderland*, "but I think I must have changed several times since then." Today, many sales reps can empathize with Alice's confusion. While the channel augmentation outcome does not eliminate the sales force or retailers, it does change their role and the time they spend performing different functions. Freed from the need to provide order status information or respond to routine queries, salespeople and resellers can concentrate on what they do best, which is to understand customer needs and interact with them face to face.

Consider Xerox, which aims to reposition itself from a company that sells copier machines to one that manages the work flow of digital document assets. How does this repositioning change the role of its direct sales force? In fact, the company actually will now need *more* employees spending time at its clients' organizations. Until now the question for customers was: How many copies do you run and how many copiers do you need? Xerox only cared about the location of the copier and how many copies it churned out. The company didn't care much about what the document contained, where it originated, what its purpose was, why it was being copied, and who the intended recipients were. Documents, after all, are vessels that contain information and knowledge. They are merely a means to an end. Thinking like a document company will require Xerox to become far more insightful about how information and knowledge flow in its customers' businesses, and to use this understanding to develop document management systems, of which copiers are only one small component. Who's going to do this? A salesperson, but a very different kind of salesperson. Instead of someone who pushes copiers, the salesperson needs to be able to analyze business processes and work flows. The copier itself may actually be sold and supported over the Net. So while salespeople are still required in a channel augmentation outcome, they need to be repositioned, retrained, and reskilled. The transactional component of the selling role may migrate to the Net, but the presales activities become qualitatively more complex, the selling situation becomes far more consultative in nature, and the consultative role takes up a far greater proportion of the salesperson's time. There is no disintermediation here—only a redefinition of roles and a shift in priorities.

Brand Augmentation

In the land of brand augmentation, the richness of the interaction the customer experiences with the physical product, the salesperson, or the atmospherics of the store is high, so the retail store experience is an essential part of the buying experience. As such, the Net may not be particularly well suited to serve as a sales channel. Nonetheless, it can become an excellent tool for communicating and enhancing brand equity. For example, the Net can be an effective channel for augmenting the brand presence of restaurants, enhancing the marketing communications programs that allow them to better serve their customers, even though people will certainly still prefer to dine in physical restaurants and place their orders with human waiters. Similarly, people are unlikely to buy spaghetti sauce or cosmetics on the Net, but the Net can still play an important role in building a dialogue with prospective customers. Not all websites need to be selling sites. Some can be telling sites.

But do customers really want to build online relationships with their spaghetti sauce provider? Surprisingly, the answer may be yes. At Ragu.com there isn't much to see in the way of bottled spaghetti sauce. Instead, a grandmotherly figure calling herself Mama welcomes visitors into her *cucina*. She invites them to take an Italian lesson and learn about Italian architecture and Italian films and to browse through her Italian cookbook. She doesn't try to sell a jar of anything, but visitors will certainly enjoy her ebullient personality, and during their next visit to the grocery store they may, in fact, think favorably of her "pure Italian" products. Ragu is just one creative approach to the problem major marketers face with regard to consumers' attention deficit. In this case, the strategy was to engage visitors in a conversation that entertains and educates, all in the context of the brand's core value proposition, with a line of sight to the point of purchase.

Arguably, most shoppers view toothpaste as an even more mundane commodity. Who in their right mind would want an online relationship with their toothpaste provider? P&G took a slightly different approach with respect to brand-building, realizing early on that an optimal strategy might be to foster a relationship not with customers, but with dentists. Today, the Crest website is one of the best information resources available to dental practitioners—no doubt influencing their product recommendations to patients. Eventually a company may succeed at creating loyalty with a particular group of users, not necessarily the end-users, and can grow a viable community around that loyalty base. Again, there is no disintermediation here. In fact, there may not be any sales at all. But the Net allows firms to enhance brand equity by moving from one-way broadcast messaging to one-on-one personalized dialogue with customers.

Channel Proliferation

In product categories and buying situations characterized by limited physical and information interactions, the Net is likely to become simply another point of presence, another way to go to market and serve customers. In these cases, the Net can be a stand-alone channel, but the physical channel also remains a viable stand-alone channel. The different channels simply respond to different buying situations. For example, a customer may choose to buy a book online if she can wait a few days for delivery. If she wants the book immediately, however, or if before committing to buy it she wishes to first sink into a comfortable chair and leaf through its pages, then she might find herself sipping an iced tea in the cafe of a bricks-and-mortar bookstore. Often, people like to browse serendipitously in a way that electronic databases don't easily allow. They like to engage in wide-angle browsing—and of course, no wide-angle browsing lens surpasses the human eye.

In the channel proliferation outcome, the online and offline channels are not substitutes. They are both essential points of presence to serve the diverse buying occasions in which customers might find themselves. The same customers may use different channels under different situations. While the introduction of an additional channel may result in some cannibalization of sales, it is generally more important for a company to create a hybrid presence that allows it to serve customers whenever and however they choose to buy in a specific situation. Most low-end shopping goods fall into this category. These include the "classic" e-retailing categories: books, music, toys, and office supplies.

Channel Deconstruction

The world has become a dangerous place for intermediaries that add little value in building and enhancing relationships, and merely serve as conduits for brokering information and transactions. The transactions and the information can easily migrate to the Net, leaving the intermediaries with little reason to exist. In these situations, the middlemen become corner solutions—adding no residual value once the information-intensive functions are migrated to the Net. Middlemen in information-intensive businesses are particularly vulnerable to this outcome. Financial services, travel, and publishing are classic instances of industries where middlemen are being forced to question their value addition, as the information-brokering role gets commoditized, and the consultative role becomes more transparent. That airline travel has already experienced an enormous shift to the Net with the rise of online businesses like Travelocity and Expedia can be traced to the fact that many travel agents add little value beyond making bookings and delivering tickets. For that matter, how much personal time and attention do you receive from the average insurance agent or stockbroker?

To survive, channel intermediaries in the channel deconstruction quadrant need to move up to the channel augmentation quadrant, by becoming advisers, consultants, and value-added service providers. Travel agents can become travel consultants, advising their clients on the best vacation packages, finding special deals that don't appear on publicly available reservation systems, being available round the clock to respond to emergencies, or negotiating with airlines and hotels for upgrades and better rates. The "agent" role morphs into a "concierge" role, where the transaction brokering function is neither important nor the source of the travel agent's bread and butter. In fact, a travel concierge might actually encourage his customers to ultimately buy their tickets from an online provider of their choice, because the transaction itself becomes a commodity. This is not disintermediation. This is evolution in the Darwinian sense. Evolve and adapt. Or die.

Taken together, these channel outcomes prove two simple points. First, the effect the Net will have on channels will depend on the richness of physical interactions and the intensity of information exchange in the buying process. Second, in a vast majority of cases the outcome is not a corner solution, where the Internet emerges as a stand-alone channel and the *only* channel the firm uses to go to market. As we argued earlier in the chapter, a corner solution rarely turns out to be the optimal solution when you blend different channels and channel functions to create bundles of service outputs that best serve different customers. In most cases the channel outcome will be a hybrid model, where channel functions are allocated across a number of synchronized channels in order to best respond to customer needs. What will these hybrid channel designs look like? Are there any general patterns we can identify? Indeed there are.

Toward Channel Synchronization: Emerging Hybrid Channel Designs

Alciato's *Book of Emblems*, first published in 1531, offers the following proverb:

> A lame man is carried upon the shoulders of one who has lost his sight. With his eyes, the lame man repays this service of his friend. In what one lacks, it is agreed, the other is superior; one man borrows eyes, the other man borrows feet.

In the context of channels of distribution, this proverb couldn't be more timely or on target. In most cases, the Net will not substitute for channel intermediaries. Rather, when we think of the Internet and existing channels (the salesperson, the reseller, the catalog, and the telephone), it becomes clear that these different channels offer complementary service outputs, which makes it unlikely that either one alone can win. Like the lame man and the blind man, they must join forces and move forward in tandem to form a hybrid model where the Net complements the traditional channels. This hybrid channel design can take on two basic types of configurations: the *front-back hybrid pattern* and the *side-by-side hybrid pattern* (see Figure 4-4).

Front-Back Hybrid Design

In this design, two independent channels, and often two independent companies, work front-to-back to create a hybrid system that serves customers. The front-end may be a "high-tech" Internet channel, while the back-end may be a "high-touch" personal channel. Consider the real estate business. In the dotcom heyday, the proponents of disintermediation contended that the Net would put real estate agents out of business. Their argument assumed that home buyers would search, negotiate, and buy houses through a Web-based home buying site, without needing to involve a Realtor. It was thought that Realtors

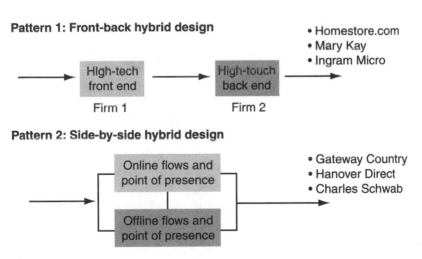

Pattern 1: Front-back hybrid design

- Homestore.com
- Mary Kay
- Ingram Micro

High-tech front end — Firm 1

High-touch back end — Firm 2

Pattern 2: Side-by-side hybrid design

- Gateway Country
- Hanover Direct
- Charles Schwab

Online flows and point of presence

Offline flows and point of presence

Figure 4-4
Hybrid channel designs

would be road kill on the information superhighway. But reality has turned out to be quite different, with numerous dotcoms in the home buying arena starting to look much more like road kill than the Realtors they set out to eliminate. Ironically, the home buying sites that are thriving actually *complement* retailers, by serving as a front-end lead generation vehicle. For example, Homestore.com operates a website called Realtor.com, which lists over 1.4 million homes for sale. These listings are drawn from over 730 Multiple Listing Services across the U.S., in collaboration with Realtors. Realtor.com channels leads to real estate agents, who then take over the relationship-oriented "back-end" of the home buying process. Realtor.com also develops customized websites, where Realtors can promote themselves and their listings. Homestore.com helps Realtors sell more homes, and it helps them sell more services to home buyers, above and beyond the home itself. These services may include home mortgages or Internet access. Again, the Net serves as a front-end channel that is technology-centric, while the Realtor serves as a back-end channel that is relationship-centric. Far from substituting one for the other, the two channels work back-to-front to complement each other.

The front-back hybrid is also proving to be the model of choice for Dallas-based Mary Kay, a $3 billion beauty and skin care manufacturer that goes to market primarily through a massive network of 800,000 independent beauty consultants who work part-time selling cosmetics. Had Mary Kay thought about the Internet in "either/or" terms, it might have set out to create a Web-based sales channel that would have ended up conflicting with its existing channel. Instead, Mary Kay realized that the sales force was its source of competitive advantage. Its army of beauty consultants have built deep relationships with end-customers and the local communities, and this level of customer intimacy could never be replicated by a Web-based channel. With this realization, Mary Kay began offering its beauty consultants the opportunity to commission their own websites, which they did. In fact, nearly 100,000 were in operation by the end of 2000. These sites allow customers to order online, pay online, and have products delivered through a third-party fulfillment agency. The Mary Kay corporate website does not sell any products directly to end-users; rather, it generates follow-up leads for the independent beauty consultants.

In this front-back hybrid, the front-end is the Mary Kay beauty consultant, while the back-end is the Mary Kay infrastructure. Similar to the Homestore.com example, Mary Kay has created a hybrid channel design where the Internet and the traditional sales channels work front-to-back to serve customers. Again, instead of an "either/or," the hybrid model is an "and." The solution to the problem was found in the shades of gray, not the black and white.

The Side-by-Side Hybrid Design

The side-by-side design paves two paths to the customer—online and offline, which coexist and jointly provide the best combination of service outputs. The side-by-side design takes into account the fact that the Net is good at some channel functions, but that other channel functions are best performed by a physical channel and real salespeople. The counterintuitive moves of Gateway, a leading PC manufacturer, offer an excellent illustration of the side-by-side design. Gateway, like Dell, has built its business on the premise that PCs need to be built cheaply and sold direct. For 15 years, Gateway has sold its computers directly to consumers, at first using call centers, and now of course the Net. But declining margins, increasing complexity of computers, and the decreasing level of computer savvy of new computer users have converged to create an important insight for Gateway: Its future lies "beyond the box" and beyond the Internet. Since 1996, Gateway has opened more than 600 Gateway Country stores and kiosks in OfficeMax locations—retail outlets where customers can test-drive computers and ultimately place orders. The stores also sell services, such as training classes, financing, and Internet access. Its suite of complementary services with high margins compensate for shrinking hardware profits. The result? More than half of Gateway's profits come from such add-ons, which could not be sold effectively without a physical presence.[16] Gateway uses the Internet and telemarketing channels to handle marketing, sales, and support, with third parties managing fulfillment. And it uses Gateway Country stores for demonstrations, returns, and to offer computer training. The channels live together in perfect harmony, side by side, like ebony and ivory on a piano keyboard.

The side-by-side pattern is also proving to be more robust than the pure play model in the financial services business. Charles Schwab provides an interesting example. Over 80 percent of all trades placed by Schwab customers are done so online. Yet an astonishing 75 percent of new accounts opened by Schwab customers are done so in its

399 branch offices spread across the country. This is the side-by-side design in action; the Net as a transactional channel, but the physical presences as the advice and handholding channel. Ironically, Schwab's "pure play" rival E*Trade, which has spent hundreds of millions of dollars telling us to "boot your broker," is scrambling to acquire networks of ATMs and open service counters in hundreds of retail stores. "Pushing our brand into the real world is the next evolution," declared the company's chief sales and marketing officer.[17] But what's the "real world"? Is a physical point of presence any more real than an online point of presence? In truth, *all* channels are real and essential.

Taking Channels Apart and Putting Them Together Again

If the case for synchronization is clear, as is the logic behind hybrid channel designs, how should a firm actually go about redesigning its existing channels? The answer: Start with your customers, and work backward to design specific go-to-market systems that mix and match all available channels, including the Net, to create a set of hybrid channels that map to specific customer segments. A key insight in this process: Channel synchronization is *not* about disintermediation of entities that are vertically integrated. Rather, it is about the reallocation of *functions and flows* across the entire spectrum of available channels, of which the Net is only one channel. The first step in the redesign process is to understand the different benefits that drive the behavior of customers in the market and determine how they respond to offerings.

To illustrate this basic point, consider 7-Eleven. Established in 1945, the 7-Eleven convenience stores were so-called because they opened at seven in the morning and closed at eleven at night. Some years later, opening hours were extended so that many stores were open twenty-four hours. The fact that 7-Elevens stayed open from early until late was widely seen as a nice benefit. However, 7-Elevens also have their share of drawbacks. These include the premium the store charges for merchandise, which is often 50 percent higher than at other retail outlets, and the selection of merchandise, which is generally limited to just a few SKUs for each product category. In summary, 7-Elevens score high on convenience but poorly on price and choice. Now, along these same three criteria, consider a "no frills" warehouse chain like Sam's Club. Because Sam's Clubs are relatively few and far between, the store performs poorly on convenience. However, owing to its buy-in-bulk discounts, the store performs well on price, and with its 3,500 items in stock, ranging from office supplies and food to jewelry and clothes, Sam's Clubs also perform well on choice. In summary, along these service outputs—convenience, price, and choice—it may be said that 7-Elevens and Sam's Clubs are polar opposites. Of course, some customers interacting with marketers through a channel may be looking for a particular set of benefits, or service outputs, other than convenience, price, and choice—for example, simplicity, quality, or support.

The next step in the exercise is to discover the sets of customers who have the same priorities and want similar benefits. This can be accomplished by creating a matrix that maps customer benefits (what customers want) against customer characteristics (who customers are). As a next step, ask: What are all the go-to-market mechanisms available to us? The Internet alone may offer several, such as affiliates for generating leads, Net-based resellers for providing online storefronts, or MRO hubs like Ariba and Commerce One for aggregating demand for indirect materials and supplies. Of course, all the existing channels—company salespeople, manufacturers' representatives, distributors, wholesalers, retailers, value-added resellers, and telemarketing channels—need to be taken into account. For each channel ask yourself: What service outputs is this channel particularly good at providing, and what service outputs is it not too good at? More than likely, each channel is currently used as a vertically integrated go-to-market mechanism that inherently involves compromises. Instead, the entire set of channel functions should be *decomposed* into their elemental components. Just as customer preferences were decomposed in terms of demand, the service outputs that channels provide can be decomposed in terms of supply. And just as it was possible to identify sets of customers that display similar benefit configurations, it's also possible to create hybrid "bundles" of channels that will provide a corresponding set of service outputs. In the spirit of the story of the vessel and the food that appeared at the beginning of this chapter, think of channels as vessels that deliver benefits. And think of the benefits, or the service outputs, as the food that is delivered. As a final step, match the "buckets of demand" with the hybrid channel designs that best serve each set of customers (see Figure 4-5).

Breaking channel functions apart and reallocating functions to channels by customer segment is far superior to the "plus-one"

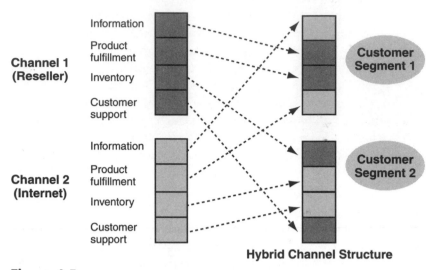

Channel 1
(Reseller)

Information

Product
fulfillment

Inventory

Customer
support

Channel 2
(Internet)

Information

Product
fulfillment

Inventory

Customer
support

Customer
Segment 1

Customer
Segment 2

Hybrid Channel Structure

Figure 4-5
Functional reallocation in channels

approach of bolting on the Internet as yet another channel silo to the existing channels. The process of reallocating functions leads to a go-to-market approach customized for each customer segment. This is the ultimate manifestation of synchronization—synchronizing customer segments with hybrid channel designs, one segment at a time. Inevitably, the hybrid design that results from this exercise will involve the Internet in every one of these bundles, but in different roles. Rarely will the hybrid designs be black and white in nature. Again, they will tend to be different shades of gray. And the hybrid designs will lead to less channel conflict.

To bring to life this process of channel redesign, consider the exercise that put Herman Miller on the right path toward e-business transformation. Before taking the plunge into e-business, Herman Miller had gone to market primarily through its network of retailers, supported by its own sales force. It was largely a single-channel company, and this channel was optimized for its core market: medium to large enterprise customers with complex needs. These customers required consultative selling, extremely high levels of customization, and a large variety of products and options. For the most part, they were well served by the existing set of channels. But as the Internet came along, Herman Miller began to think deeply about how it could incorporate the Net into its existing channel structure. According to Gary Vanspronsen, Herman Miller began with the simple questions: What sets of customers do we serve, including those we don't serve too well today? And what are the *key priorities* for each set of customers?

By mapping a set of possible customer priorities (convenience, speed, selection, customization, performance, flexibility, cost) against different types of customers, Herman Miller came up with four distinct value propositions and matching channel systems for each value proposition. For instance, one segment that Herman Miller serves is large enterprise customers with 500 or more employees. The characteristics of these customers are: multiple locations, highly specialized needs, extremely high performance requirements, and a high priority on customization of work spaces as dictated by the company's corporate vision and values. For these customers, Herman Miller uses a "technology-assisted selling" model, where the sales force and retailers collaborate to sell directly and in person to customers. Salespeople are supported by a Web-based sales assistance system that provides product specifications, demonstrations, availability, and order status while they are on sales calls at customer premises. Retailers and salespersons are also supported by an innovative system called Z-Axis, which allows customers to lay out their work spaces using a visual layout tool, to store their designs, and to order all the pieces of furniture that make up the work space. And customers can look up their order status online on the Herman Miller website. To serve this segment, Herman Miller uses the salesperson to understand customer needs and to demonstrate the offering, uses the reseller to do the installation and maintenance, and uses the Net to communicate order status information and customer support. All channels work in tandem, but in a very specific configuration (see Figure 4-6).

Herman Miller also identified a segment that it had traditionally failed to serve well: fast-growing, smaller companies that value speed and convenience over performance and customization. These are customers who "won't take slow for an answer." They are passionate, high-energy companies that, according to Gary Vanspronsen, want furniture to "look and feel like an iMac—cool, doable, and convenient." This customer wants furniture to be simple, affordable, and easy to buy. As we discussed in Chapter 2, Herman Miller created an entirely new business system to serve this segment, called Herman Miller RED. Accessible through its website, this channel involves selling directly to

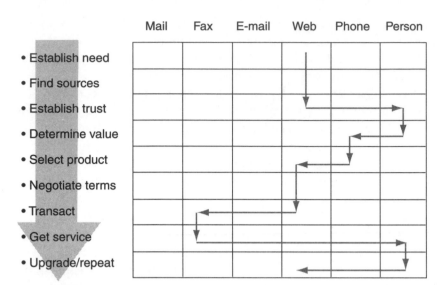

Figure 4-6
Toward the seamless company

customers over the Net, with dealers handling just installation and maintenance. The products themselves are easy to order and easy to configure.

But new products and new channels were not enough to deliver on the value proposition of speed. Therefore, Herman Miller took the necessary steps to slash its lead times from four to six weeks down to between five and ten days, with an eventual target of same-day manufacturing. To get to this goal, it has designed an entirely new manufacturing facility, where manufacturing is done by the *customer order*, not by product. The order, which might include chairs, desks, and partition panels, moves together through different stations in the assembly line. Workers are cross-skilled to make it easier to maximize flexibility and speed. Suppliers deliver components daily, and components are also batched by customer order. A central manufacturing control system synchronizes all the activities on the shop floor, and it allows last minute changes to be made very easily by rerouting the orders through the cellular assembly line. The entire system—from the website to the configuration engine to the product design to the manufacturing system to the suppliers—is optimized for speed and flexibility. In this synchronized system, the Internet serves as the primary sales and support channel, while the retailer still does the installation and maintenance. The sales force does not play a significant role in this design. Again, Herman Miller RED is a hybrid design, blending the best the Net has to offer with the best that other channels have to offer, to create a dramatically different value proposition and open up completely new revenue streams. A compelling piece of evidence of market expansion: Only 5 percent of Herman Miller RED customers had ever bought furniture from the company.

The logic of hybrid designs and channel synchronization can be summarized in terms of four axioms:

1. Customers differ in the benefits they desire and the priorities they place on different service outputs.
2. Every channel provides a bundle of these service outputs, but with a varying degree of effectiveness across the service outputs.
3. You can break apart the functions performed by vertically integrated channels into functional components, so that you can mix and match functions across channels.
4. You can reallocate these functions across existing channels, as well as the Internet, to create sets of hybrid channel designs that synchronize with different customer segments.

Only in the rarest of cases will a company end up with a one-to-one match between one vertically integrated channel and one set of service outputs desired by a particular customer segment. In most cases the optimal configuration will tend to cut across channels and will rarely eliminate any existing channel entirely. However, the corollary is that it will be equally rare to find that the optimal allocation of functions to channels will be the same as it is before the redesign. So, in the hybrid world, every channel will have to adapt and change.

Whose Job Is It, Anyway?

Achieving synchronization is a difficult challenge because the customer experience impacts all levels of the organization, from senior management to customer service reps, and all departments, including marketing, technology, design, human resources, and purchasing.

Like *quality*, the customer experience should be everybody's job. Yet it can just as easily become nobody's job.

To break down external and internal silos that fracture the customer experience, it is important to have a single point of accountability. Enlightened firms are appointing a new breed of senior executive who is accountable for the quality of customer experience. This "Chief Experience Officer" should be the keeper of synchronization and the slayer of boundaries. He or she should be an insider looking from the outside in, adopting the perspective of the customer to look across products, business units, geographies, channels, departments, and at different levels of the organization. The Chief Experience Officer needs to identify disconnects and inconsistencies in the way customers experience the firm across all of its touch points and all of its faces. He needs to chip away at any disconnects and synchronization lapses one at a time, to push the firm along its journey to seamlessness and synchronization. And he needs the force of personality and the authority to make things happen, because the nature of the job requires him to cross turf boundaries.

At Hewlett-Packard, Ann Livermore, one of the most senior executives, is responsible for managing and improving the total customer experience for the company's enterprise and commercial customer segments. She manages the professional services and financing businesses—all enterprise sales, service and support, and commercial sales. She also manages HP's country general managers, which allows her to synchronize across geographies. As synchronization becomes a more salient issue, we foresee many more Ann Livermores in large multidivisional firms. A sobering thought: Who's responsible for the customer experience in your company? If you don't know precisely, you are going to find it hard to break down the boundaries that impair the customer experience.

Achieving synchronization requires strategic thinking, process redesign, and technology infrastructure. The tools that make synchronization ultimately happen are the databases, the software applications, and the hardware that keep the modern enterprise humming. To understand how all this works, you need to look under the hood. And you need to understand how the infrastructure that enables e-business is evolving as technology advances. This is the topic we turn to in the next chapter.

5

E-INFRASTRUCTURE: OPENING THE HOOD

Make things as simple as possible—but no simpler.
— Albert Einstein

A CLASSIC TALE about Henry Ford tells of how he was badgered by a lawyer when he took the witness stand in a court case. The lawyer was attempting to discredit Ford's testimony by pointing out his lack of education. He was asked several simple questions about American history that any schoolchild should have been able to answer. When he was unable to produce the answers, his credibility as a witness appeared to have been severely shaken. Not one to be so easily outwitted, Ford responded to the lawyer's chiding by pointing out that he had no real need for such information in the first place. But should such a need present itself, he could simply press a button on his desk and someone would quickly get him the answer.

The Henry Ford anecdote serves to remind line managers of their role within the realm of e-business technology design and architecture, or *e-infrastructure*. Just as car owners are not required to grasp the functional intricacies of dual overhead cams or variable valve timing in the design of internal combustion engines, line managers are not required to have at their command a deep and comprehensive understanding of the company's e-infrastructure. But while they may be excused from getting their hands dirty under the hood, they *do* need to have gained *strategic fluency*. This means being able to speak intelligently about the e-infrastructure and ask the right questions of the technology architects, just as car owners would want to do of their mechanics. To this end, line managers need to understand the basic building blocks of e-infrastructure and know how to map the blocks to the enterprise business processes. Moreover, they need to understand the myriad business possibilities that a state-of-the-art infrastructure platform enables, as well as the key themes and trends that are shaping the evolution of e-infrastructure. Armed with this knowledge, line managers can then collaborate in a meaningful way with the internal technology team, technology consultants, and technology vendors to convert the blueprint of strategy into the realities of technology-enabled business processes.

This chapter does not set out to train mechanics or provide technology architects with a user's manual. As we pointed out in the preface, the world suffers from no shortage of how-to books on implementing e-business applications or e-enabling core business processes.[1] Most of these books are replete with detail and dense with analysis, and every few months, like clockwork, a new set of applications, vendors, and how-to books bursts forth on the scene. Keeping up with the rapid pace of innovation around enterprise applications is difficult for experts, and nearly impossible for business managers who struggle to keep their heads above water, just given the day-to-day demands of their jobs. In our view, the antidote for complexity is a sense of perspective. Rather than become immersed in the cumbersome details of vendors and platforms, we believe that business managers would be better advised to concentrate on the big picture, drilling down to the nitty-gritty only when it becomes absolutely necessary. Consequently, our discussion of e-infrastructure tends to hover at the strategic and thematic level, where we focus not on technologies and vendors but on concepts and trends.

Also important to our discussion are evolutionary themes. Only with a solid understanding of how enterprise applications have evolved over time can managers fully comprehend the legacy issues they are likely to face as they e-enable their systems, and the trends that will likely shape the evolution of enterprise applications in the years ahead. Therefore, we embark upon our journey with a brief historical overview of the various waves of corporate information automation, starting with the mainframe era and culminating in the age of network computing and the Internet.

The Evolution of Enterprise Applications

The history of corporate automation dates back to the 1960s, to the advent of mainframe computing. Commonly called the era of "departmental computing," this period saw the creation of software applications for back office functions like general ledger, accounting and manufacturing resource planning (MRP). These applications were internally focused and intended to automate and improve the performance of individual departments within the enterprise. Departmental applications, as the name suggests, were accessible only by a functional department. Geographically and organizationally dispersed business units, departments, manufacturing plants, and sales offices could not access the same departmental applications. Furthermore, while divisional or departmental employees could access and share information electronically, all external-facing communication occurred manually. Human beings acted as intermediaries between the applications and the external entities that interfaced with the enterprise.

The next major era in corporate automation can be traced to the introduction of the client/server architecture and the creation of enterprise resource planning (ERP) systems in the 1980s. The client/server architecture separated the *application* logic from the *database*; as opposed to the monolithic mainframe applications, where the applications and databases were designed in unison and tightly coupled. This architecture, together with the development of relational database technologies, allowed information to become centralized and shared across multiple functional areas and geographies. As a result, employees dispersed across the enterprise could now access the same functional applications in real time. The major advance from ERP systems was to provide an integrated view of the core business processes to all employees, tied together by an integrated database. The ERP system became the transactional backbone of the enterprise, tracking enterprise resources (e.g., raw materials, cash, and production capacity) and the status of commitments (e.g., customer orders, payments, and inventory), regardless of whether the data was entered by the accounting, manufacturing, sales, or purchasing departments. These systems made it possible to digitally record every event that changed the status of resources and commitments. For the first time, every employee could operate on the same platform with the same information, seeing changes in real time. This represented a major advance over the disparate, homegrown applications of the mainframe era.

While ERP systems played an instrumental role in breaking down the information silos within the enterprise, they did little to penetrate the walls that separated the enterprise from its external constituents. Designed to be internally focused, ERP systems could be used to manage only those operations that took place within the four walls of the enterprise. Because they were unable to access ERP applications directly, customers and suppliers instead had to exchange information manually, using telephones and fax machines. At that time, the only electronic form of communication between enterprises was Electronic Data Exchange (EDI), a highly structured and inflexible standard that could be used to transmit business data, like invoices and purchase orders, over closed networks. The fundamental limitation of the client/server architecture and the EDI protocol was rooted in their need for proprietary networks and proprietary client-side software. Consequently, information could be exchanged only on a point-to-point basis. Ad hoc interactions with external entities could not be supported. Given the high upfront expenditures for EDI infrastructure, deployment was limited to large suppliers and large customers.

The third phase of corporate automation saw the rise of software applications that extended the ERP systems beyond the boundaries of the enterprise. These "extended enterprise" applications connected the ERP systems to suppliers and customers. The fundamental difference between the inward-facing ERP systems (and legacy mainframe applications) and the newer external-facing applications lay in the fact that inward-facing applications were *function-centric*, while outward-facing applications are *entity-centric*. For instance, ERP systems are typically organized in terms of functional area modules (payroll, accounting, sales, manufacturing), whereas the newer applications are organized by entity (customer management, supplier management, and partner management). The earliest categories of outward-facing applications were supply chain management (SCM) applications on the supplier side, and customer relationship management (CRM) applications on the customer side. While still employing the client/server architecture, these applications focused on connecting customers and suppliers with the enterprise.

On the supplier side, software firms like i2 Technologies, Manugistics, and Oracle created systems for supply chain planning and execution for direct materials procurement. These SCM applications were followed by software applications from firms like Ariba and Commerce One for automating and streamlining indirect materials procurement. Called Operating Resource Management (ORM) solutions, these indirect materials procurement applications allowed enterprises to centralize and automate the purchasing of operating supplies. On the customer side, firms like Siebel, Silknet, Inference, Clarify, Remedy, and Vantive, to name just a few, created applications for managing interactions with customers, as well as for automating the activities of the sales force in its interactions with customers. These sales force automation and customer interaction applications have gradually been augmented with analytical applications for customer profiling and data mining, to create full-fledged CRM suites.

The emergence of the World Wide Web marked the fourth phase of corporate automation. This phase, still very much in its infancy, introduced network-centric applications deployed over the public Internet infrastructure. Unlike client/server applications, these Web-native applications can be accessed by anyone with a Web browser, an Internet connection, and the appropriate security password, meaning that users need not invest in proprietary software or a proprietary network infrastructure. Enterprises can now connect seamlessly with any external entity, regardless of whether they had a preexisting relationship with the entity. This *open architecture* is particularly useful for end-customers, as well as smaller suppliers and resellers, who can interact directly with enterprises. In fact, the concept of *direct e-commerce*, where customers transact with enterprises over the Net, would not be possible without this open architecture. Unlike the earlier classes of applications that were used by a few thousand employees and trusted business partners, Web-based applications can be used by millions of customers and other external entities. With open access, scalability (the ability to support large user bases), and security (the ability to protect the confidentiality of transactional data over the network) assume far greater importance in the design of enterprise applications. Web-based applications offer another important advantage: Their physical location no longer needs to be within the walls of the enterprise. Applications can now be hosted remotely, and offered as services to enterprise clients. As we've discussed in earlier chapters, the rise of Application Service Providers (ASPs) and e-services (applications delivered as services) is a direct consequence of location flexibility.

While open access and deployment flexibility are two characteristics of the current phase of the e-infrastructure evolution, another important trend is the emergence of a *hub-based* application architecture designed to centralize and coordinate interactions across the business web that surrounds the enterprise. This application architecture differs significantly from the linear *chain-based* architecture that characterized the early generations of extended enterprise applications. The hub-based architecture stems from the broadening and deepening of connectivity between the enterprise and its external constituents. This enhanced connectivity is changing the very nature of business processes, which have traditionally been conceptualized at the enterprise level, with clear inputs and outputs to external entities. For instance, a purchase order is an "output" to suppliers, while an invoice is an "input" for customers. In fact, the fundamental concepts and metaphors that anchor e-business applications are all grounded in this linear input-output thinking. The concepts of "supply chains" and "demand chains" reflect the basic assumption that the enterprise exists as one link along a linear chain of entities that serve a set of customers. But this linear chain no longer needs to be the anchoring metaphor for e-business applications, and the walls of the enterprise no longer need to be the logical boundaries of a business process. In fact, most business processes are by nature *interenterprise processes*. Capacity planning, order processing, logistics management, sales promotion management, and new offer development all require that multiple entities closely collaborate, in a networked manner. To optimize performance, these interenterprise processes need to be designed and managed at the level of the entire business web, and not at the level of individual enterprises.

Interenterprise processes represent one of the most important arenas for finding new levels of efficiency in business-to-business commerce. So it is not surprising that a number of new e-infrastructure applications have been announced with the "hub" instead of the "chain" as their central metaphor, and the *value network* as the level of deployment, not the linear supply or demand chain. On the supply side, firms like Agile Software, Atlas Commerce, i2 Technologies (with

TradeMatrix), SAP (with MySAP.com), and Bowstreet are creating hub-based architectures that enable a virtual network of partners to collaborate in managing product design, sourcing materials and components, product manufacturing, and product changes. On the demand side, firms like Asera, ClickCommerce, Intershop, Oracle, and Broadvision are creating hub-based applications for managing interactions and transactions between an enterprise and its resellers, distributors, sales force, and customers.

The hub-based applications architecture places the enterprise at the center of a sourcing or distribution network that includes all external members of the business web. It also extends visibility beyond a single link in the supply or demand chain, creating end-to-end visibility across the entire business web. This end-to-end visibility allows enterprises to more tightly orchestrate information flows, physical flows, and payment flows. Hub-based architectures and interenterprise business processes are certain to play an important role in the continued evolution of e-infrastructure over the next few years. We discuss the implications later in the chapter by highlighting the trend of moving from sequential information transfer between enterprises to synchronized information sharing among the members of the business web. The real-time synchronized network is the ultimate goal of any enterprise. But to get there, it becomes important to first understand the individual building blocks of the applications infrastructure.

The Four Building Blocks of E-Infrastructure

At first glance, the landscape of technology solutions that constitute the building blocks of the e-infrastructure seems impossibly complex. It would take multiple volumes, dense with jargon, buzzwords, and acronyms, to do justice to describing the lay of the land. So where do we begin? By taking a cue from Winston Churchill, who made the observation: "Out of intense complexities, intense simplicities emerge." Quite simply, our approach is to reverse the vantage point from *solutions* to *problems* and from *means* to *ends*. Instead of cataloging the universe of technology vendors and solutions, we focus on the entities with which these applications connect and the business goals they seek to support. The reason is simple: *There are far fewer problems than there are ways to solve these problems.* The solutions space is always more diverse and complex than the problems space. There are far more software platforms, vendors, and solution approaches than there are categories of entities in the business web and the business processes that are enabled by the platforms and tools.

Adopting this problem-centric frame of reference, we can define the building blocks of e-infrastructure in terms of the *key entities* with which the enterprise interacts and transacts. As we noted earlier, a major development in the enterprise applications arena is the fundamental shift from functional applications to applications that focus on specific entities, such as customers, suppliers, partners, and employees. These entity-centric applications share a common goal: to make the interactions between the enterprise and these entities more efficient and more profitable.

The entity-facing applications that constitute the building blocks of e-infrastructure can be broadly classified into four "faces" that correspond to the four key sets of entities with which the enterprise connects. These entities are:

* Customers
* Suppliers
* Partners
* Employees

Customers are the individuals or the businesses that the enterprise serves. Suppliers include the entities that supply direct materials, such as raw materials and components, as well as the entities that provide indirect materials, such as operating supplies and services that support the operations. Partners may include a diverse set of distributors, retailers, affiliates, and complementors that help the enterprise get its offerings to market and augment the offerings with complementary products and services. Employees are the individuals who work for the firm on a full- or part-time basis.

The four corresponding building blocks of e-infrastructure—customer management, supplier management, partner management, and employee management—connect and extend a company's core ERP systems. Each set of applications is designed to enhance and optimize a specific set of entity relationships. And each application mirrors a key business process. Putting it simplistically: An enterprise buys, makes, sells, collaborates, and learns. Supplier-facing applications help the enterprise to buy more effectively. Customer-facing applications and partner-facing applications help an enterprise to sell more effectively.

ERP applications help an enterprise to make more effectively. And employee-facing applications help the enterprise to communicate, collaborate, and learn more effectively. As shown in Figure 5-1, these four external faces of e-infrastructure, along with the ERP transactional backbone, constitute the information infrastructure, or *e-infrastructure*, for the modern enterprise. Table 5-1 provides a more detailed view of the specific functionalities that constitute the end-to-end commerce chain of sourcing, planning, making, selling, settling, and supporting customers, and a representative list of software vendors that compete in some of the specific arenas.

The Customer Face: Marketing, Sales, and Customer Service

Just as the customer should be viewed as the North Star that guides a firm's value creation activities, the most important entity relationship applications of the enterprise are those that face the customer. Increasingly, all other external-facing applications (i.e., partner, supplier, and employee) should be driven by and tightly integrated with

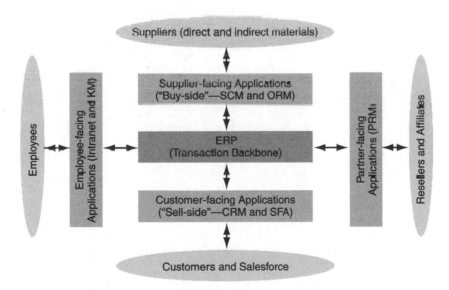

Figure 5-1
Toward an entity-centric infrastructure

Table 5-1
The Vendor Landscape in E-Infrastructure

Applications arena	Business functions enabled	Key players
Indirect materials (MRO) procurement	Procuring of nonproduction inputs from strategic suppliers and online marketplaces	Commerce One, Ariba, Rightworks
Direct materials procurement and supply chain management	Collaborative sourcing and planning with suppliers to optimize production, delivery, demand forecasting, transportation, and manufacturing	i2, Manugistics, Atlas Commerce, Logility, WebPlan
Collaborative design and product management	Enabling multiparty collaboration for design, launch, and modification of new products	Agile Software, MatrixOne, NexPrise, i2, (Aspect Systems)
Content and catalog management	Managing the production, distribution, maintenance, personalization, translation, and syndication of content and product catalogs	Vignette, Requisite, Cardonet, Saqqara, Cohera, Mercado, Viveca
Configurators	Managing product configuration information and enabling online configuration of products	Calico Commerce, Trilogy, Selectica, Firepond
Integrated marketplace transaction platforms	Executing core market-making and transaction, using platforms with multiple trading mechanisms (static/dynamic) and front/back end transaction backbone for marketplaces	Ariba, Commerce One, Oracle, VerticalNet, Idapta, i2, Asera

continued on next page

Table 5-1
The Vendor Landscape in E-Infrastructure (continued)

Applications arena	Business functions enabled	Key players
Direct sales (e-commerce) platforms	Enabling direct sales platforms for catalog sales to end-customers	Broadvision, ATG, Intershop, Open Market, Blue Martini
Indirect sales (partner sales) platforms	Enabling indirect sales through channel partners and management of relationships with selling partners	ChannelWave, Partnerware, Click Commerce, WebRidge, Intershop, Asera
Logistics and distribution management	Coordinating outbound logistics and distribution	i2, Celarix, GoCargo, Yantra, SubmitOrder, iFulfillment, CarrierPoint
Payment and settlement management	Managing posttransaction payment and settlement flows	VeriSign, iEscrow, eCredit.com, Aceva, OrderTrust
Customer relationship management	Capturing and managing customer acquisition, customer profiling, merchandising, and customer support activities	Siebel, E.piphany, Kana, Blue Martini, Synchrony, Pivotal, Comergent, Quintus, Annuncio
Customer analytics and marketing automation	Analyzing customer transactional data and automating/optimizing marketing programs	E.piphany, Cognos, DoubleClick, Net Perceptions, MarketFirst, Aprimo, MarketSwitch, Paramark

the customer-facing applications. The customer face includes the end-to-end business process that begins with demand creation and culminates in customer support. The process includes three major stages: *marketing*, the range of functions associated with presales activities, including marketing communications and branding; *sales*, the actual selling and distribution of products and services; and *service*, which includes all of the ongoing support and customer interaction activities.

Customer-facing applications are the technologies and services that an enterprise employs in order to better understand its customers, more effectively go to market with its offerings, and build more profitable customer relationships. These applications span the marketing activities that precede the transaction, the sales activities that consummate the transaction, and the support activities that follow the transaction. These applications also span a diverse set of channels that the enterprise may use to connect with its customers. And they include the operational aspects of interacting and transacting with customers, as well as the analytical aspects of modeling and optimization to improve the profitability of customer relationships. Ideally, customer-facing applications should enable the enterprise to evolve its customer interactions from fragmented silos of activities and information to an integrated solution that spans all the company's transaction and communication channels. In addition, customer-facing applications should enable the enterprise to evolve its marketing resource allocation process from one that is judgment-based to one that is fact-based and which promotes financial accountability of customer-facing activities.

The growth of customer-facing applications is the story of an increasing diversity of customer touch points and an increased use of technology to mediate interactions between enterprises and their customers. Consider that in the days of craft production there was only one touch point, and "customer relationship management" meant person-to-person interaction. When commerce was localized and isolated, the corner grocer knew most of the townspeople by name, and customers enjoyed personal relationships with the vendors with whom they interacted. Then came the Industrial Age and with it the growth of enterprises and transportation that led to a shrinking of the world as one marketplace. The geographical scope of markets came to transcend the immediate geography of the producers. With widespread trading taking place across borders and into a much more widely dispersed area, firms could no longer connect with customers on a one-to-one basis. Instead they came to rely on middlemen that could distribute their products and messages to a large base of customers. These middlemen included mass media vehicles that mediated marketing communication flows between firms and their customers, channel intermediaries that mediated product and payment flows, and contact management channels that mediated service and support flows.

Industrial Age marketing relied on print and television advertising to communicate marketing messages to customers. These mass media channels replaced personalized interaction with impersonal messages. Marketers could personalize their messages only by targeting specific customer segments through different media vehicles—a crude technique at best. Direct mail catalogs and telesales offered a way to communicate directly with customers, but with limited effectiveness and primarily in one direction. The advent of the Net has created several new possibilities for direct marketing and personalized promotions. E-mail can be an effective permission-based marketing tool for outbound communications. The website can also be an effective channel for communicating product, brand, and company information in a personalized manner. The creation of Web-based personalization technology has allowed marketers to create messages that adapt to customer profiles and behavior. Personalization can be based on correlating customer behavior with that of similar customers, or by inferring preferences, based on an extrapolation of a customer's past behavior.

Beyond personalization lies a vision that is only now beginning to gather steam: *marketing automation*. The term describes the electronic execution of marketing programs through the use of data warehouses, data mining techniques, campaign execution tools, and response management tools. The data warehouse stores all customer interactions. Data mining techniques are used to identify patterns, which can be used in support of designing personalized offers for customers. Response reporting analyzes the results of marketing campaigns and fine-tunes the execution for future campaigns. Unlike the batch process that characterized the planning and execution of marketing programs in the offline world, marketing automation permits campaigns to be designed, executed, and adapted in real time. The promise of *real-time marketing*, long envisioned by experts like Regis McKenna, who imagined a future "when action and response are simultaneous," is finally edging toward reality.[2] For example, by employing outbound e-mail programs, a company can unleash hundreds of thousands of marketing messages in one fell swoop. These messages can produce quick results, making it possible to fine-tune and launch the next round of promotional offers in a rapid-fire manner.

The adaptive nature of real-time marketing serves as the foundation for the next evolutionary level: *marketing optimization*. This term describes the layering of algorithmic tools on top of an automated marketing process to maximize the financial returns on marketing campaigns. The result can be the Holy Grail for any major marketer: *delivering the right offers to the right customers through the right channels at the right point in time*. Marketing optimization allows firms to define their marketing goals, such as customer relationship profitability or customer acquisition cost, as well as the constraints of the marketing campaign. The optimization algorithms then determine the best possible match between offers, customers, and channels.

The combination of automation and optimization allows marketing interactions with customers to evolve from a batch process to a real-time process, and from a single-product, single-channel process to a multiple product, multichannel process. Marketing optimization also allows customization to be carried out at an individual customer level and not merely at a segment level. Given the benefits, it's no surprise that a large number of firms today are creating technology solutions that promise to improve the productivity of marketing investments through optimization.[3]

Technology has also transformed the *sales* stage of customer-facing applications. Until the mid-1980s the sales function had little to do with technology, and everything to do with personal relationships and salesmanship. To close sales, reps could count only on their own individual selling ability and knowledge of products, customers, competition, and the marketplace. This began to change with the advent of Sales Force Automation (SFA) software, which enables enterprises to dramatically improve sales force effectiveness. How? By allowing sales reps to quickly develop quotes and proposals; by providing them with real-time access to product, configuration, pricing, and promotion information; by allowing them to prioritize their efforts by analyzing customer account potential and profitability; and by improving their ability to demonstrate products in customer-facing situations. However, early generations of SFA software also had their share of limitations. For example, they could be accessed only by sales personnel employed by the firm, and they typically used proprietary client/server architecture.

But now the Internet has opened up new vistas for technology-assisted selling. Tools previously available only to the sales force can now be leveraged to link third-party selling partners (e.g., manufacturer's reps, distributors, value-added resellers, and retailers) to other inside sales channels like telesales and retail sales reps. In addition, technology makes it possible to sell directly to customers, through channels like the Net, kiosks, and wireless devices, obviating the need for a human sales rep. Technology-assisted selling allows enterprises to improve effectiveness, as well as optimize resource allocation, across all of their sales channels. As it shifts qualitatively from playing a *supporting* role to an *enabling* role, technology-enabled selling will be used increasingly to synchronize and integrate all selling channels used by the enterprise, including telesales, the Net, resellers, and the direct sales force, through the use of a common customer relationship repository, a common applications infrastructure, and a shared business process.

Of course the role of technology does not end with the sale. In fact, some of the biggest advances in customer-facing applications are occurring in the arena of customer service and support.

Returning to our history lesson, note that with the end-customer disconnected from the manufacturer it became important to put technology in place to maintain that connection. Ultimately, the creation of indirect channels, the fragmentation of markets, and the increase in geographic scale led to the need to build "customer relationship management systems," the earliest iteration of which was mail-based customer support. Made possible by the U.S. Postal Service, and supported in most companies by a dedicated front line, incoming customer mail either got sent up the ranks to management, or was addressed on the spot with standard form letters. For decades, customers could write a letter to a company and actually expect to receive a personalized reply.

The call center represents the next big advance in customer relationship management. Located either on-premises or outsourced to a third party, the call center entails banks of people serving customers through the infamous 1-800 number. Until just a few years ago, customer support was synonymous with customer service reps fielding phone calls over toll-free lines. And then, of course, came the Net. With its growth, connectivity between companies and customers has gone up by orders of magnitude in terms of frequency and diversity.

Today, the channels through which customers can communicate with companies include e-mail, fax, phone, voice-over-IP, and even video — a reality that, as we discussed in Chapter 4, seems to have caught many companies completely off guard.

In the early days of the Net, companies putting up a website would, as a matter of course, post a button that invited their customers to "e-mail us." And customers did send e-mail, in some cases by the tens of thousands. Unfortunately, owing to a lack of infrastructure and personnel, most companies were ill-equipped to handle such large volume. This led to the emergence of outsourced e-mail management services and chat-based customer care solutions. As we discussed, these additional channels for customer contact created a new problem; insomuch that these point solutions were often channel-specific, they ended up creating data silos that were poorly integrated with the legacy call center operations.

A recent trend in customer contact management is the emergence of unified *customer interaction management* systems.[4] These systems integrate all channels of customer interaction on a common platform, and capture all customer interaction sessions on a common knowledge base. In these systems, all customer calls get routed through a common queue, regardless of the channel through which the contact originated. Moreover, all calls get routed in a context-sensitive manner to the most appropriate customer service rep based on the importance of the customer relationship and the nature of the call. Customer interactions can be progressively categorized and analyzed to identify and respond to frequently asked questions (FAQs), to detect problems with products, and to identify cross-selling and up-selling opportunities.

Software applications that support the three stages of customer-facing activities — marketing, sales, and service — have traditionally evolved somewhat independently, with little integration among these stages. Sales force automation software vendors like Siebel, Onyx Software, Pivotal, Applix, and Saratoga Systems evolved along the technology-assisted sales dimension. Call center and help desk software vendors like Clarify, Quintus, Remedy, Vantive, and Silknet evolved along the customer service and support dimension. And analytics vendors like Cognos, Microstrategy, Brio, SAS Institute, and Business Objects evolved along the business intelligence and data mining dimension.

These different dimensions are overlapping and converging into one catchall applications arena: CRM. Today, CRM has practically as many definitions as it does vendors. While most would agree that the basic objective is to use technology and supporting business processes to help enterprises attract, retain, and serve their most profitable customers, there is considerable divergence as to how this translates operationally in terms of software applications and approaches.

In our view, customer-facing applications simply allow an enterprise to link marketing, sales, and customer service processes through an integrated infrastructure, to create a seamless end-to-end customer experience. The applications ideally capture, monitor, and analyze every customer interaction to progressively improve customer satisfaction and profitability.

At the heart of every customer facing applications platform is the database that holds all information related to customers, called the *customer relationship repository* (CRR). This repository is the central memory of the enterprise, recording information about every customer contact in a single physical data warehouse, or in a virtually integrated environment that pulls together all customer data from across the enterprise. The CRR is the foundation upon which customer-facing applications are built. The applications themselves may be a combination of many components needed to achieve a one-to-one marketing capability, as well as interfaces between ERP systems and customer-facing systems.

If the customer relationship repository is the record keeper of customer-facing applications, the *campaign manager* is the choreographer who directs the operations backbone of marketing program design and execution. The campaign manager includes the tools that allow the enterprise to profile and segment customers, design marketing campaigns, develop customized offers for customers, and evaluate the results of marketing programs. The operational foundation of the campaign manager is complemented by a set of *analytical tools* that allows the enterprise to analyze customer data to identify patterns, to interpret these patterns, and to use the patterns in fine-tuning marketing programs. These analytical tools are invaluable for sifting through the data in an automated and efficient manner—the so-called process of *data mining*—to discover nuggets of insight. Traditionally, the analytics have been a batch process, meaning that the analysis of results and the adaptation of campaigns have proceeded sequentially. However, with the availability of online customer information and analytical processing tools, the analytics can evolve into a real-time process, with execution, analysis, optimization, and adaptation becoming part of a continuous automated loop.

If the campaign manager directs the backbone for marketing operations, the *channel manager* directs the backbone for customer interaction management in a customer-facing applications suite. The channel manager ties together the various touch points for customer interaction, and links to the sales force automation system, the call center, and the Internet-based customer interaction channels. The channel manager enables an enterprise to capture information from every customer touch point, to pass it on to the customer relationship repository, and to retrieve outputs from the analytics modules to every touch point for execution. The channel manager should also enable the enterprise to view the activity and performance of all customer interaction channels simultaneously.

Located between the execution of demand-creation programs by the campaign manager and the service-related operations by the channel manager are the *sales automation* applications that form the operational core of the selling function. These sales automation tools should support the automation of sales through multiple channels: sales through the enterprise sales force, sales through partners, and direct sales to customers through the Internet. In other words, sales automation applications should include tools for selling directly "to" customers, as well as selling "through" partners to customers. The specific types of sales automation applications include *lead management tools* for following up on sales leads; *sales configuration tools* for configuring products, prices, financing, and service packages; and *personalization tools* that permit offers and products to be customized for specific customers.

Content management tools provide the final element of functionality in the customer-facing suite of applications. Content can include product catalogs, brochures, and all of the marketing collateral materials that may be needed by the sales organization, the marketing organization, or any of the external entities that collaborate with the enterprise to create marketing, sales, and service programs. Content management systems ensure that all of the customer communications materials remain centralized, current, consistent, and easily accessible.

In summary, an integrated set of customer-facing applications starts with the customer relationship repository at the core, and is complemented by three sets of operational applications: the campaign manager for marketing activities, the channel manager for customer interactions, and the sales automation tools for selling activities. It also includes a suite of analytical tools that support querying, analysis, and reporting of customer data, as well as content management tools for storing and disseminating product and marketing-related information.

Do such integrated customer-facing applications suites exist? Unfortunately, today the answer is no—despite the marketing hype from leading vendors like Siebel, Oracle, Kana, and E.piphany. No single vendor, and no single set of applications, can offer all elements of functionality, due to the diverse nature of the applications and the legacy that each vendor brings. In practice, most large enterprises will have to cobble together their customer-facing applications architecture by starting with a core platform from one of the leading vendors and layering on additional best-of-breed components that need to be integrated with the platform, using middleware applications. While complete solutions may still be years away, it is important to have a clear vision of the ideal customer-facing applications suite and to work toward this unified vision.

Of course, the pathway to the end-goal will vary according to industry and organization. As with the prioritization of e-business initiatives, which we discussed in Chapter 2, the trick here is to "know thyself." For instance, multichannel enterprises may choose to begin with the channel management piece to streamline customer interactions, and then work their way "outward-in" to the analytical and marketing automation elements. On the other hand, organizations that have customer data strewn across many different divisions and systems may benefit tremendously from embarking on the creation of a centralized data warehouse to create one view of their relationships with customers. Other enterprises with a strong history of sales force automation may choose to use the SFA tools as the foundation for automating their sales channels. And yet other enterprises may begin with e-commerce systems that over time can become integrated backward into the legacy ERP and customer support systems. There are many roads to integrated customer-facing applications, but for each of them the goal is the same: better management of the most important asset of the enterprise—its customers.

The Partner Face: Collaborative Selling and Distribution

Despite the unbridled enthusiasm for the Net as a channel for direct selling to customers that besets many companies, the fact remains that most selling activity still takes place through partners. Even in the high-tech industry, often held out as the exemplar for direct commerce, with firms like Dell, Cisco, IBM, and Intel leading the pack, partners still account for over 50 percent of sales. In fact, the importance of partners in the selling process is increasing, not decreasing, as firms trim their direct sales forces and seek to leverage the assets and relationships of partners. The growing importance of partners has given rise to a new class of partner-facing enterprise software applications. A host of new vendors have emerged to offer software and services for partner relationship management.[5] In addition, traditional enterprise software vendors like Siebel, Oracle, and PeopleSoft are rapidly extending their applications to include partner-facing functionality.

Partner-facing applications streamline interactions between enterprises and their channel partners and improve the financial return from partner relationships. These applications encompass three primary areas of functionality: *resource allocation tools, opportunity management tools*, and *sales productivity tools*. Resource allocation includes functions like partner profiling, channel funds allocation, and return on investment (ROI) monitoring from partner programs. Opportunity management involves sourcing and managing customer leads for partners, and tracking the performance of partners in converting leads to sales. Sales productivity tools help the enterprise to distribute product information, product updates, marketing collateral, and support and training materials—all with the express purpose of assisting partners in demonstrating, selling, and supporting the firm's offerings.

Partner-facing applications overlap significantly with customer-facing applications, as both seek to improve the firm's go-to-market strategy in terms of performance and profitability. The key difference lies in the fact that customer-facing applications traditionally have assumed a *direct* connection between the enterprise and the customer, either through a telemarketing or Web-based sales channel, or through a direct sales force. In contrast, partner-facing applications focus on automating and optimizing *indirect* channels of distribution that involve one or more layers of partners between the enterprise and its customers. Unlike the sales force, partners do not work for the firm and are not bound by the firm's standards for technology. Consequently, partner-facing applications need to be far more flexible than the client/server technologies that have traditionally served as the foundation for sales force automation software. Furthermore, partners generally do not generate demand by themselves, so the firm has to take a proactive stance in generating leads and managing follow-up.

Partner-facing applications bring accountability to channel partner performance by allowing the firm to track the status of every lead. The performance of partners can be monitored accurately and in real time. In addition, these applications extend the benefits of SFA, CRM, and ERP applications to channel partners. Partner-facing applications also improve the quality and speed of communications with resellers, by creating a platform for information dissemination, training, competitive monitoring, and updates on new products. Cost savings can be significantly reduced by replacing the reams of paper-based marketing and support materials flowing from the firm to its partners.

The foundation of every partner-facing application is the system that stores partner profiles. The system is the analog of the customer relationship repository that lies at the heart of customer-facing applications. The *partner profile* is a complete view of every partner relationship, including contact and firmographic information, commission structures, and the partner's performance history. The partner profile centralizes and standardizes information across the firm's entire base of partners, thereby allowing the firm to segment its partner relationships and to target its communications and leads more accurately. The partner-facing system includes the following key elements.

Adaptive lead management This functionality allows enterprises to distribute leads to the appropriate partners and to monitor the results of leads generated from various sources. The adaptive aspect of the lead management system means that partner performance and lead productivity can be used to fine-tune the lead generation, distribution, and follow-up process. An effective lead management system should improve the close rate by better qualifying, routing, and following up leads as they work their way through the sales cycle.

Content management This functionality allows firms to distribute content such as product information, product updates, support literature, and competitive information to partners quickly and cost-effectively. Content management should include personalization capability, so partners receive content customized to their context. Content can also include training materials that can assist partner sales and support personnel to be trained on new offerings using an assisted or a self-guided learning model. Content management allows partners to improve their sales productivity and to get up to speed faster with new products and product updates.

Promotion management This functionality seeks to optimize the effectiveness and ROI of partner-facing promotional programs. It includes a resource allocation capability that determines how the firm allocates marketing funds to its partners, and a monitoring capability to evaluate the results of each promotional activity and each partner. Promotion management improves the productivity of co-operative marketing spending and helps improve the accountability of partners as they execute promotional campaigns.

Order/quote configuration This functionality allows partners to respond to customer inquiries for quotes, and to configure products and services to the requirements of customers. Configuration capabilities are particularly important for assembled and modular products that can be configured in a myriad of ways and priced and bundled in many different permutations. Configurators also check for logical inconsistencies in the configuration and eliminate those that are not feasible or available. As a result, error rates can drop, and the firm's offerings can be more accurately customized to partner and end-customer needs.

Consultative selling Interactive selling tools allow partners to demonstrate the firm's products and services to end-customers by combining content and configuration capabilities with an intuitive user interface that presents the firm's offerings in an appealing manner. These tools are similar to the interactive selling tools found in sales force automation software.

E-commerce storefronts A firm's partners will often want their own e-commerce presence to sell directly to their customers. It is in the interest of the firm to ensure that the partners adopt a common technology platform and consistent user interface to present to end-customers. And it is in the interest of the firm to provide this infrastructure to its partners, so that the partners' retail presence is tightly integrated with the firm's e-commerce platform and ERP systems. Therefore, partner-facing applications often include ways for partners to create their own retail storefronts, using a common back-end infrastructure and a consistent front-end look and feel. A shared platform distributes the infrastructure costs over a large base of partners. It also promotes the integrity of the firm's brand by ensuring that end-customers have a consistent experience, regardless of the partner with whom they choose to do business. The firm can also provide shared value-added services to its partners, including financing, logistics, and customer support.

Forecasting and planning   Planning functionality allows partners to formulate demand forecasts and sales plans based on information about end-customer demand, as well as the firm's own capacity and production plans. These tools permit partners to collaboratively plan and forecast, and they allow the firm to generate demand forecasts for sales through partner channels.

In summary, partner-facing applications permit enterprises to transform their overall approach to partner management, shifting from processes that are ad hoc and tactical to ones that are strategic and rely on real-time data to improve the planning, analysis, execution, and optimization of partner-focused programs. The firm and its partners can set joint goals, make joint plans, and implement joint marketing strategies. Partner-facing applications will continue to gain momentum as firms increase their reliance on partners to leverage their assets and broaden their reach.

The Supplier Face:
Collaborative Sourcing and Procurement

Supplier-facing applications are the mirror image of partner-facing applications. They are designed to improve the efficiency and effectiveness of interactions between the enterprise and its suppliers. These suppliers may be of three types: *direct material suppliers, indirect materials suppliers,* and *services suppliers.* As we've said, direct material suppliers provide the firm with raw materials, components, and subassemblies that go into the products that the firm manufactures. Indirect material suppliers provide the firm with operating supplies for maintenance, repair, and operations that support the activity of manufacturing. Services suppliers are a diverse lot and can include transportation services, IT services, human resource services, marketing services, and management consulting services, to name a few. Supplier-facing applications are generally classified into three categories: operating resource management (ORM) applications, supply chain management (SCM) applications, and services procurement applications. These distinctions are necessary because the procurement process is quite different for each.

Procurement of indirect materials (i.e., operating supplies) is typically a logical place to start in the world of supplier-facing applications. Why? First, operating supplies tend to be "horizontal" in nature, which means that businesses across several industries will often use the same kinds of operating supplies.[6] For instance, most businesses buy computers, office furniture, and travel-related services. The horizontal nature of operating supplies makes it easier for software vendors to create a common catalog of suppliers that can serve a number of industries and can be easily customized to the needs of specific enterprise customers.

Second, indirect materials are not used in manufacturing the product, so operating supplies tend to be sourced nonstrategically. Sourcing does not generally depend on the production, capacity, and demand planning functions that characterize direct materials procurement. This means that the processes for procuring operating supplies can be less tightly integrated with the firm's internal systems. Also, the software systems for operating supplies procurement do not need to include decision support or collaborative planning features.

The third reason that operating supplies procurement may be a logical place to start is that the procurement process is typically ad hoc and plagued by uncoordinated "rogue purchasing." Automating the procurement process generally results in cost savings due to automation, demand aggregation, and improved access to suppliers. For all of these reasons, leading firms in the operating supplies procurement space have enjoyed rapid acceptance of their solutions by large enterprises. These software vendors have been able to demonstrate quantifiable and quick savings, with direct impact on the bottom line.

The sourcing of direct materials—again, also called *supply chain management*—represents a whole different ball game. Direct materials are strategically sourced, and are far more "vertical" or industry-specific than are operating supplies. For instance, the direct materials requirements of an automobile manufacturer are very different from those of a plastics or electrical equipment manufacturer. So, too, does the *structure* of the supply chain differ significantly by industry. In the electronics manufacturing sector, for example, outsourcing procurement extends to outsourcing the entire manufacturing process, through virtual manufacturing firms like Solectron and Flextronics. On the other hand, Original Equipment Manufacturers (OEMs) in the automobile sector perform final assembly, but source components and subassemblies from a multitiered network of suppliers. The industry-specific nature of direct materials explains the difficulty of creating one-size-fits-all software platforms for managing the sourcing of these materials. Design of supplier-facing systems for direct materials demands significant domain expertise, and significant customization for each industry. These supplier-facing systems also need to interface closely with the firm's product development and manufacturing process. For instance, every time a firm introduces a new product, suppliers need to be involved in defining product specifications, managing product design and development, managing changes in product definition, creating manufacturing capabilities for the new product, and identifying upstream materials and components suppliers. Similarly, in product manufacturing, suppliers need to have ongoing visibility into the end-customer demand, capacity constraints, production plans, and cost targets for the firm's products. Collaborative planning and execution is essential for optimizing the procurement of direct materials, and software systems that connect firms with direct materials suppliers have to support joint planning, forecasting, and optimization of the end-to-end sourcing system.

While the procurement of services may be the least well-defined piece of the supplier-facing agenda, it's the one that potentially holds the most promise. As pressures mount to focus on the core business, companies are growing increasingly dependent on third-party services firms to supplement their own capabilities. These firms may serve any functional department. Marketing firms provide advertising and marketing communications services. System integrators provide IT-related services. Human resource firms provide recruitment and outplacement management services. Traditionally, services procurement has been a manual process that relies heavily on personal relationships and personal selling. For this reason, traditional systems, geared to product procurement, are not well suited to the procurement and management of outsourced services. But with the advent of Web-based solutions for a variety of outsourced services needs, the services procurement process stands at the precipice of transformation.

Consider the complex and dynamic IT professional services marketplace. IT projects generally involve multiple entities in a professional services supply chain, including software suppliers, hardware suppliers, connectivity suppliers, consultants, and system integrators. While this supply chain encompasses all activities needed to plan, procure, and deliver professional services, it remains inefficient and prone to failure due to poor communication of project expectations by buyers, and the inability of firms to objectively evaluate IT services suppliers. New entrants into the services procurement marketplace are creating management platforms and professional services marketplaces to match suppliers with buyers of IT services and to facilitate the ongoing interactions between firms and their chosen suppliers as projects get under way. These platforms lower procurement costs by increasing the number of competitive bids and by automating the procurement process. In addition, they guide buyers in selecting the best suppliers by providing independent research and evaluation metrics.

Services procurement solutions are also emerging in other areas, like human resource management and marketing communications. Consider a direct mail marketing brochure. The process of creating a brochure requires interaction among the sales department, the marketing department, the creative agency responsible for the design, the printer responsible for the production of the brochure, and the catalog fulfillment agency responsible for mailing the brochure. The procurement process involves identifying the best suppliers for all of these elements of the solution and coordinating the activities of a number of different suppliers. New firms, like Collabria, are developing collaborative printing solutions that streamline and automate the end-to-end procurement and production process for printed materials. Advertising, public relations, event management, and conference management are other services that can be automated and streamlined by third-party solutions providers. For instance, Niku, an early leader in the professional services automation marketplace, creates marketplaces that allow services firms to streamline their interactions with buyers in a number of arenas, including IT services, advertising, law, financial services, and healthcare. Eventually, every enterprise will need to have a common platform for procurement of people-intensive services across the enterprise as services become more strategic and consume a greater proportion of the overall procurement budget.

The neat distinctions that have characterized the supplier-facing applications arena are dissolving, with the indirect materials procurement platform vendors (e.g., Ariba and Commerce One) starting to acquire capabilities in direct materials procurement, and the supplier-facing platform vendors (e.g., i2 Technologies, SAP, and Manugistics) allying themselves with the indirect materials procurement vendors. Such convergence is inevitable, given that firms desire a unified platform for managing all of their sourcing needs. The unification of platforms, in fact, transcends individual firms. Several industrywide initiatives have been announced to create shared platforms for procurement, sponsored by consortia of key suppliers and buyers. These initiatives are motivated by the need for a common vocabulary, common standards, and shared infrastructure across firms, to create efficiencies at the industry level. While industrywide initiatives will no doubt play a significant role in enterprise procurement strategies, we nonetheless believe that most enterprises will continue to develop and operate private networks that connect their web of strategic suppliers with the enterprise at the center of the network.

The supplier-facing applications arena will see the continued growth of public as well as private networks that transform linear and inflexible supply chains into nonlinear and dynamic fulfillment networks. These networks will feature different mechanisms for sourcing, including catalog purchasing, auctions, reverse auctions, negotiated bid/quote mechanisms, and exchange mechanisms. They will permit enterprises to buy on a systematic and prenegotiated relationship basis, as well as on an ad hoc and transactional basis from suppliers. Firms will be able to choose the sourcing mechanism, as well as the suppliers, that best meet their demands. They may be able to liquidate excess inventory through an auction, buy components from a supplier catalog, conduct reverse auctions for procurement of commodity raw materials, or negotiate contracts for manufactured parts with strategic suppliers, all over a common enterprisewide (or even industrywide) platform.

Supplier-facing applications will also evolve along another dimension: from automation and integration of supply chains to collaborative sourcing, planning, and design across their supplier networks. Traditionally, enterprises and their suppliers have retained ownership over key planning and operational information, as well as the databases and applications that stored and manipulated this information. These islands of information resulted in multiple competing plans and forecasts and eventually increased levels of inventory in the supply network as a hedge against errors in demand forecasts. With the increased adoption of supply chain planning and execution systems, enterprises are coming to realize the value of planning done in collaboration with their suppliers, channel partners, and customers, with the open sharing of sales, production, and capacity data. Web-based collaborative planning tools allow enterprises to exchange forecasts and production information with suppliers, and to eventually move beyond exchanging information to operating on a common, shared data and information repository. We discuss the migration from sequential to shared processes later in the chapter, as we explain how the trend is shaping the evolution of supplier-facing applications from a linear supply chain design to a nonlinear and dynamic hub-based architecture.

Another emerging theme in the evolution of supplier-facing applications is the development of capabilities for collaborative design of new products with suppliers. Traditionally, firms have included only a few key suppliers in the process of designing new products. But shrinking product life cycles and increased reliance on key suppliers have resulted in a need for closer collaboration in the new product design and development process. Firms are responding to this need by creating real-time linkages among their suppliers, their engineering teams, and their marketing teams. Companies like Hewlett-Packard and National Semiconductor are creating "design portals" that allow customers and suppliers to collaborate in the early stages of design for new products. Collaborative design can significantly reduce time-to-market for new products, improve the quality of the end-product, and reduce inventory in the supply chain by designing products that are "supplier friendly."

The Employee Face: Internal Communication and Collaboration

The discussions taking place today with respect to e-infrastructure tend to focus on applications that connect the enterprise with its external constituents: customers, suppliers, and business partners. However, there is an equally important class of applications that facilitate interaction *within* the enterprise — between the firm and its employees, and among teams of employees. These applications allow employees seamless access to information and services, and they improve collaboration and knowledge management within the enterprise. Employee-facing applications can be classified into two overlapping categories: *enterprise portals* and *knowledge management applications*. These applications typically run on the intranet within the enterprise, although they can be gradually extended beyond the walls of the enterprise to include key partners, customers, and suppliers.

Enterprise portals are corporate incarnations of the consumer portal concept (e.g., Yahoo!, Excite, and About.com). The enterprise portal provides a single point of access to all sources of information, data, people, and business applications. There, employees can search for information and people, publish and retrieve content, establish and participate in communities, subscribe to news and information sources, and personalize their interface to the corporate intranet. In addition, the enterprise portal may offer links to internal websites, interfaces to internal applications, information on competitors, and links to industry associations and business partners. It can also be used to organize internal documents and information, to replace paper forms and manual employee-facing applications with electronic versions, and to present information from internal enterprise applications in a user-friendly manner. Enterprise portals represent the logical evolution of the intranet concept, which began with homegrown Web pages set up by different departments. These intranets are gradually giving way to robust enterprise portal applications.[7]

The functionalities of an enterprise portal can be organized in a layered or hierarchical manner. At the lowest or most fundamental level, an enterprise portal must provide *integration* with both internal and external information sources. The integration layer is the functional foundation for information access, without which an enterprise portal would fail to achieve its basic goal of opening a single window into a diverse information space. The integration capabilities must include the ability to handle structured data from enterprise applications, and unstructured information like documents, as well as processes and events. Next, the enterprise portal must have *indexing* capabilities—the ability to organize and categorize information so it can be viewed and retrieved in different ways by different users. A well-designed enterprise portal should support categorization schemes that are unique to different employee roles and different work groups within the enterprise.

Related to indexing is another key functionality; a robust *search* capability that allows employees to locate information regardless of format or location. Search capabilities should also be flexible, allowing users to look for information in different ways, including concept searches, natural language queries, and even human-assisted searches. An enterprise portal should also allow end-users to *publish* and *distribute* content to the central information repository. This process should ensure that content is easy to publish, accurate, and timely. This usually requires a human filter to ensure quality and consistency of information. Finally, an enterprise portal must support personalization, allowing employees to customize the enormous volume of information available within the enterprise to their context. Users should be able to select the information and business processes to which they wish to gain access, and customize the look, feel, and placement of information.

While the first generations of enterprise portals will focus on information communication, organization, search and retrieval, these versions will quickly evolve into a higher level of functionality, supporting *workflow* and *collaboration*. Functioning in this capacity, an enterprise portal becomes much more than a static "information kiosk." Rather, it becomes an enabler of community and collaboration between teams of employees, and eventually among employees, customers, partners, and other external entities. At this stage, the enterprise portal starts to take on the characteristics of knowledge management applications designed to improve collaboration among employees and the ability of the enterprise to capture, archive, disseminate, and update knowledge. While client-server groupware applications like Lotus Notes have been used for over a decade as platforms for knowledge management (KM), the growth of the Web has accelerated the adoption of KM applications, greatly expanding their reach and flexibility.

Knowledge management applications and enterprise portals share a common goal. Both act as "central nervous systems" that seek to improve the quality of information flow within the organization. However, some key differences exist. For example, while enterprise portals focus on improving *communication* by aggregating, organizing, and presenting digital information to individual employees, knowledge management initiatives focus on improving *collaboration* between teams of employees by improving the process of acquiring, creating, archiving, disseminating, and deploying knowledge. Like enterprise portals, KM applications include functionalities like information, storage, indexing, navigation, and personalization. However, KM applications also focus on sharing, collaboration, synthesis, and dissemination of information to appropriate decision makers. While enterprise portals improve the productivity of individual employees through better access to information, knowledge management initiatives make teams of employees more productive through improved collaboration and use of the organization's knowledge assets.

The fact that knowledge management requires individuals to work collaboratively toward a team goal means that KM initiatives need to be supported by cultural change, incentive alignment, and business strategy alignment to a much greater extent than the implementation of an enterprise portal. After all, what is knowledge but information that is deeply embedded within the specific context of the enterprise? This context includes the strategy, values, culture, and organizational structure of the enterprise. In addition to software, KM initiatives require a generous dose of "peopleware": people who identify and filter content sources, people who create knowledge taxonomies and link content (as well as other people) to the taxonomy, and people who maintain and nurture knowledge communities.

The distinction between enterprise portals and knowledge management applications is quickly disappearing, as enterprise portals begin to offer work flow and collaboration features that were once only found in sophisticated groupware applications, and as groupware applications begin to evolve beyond the rigid client/server architecture and offer improved capabilities for publishing and integration with legacy business applications. The eventual goal of employee-facing applications is to offer employees an integrated platform and a unified interface for information access, work flow automation, learning, and collaboration.

Beyond the Four Faces: The Colliding Universes of Enterprise Applications

"Everything in this book may be wrong," cautions Richard Bach in his profound tale of a reluctant messiah in *Illusions*. And this caveat may be the best way to summarize our discussion of the four external faces of the enterprise. The faces are boundaries that have been created for reasons of legacy and convenience. But like all boundaries, the distinctions are ultimately artificial and limiting. It is useful to conceptualize e-infrastructure in terms of the various key entities that surround the enterprise. But having done so, it is equally important to note that these entities, and therefore the applications that connect enterprises with them, are inextricably linked. The business processes involved in managing relationships with customers, partners, suppliers, employees, and other stakeholders are interconnected and interdependent. Therefore, the software applications and tools that enable these business processes must also be integrated and interdependent.

Let's consider some of these artificial boundaries. We've said that the distinction between customer-facing applications and partner-facing applications is that customer-facing applications support selling directly to customers through the Internet or a direct sales force, while partner-facing applications focus on indirect selling through channel partners. On deeper examination, the distinction between direct and indirect sales is meaningless, because both channels share the same goal: to improve how the enterprise goes to market and builds relationships with customers. Similarly, in discussing employee-facing applications, we argued that enterprise portals were different from knowledge management applications because enterprise portals focus on improving communications, while KM applications focus on improving collaboration. Again, this is a false distinction, because communication and collaboration are both aspects of the larger issue: improving productivity of knowledge workers by automating information and knowledge flow within the enterprise. We also distinguished between supplier-facing applications and partner-facing applications by observing that the former support collaboration and interaction with upstream suppliers in the "supply chain," while the latter support collaboration with downstream suppliers in the "demand chain." Again, the distinction between the supply chain and the demand chain is meaningless, because the upstream and the downstream partners are all part of the end-to-end value network that supports the fulfillment of customer demand. Other distinctions in the enterprise applications domain are equally meaningless. The intranet, the extranet, and the Internet, for instance, are simply different levels of information access provided to different constituencies.

So, despite our assertion that the universe of enterprise applications can be segmented into four distinct entity-centric faces of the enterprise, the fact is that the enterprise may ultimately present a unique face to every entity and every individual that interacts with it. Each face is nothing more than a context-specific view into the same unified repository of enterprise information on customers, partners, suppliers, and products. This vision of the unified enterprise (see Figure 5-2) suggests a unification of all databases that store information about external entities and all applications that connect different entities to this information. In the unified enterprise, the enterprise information and knowledge repository sits at the hub of an integrated network of applications. In the unified enterprise, there is no distinction between employee portals, partner portals, and customer portals. They are all windows into the same repository of information, differing only in the roles that are defined for each user, the interactions that are associated with each role, and the level of access permitted for each role. Again, the Internet, intranet, and extranet simply become different levels of secure access to the applications and content objects that constitute the enterprise infrastructure.

As we suggested in the previous chapter, the journey to the unified enterprise can be a long and difficult one, because the applications that constitute different elements of the unified framework have evolved independently and have not been designed to work together.

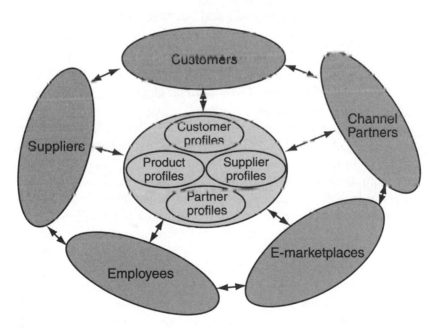

Figure 5-2
The unified enterprise

Therefore, integration generally involves gluing together pairs of applications with middleware, so that they can exchange data and information with each other. This middleware approach is a far cry from a unified platform designed ground-up with a common applications architecture and a shared database. A compromise approach may be to develop a component-based architecture that combines legacy external-facing applications with best-of-breed components of newer Web-native applications on a common platform. We discuss the emergence of such platforms in the next section.

With the basic building blocks of e-infrastructure in view, we now turn to broader trends that are shaping the evolution of e-infrastructure. These trends are important to understand, because they point out the directions toward which every enterprise must think as it overhauls its applications infrastructure to capitalize on Internet technologies. Like the force of gravity, these trends are inescapable. A deep understanding of them can help guide managers as they oversee capital investments in enterprise applications.

Modularity: From Integral Architecture to Component-Based Architecture

In the realm of strategy, we proposed that the business architecture be thought of as LEGO blocks of business processes assembled in flexible and creative ways to serve customers. In the realm of e-infrastructure, there is a similar move afoot: To think of applications infrastructure in terms of modular components that can be assembled like LEGOs to create complete software applications. Components are self-contained packages of functionality with clearly defined interfaces. That way, software architects can glue them with other components to rapidly create complex software applications. Components draw a clear line between software *construction* and software *assembly*, because the software architect can assemble components without needing to know the internal function of each component. This separation allows software architects to evolve from the "craft" method of developing software applications from scratch, to a "software factory" method for developing applications by reusing and assembling existing components.

Component-based architecture allows software architects to respond to the demands of flexibility and speed imposed upon them by the dynamic world of e-business infrastructure. It also serves as an effective design strategy to deal with complexity in software applications development. When software applications were relatively simple, they could be written as integral applications—a "black box" with individual elements of functionality tightly coupled. As their size and complexity increased, however, the integral architecture proved to be inflexible and inefficient. Software applications were difficult to design, because they needed to be written from scratch each time. And they were difficult to adapt, because of the tightly interwoven nature of individual functionalities within the applications. In addition, because the applications were not meant to operate as independent components, it was difficult to reuse pieces of software code to build new applications. By the late 1980s the software industry began to get seriously bogged down by complexity, and it began to search for an alternative approach for designing software. The answer was object-oriented programming (OOP).

Object-oriented programming relies on *abstraction* and *loose coupling* as tools for managing the complexity of software design and development. The central insight of this approach is to build small, self-contained bits of code that correspond more closely to how the program mirrors the real world. The concept of the *object* is central to this approach. Objects are little black boxes of functionality that are fully independent of any code that references or uses them. Objects are defined in terms of their properties (what they are) and their behavior (what they do). The beauty of objects is that a programmer can use them even without knowing what's inside the black box. Details of how the object is defined and how its functions are implemented don't need to be known to anybody except the object itself. These details are encapsulated within the object. Encapsulation makes it easier to modify software applications because you only need to deal with small pieces of code at any time, and you can insulate yourself from the inner workings of these pieces of code. You can concentrate on using the objects and designing systems that use the objects instead of rewriting software code from scratch each time. Furthermore, if you come across an object that is "mostly" what you need, you can easily add new features without breaking the old ones or even understanding how the old ones work. In short, object-oriented programming permits quantum leaps in flexibility and reusability.

Yet even the object-oriented programming approach, while conceptually elegant, swiftly becomes unwieldy when used to develop complex enterprise software applications. What is needed is a higher level of abstraction of this concept. *Component-based* architecture is this higher level of abstraction, because software components are nothing but aggregations of objects that provide chunks of application functionality as *services* to other components, and they can be assembled to create complete software applications.[8] Component-based architectures combine legacy software applications that have been "wrapped" to appear and behave like components with newer components developed as part of a distributed component platform. Figure 5-3 illustrates how legacy applications and newer components can be combined in a tiered fashion to create e-business applications. The development process then becomes one of assembly and adaptation, where the specific business rules for the enterprise are incorporated in the way the components are *configured* and assembled. The competitive differentiation of the enterprise is therefore based not on what the individual components are and what they do, but, rather, on how the components are put together and adapted. This separation of manufacturing from assembly allows the enterprise to combine the benefits of using stan-

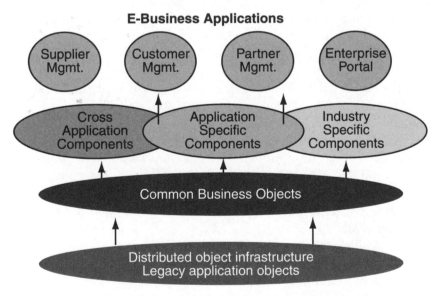

Adapted from: Enterprise E-Commerce *(Fingar, Kumar, Sharma, 2000)*

Figure 5-3
Component-based architecture

dardized best-of-breed components that do not need to be built from scratch, with the proprietary business logic that sets the enterprise apart from competitors.

Component-based architecture would be difficult to implement without a robust platform that integrates all of the best-of-breed components into a unified applications framework. Why? Because the components are developed by a multitude of vendors and are designed to operate independently of each other. Each component typically works on its own data, with its own definition of users, privileges, authorizations, and features. Without a common software foundation for e-business applications, the integration challenge of cobbling together the components becomes a daunting task. In response to this problem, e-infrastructure firms are developing platforms that allow best-of-breed components to be integrated into a unified framework.

An example that we mentioned in Chapter 1 is the e-service platform developed by Asera, which uses a "layered" approach to abstract core infrastructure functions like session management, load balancing, and messaging. It then makes these functions available as services to the applications.[9] The platform supports dynamic integration of best-of-breed software applications from independent vendors, along with existing enterprise applications, into a unified e-business applications framework. Users can decide which applications they want to subscribe to, and add/delete/modify individual applications from the framework without engaging in complex system integration. The applications in the e-business platform include _commerce_ applications for selling through various channels and through various mechanisms (auctions, RFQs, catalogs, reverse auctions); _community_ applications, which enable employees, customers, and partners to interact and collaborate; _content_ management applications, which automate the management and distribution of content across the enterprise; and _partner-facing_ applications, which enable sales and marketing services to be provided to partners. These applications encompass most of the four external-facing applications we discussed. In addition, the platform provides an integration framework that allows applications to work together seamlessly. At the user interface level, this integration translates into a uniform look and feel, Web-based access to all applications, and a single sign-on across all applications.

The Asera e-service platform is one instance of a move toward modular platforms that rely on abstraction and loose coupling to integrate component-based applications into a unified e-business platform. A host of other vendors, such as Ariba, ATG, BEA Systems, Sun, Microsoft, IBM, and Oracle, are also developing e-business platforms with "solution stacks" that consist of a connectivity layer, a hosting layer, a platform layer, an applications layer, and a presentation layer. While these modular and component-based architectures represent an important trend in the design of e-business platforms, the integration challenge is a difficult one. After all, components that were designed by independent software vendors were not meant to work together, and no integration framework can make this issue go away.

To illustrate the problem with modular architecture, consider an analogy from the computer world. An Apple Macintosh computer system always works better *as a system* than a Windows-based computer system, because the Apple system was designed by a single vendor and designed to work as an integrated system. In contrast, a Windows-based computer uses software, components, and peripherals from a diverse set of vendors, held together with a common set of standards, protocols, and the Windows operating system. But as any Windows user will readily attest, the integration of these components is far from perfect—at times even bringing to mind the old joke about the camel looking like a horse that was designed by a committee!

The trade-off between modular and integral architectures is simple. Modularity fosters flexibility, adaptability, and the use of best-of-breed components, but it suffers from poor integration and poor performance as a system. On the other hand, integral architectures promote better system performance and tighter integration, but they suffer from the "jack-of-all-trades and master of none" problem and promote excessive dependency on one vendor for all enterprise applications. So companies face the difficult choice between an integrated "suite" of applications from one vendor like Oracle or IBM (which promise tight integration but less flexibility) or a best-of-breed components approach like Asera (which permits greater flexibility and adaptability, but leaves something to be desired in terms of integration and seamlessness). On balance we believe that the pace of innovation in e-business applications is so quick, and the diversity of functionality increasing so fast, that component-based architectures would seem to have the upper hand in the modular versus integral architecture battle. However, this battle is far from over.

Synchronization:
From Sequential to Shared Processes

As the old saying goes, a chain is only as strong as its weakest link. The reason is not hard to find for those of us who as children played the game of Telephone. Information that is transmitted sequentially from person to person in a chain usually ends up severely distorted by the time it reaches the end of the chain. What is true of the game of Telephone is also true of how business applications and enterprises share information. Whenever information propagates linearly between a set of software applications or a set of entities that are chained together, it will be subject to delays and distortion because the "state" of the system is only visible to the next application or the next entity in the chain. This lack of end-to-end visibility makes it very difficult to coordinate the actions of the individual applications or entities, especially when other applications or other entities change the state of the system. The coordination problem becomes worse when information needs to be transmitted back and forth several times to complete a business process or transaction, because sequential information transfer usually moves in only one direction.

The problems that arise from sequential information transfer are well known, particularly in contexts such as new product development and supply chain management. The new product development process was traditionally managed as a set of sequential stages, with each upstream stage providing a set of outputs for the next downstream stage. Information flowed from one stage to another, in a sequential fashion and in one direction. Called the *waterfall model*, since water flows from one upstream level to the next downstream level, and only in one direction, this model does not allow for synchronization of information across stages, because information is transmitted linearly and sequentially. This creates coordination problems, because every upstream stage creates constraints for downstream stages, but the upstream stages do not know whether the downstream stages can accommodate these constraints. For instance, the design phase for a new product may require the selection of materials and manufacturing processes that may not be available or feasible when the product design is thrown "over the wall" from design to manufacturing.

To overcome the problems of sequential information transfer inherent in the waterfall model, several next-generation models have been created for new product development. One example is the *synchronize and stabilize model*, employed by firms like Microsoft and Netscape to bring new software products to market in a fast and flexible manner.[10] In the synch-and-stabilize model, product developers use daily product builds, two or more project milestones, and early, frequent alpha or beta releases. Individual programmers or small teams effectively act as one large team, building large-scale software products relatively quickly and efficiently while adapting to new technologies, feature changes driven by competition, or uncertainty in user requirements. The important difference between the synch-and-stabilize model and the waterfall model is the nature of information sharing across stages of development. The daily build process, a central feature of the synch-and-stabilize model, requires the *synchronous* sharing of information across different stages, because it requires the new product to be tested as a system at one point in time, as opposed to the *sequential* transmission of information from one stage to another in the waterfall model.

The insights gained from moving from sequential to synchronous information sharing have also been applied to improve the performance of supply chains, by eliminating the so-called bullwhip effect.[11] This effect is the phenomenon of progressively worsening distortion of demand information as it propagates sequentially from customers to retailers to manufacturers to suppliers. Because suppliers are the farthest removed from the end-user demand, they see the worst distortion. The antidote for the bullwhip effect is information integration, made possible by collaborative planning, forecasting, and replenishment among the participants in the supply chain. Information integration is the basis for supply chain integration, because it ensures that participants are acting upon synchronized information. The greater the extent of information sharing and information synchronization, the lesser the potential for the harmful bullwhip effect. The key idea is the same as in the synch-and-stabilize model for new product development—replacing sequential information transfer with synchronized information sharing among entities.

This points us to another theme in the evolution of e-business applications. As we discussed earlier in this chapter, the evolution of enterprise applications involved moving from *functional* applications, sequentially chained together, to *enterprise resource planning* applications, which share a common database and architecture. Before the introduction of ERP software, each functional area in the enterprise was served by an application that was function-specific. These applications could communicate information with each other only sequentially, and this limitation greatly inhibited the ability to share information within an organization (see Figure 5-4). With ERP applications, however, it was now possible for functional applications to share a common database. This shared database, the foundation of every ERP system, permitted the synchronization of data across all of the functional silos in the enterprises. An event that triggered a change in one functional area could instantly propagate across other functional areas.

While ERP systems allowed for synchronization of data and business processes within an enterprise, they did not allow for synchronization of data *across* enterprises. Currently, interenterprise business processes like supply chain management still rely on sequential transmission of information from the manufacturer's ERP system to the supplier's ERP system (upstream in the supply chain) and to the reseller's ERP system (downstream in the demand chain). Even collaborative planning and forecasting in supply chain management rely on sequential information transfer, because the different entities in the supply chain operate autonomously, and operate their own business processes.

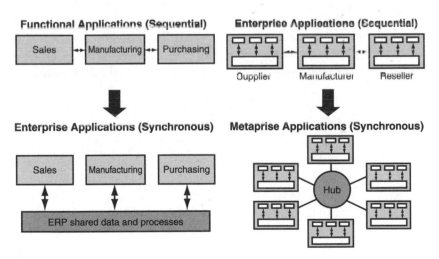

Figure 5-4
From sequential to synchronous applications

In fact, the very concept of the supply *chain* evokes a linear and sequential view of information coordination among enterprises. Just as ERP systems required the creation of shared data and shared processes within an enterprise, the creation of true synchronization among enterprises and their trading partners is the driver of next-generation application architectures that will transcend the enterprise and span the entire community of trading partners. These next-generation software platforms will enable the creation of shared business processes and shared databases *across* a community of trading partners, managed centrally by an intelligent hub. This is the logical next stage in the evolution of software applications—moving from enterprise applications to "meta-enterprise" applications.

An early example of a software company that is building such a software platform is Atlas Commerce. Dan Tiernan, the firm's CEO, foresees the creation of *Metaprises*—a community of collaborative enterprises that shares business processes and databases, and is synchronized by a central coordinator.[12] Instead of transmitting data sequentially between enterprises in the supply chain, data and business processes are inherently shared in the Metaprise. Consider how Metaprise software might help transform the supply chain in the plastics industry. An OEM like Motorola may order a plastic case for a cellular phone from a contract manufacturer. This order triggers a series of events that ripple sequentially through the supply chain. The contract manufacturer may place an order with an injection molder, who in turn may order plastic resin from a resin manufacturer, and from a specialist compounder who manufactures plastic compounds to the OEM's specific requirements. Despite the fact that these events are integrally linked and constitute a single end-to-end business process that cuts across enterprise boundaries, the process cannot be effectively coordinated if the demand signal travels sequentially in the supply chain. In this case, the resin manufacturer cannot efficiently plan production simply because it does not have advance visibility of upstream orders.

In the Metaprise model, by contrast, the OEM serves as the *channel master* for its community of suppliers, orchestrating the flow of information among the community through a central intelligent hub with a shared transaction engine and database for the supply management process. In this scenario, the purchase order from the OEM would be sent to the central transaction engine, which would *simultaneously* trigger a series of linked events. These would include issuing a purchase order to the contract manufacturer's sales order processing system, using the bill-of-materials information maintained centrally to generate a purchase order from the contract manufacturer to the injection molder's sales order processing system, and in turn generating orders from the injection molder to the resin manufacturer as well as the compounder. All of these events are triggered by a single event initiated by the OEM. There is instant visibility of orders for all participants, because the databases and information are shared, not sequential. The OEM can manage an interenterprise business process that cuts across the entire supplier community and that is inherently nonlinear in nature. The OEM can eventually also provide shared services to other members of the business web, including quality testing, logistics management, and credit/financing.

The Metaprise concept is one instance of a broader theme—the evolution of *business operating systems* to coordinate and synchronize the activities of multiple entities in a business network. Just as an operating system coordinates the activities of applications and peripherals in a computer system, business operating systems will emerge to coordinate the activities and business processes across enterprises. The Metaprise concept is a business operating system at the *enterprise* level—a "private hub" managed by one enterprise and closed to the external world. However, we are also seeing the emergence of operating systems at the *industry* level—public or semipublic marketplaces operated by a consortium of established industry players.[13] These consortia include Covisint in the automobile industry, Exostar in the aerospace industry, Transora in the consumer packaged goods industry, and Elemica in the chemicals industry, to name a few.

The basic functionality that these industry operating systems provide is a shared platform for automation of procurement and supply chains. But the true benefits of industry operating systems extend beyond the automation stage. The major payoffs will come from the enabling of *collaborative commerce*—shared business processes that are centrally managed across enterprises, and the creation of multienterprise software functionality.[14] The key idea is the same as in the Metaprise—pushing single enterprise functionality from within the walls of the enterprise to the business web and sharing multiple enterprise functionality with other enterprises in the industry, including customers, suppliers, business partners, and even competitors. The benefit, besides lower infrastructure costs and increased economies of scale, lies in the integration of information in the industry supply chain and the consequent reduction of inventory in the industry as a whole. Information replaces inventory, and synchronization of information replaces sequential information transfer. The industry operating system architecture recognizes that business processes like order processing are inherently multienterprise in nature, involving customers, manufacturers, distributors, suppliers, financial institutions, transportation providers, and the government, among others. The only effective way to coordinate these business processes is to create a shared platform, a common set of standards, and a common information backbone to connect all entities in the industry ecosystem. This shared platform allows batch processes to be transformed into real-time processes, and autonomous entities connected sequentially to be transformed into distributed networks of entities connected synchronously. Industry operating systems include software applications for managing both customer and supplier interactions, as well as buy-side and sell-side commerce transactions.

While the private hub model (the Metaprise architecture) and the public hub model (the Industry Operating Systems) share the idea of replacing a sequential "chained" architecture with a synchronous "networked" architecture, there is a significant difference. Private hubs are proprietary by design, while public hubs are open and shared across competitors. The benefit of the private hub or exchange is the ability of enterprises to preserve their proprietary business logic and business processes to gain competitive advantage. The disadvantage is that a single enterprise has to bear all of the infrastructure costs by itself, without benefit from economies of scale gained by collaborating with its competitors for sourcing inputs from suppliers. On the other hand, the public hub or industry operating system model has the advantage of scale, because it involves a larger community of suppliers, resellers, and customers. Furthermore, an industry-level entity is in a much better position to enforce interoperability among the business processes and applications of various industry participants.

In reality, Industry Operating Systems are highly ambitious and complex initiatives. Why? Because they require that competitors work together and collaborate on decision-making. As a result, implementation is likely to take a long time, and be fraught with conflicts among the founding partners. Moreover, with competitors sharing the same applications architecture for sourcing and going to market, there is a risk of erosion of competitive advantage leading to proprietary supplier and channel management.

So what should an enterprise do? Create its own private hub, or participate in an Industry Operating System? To answer this question requires another "Know thyself" question: Do we see supplier and reseller management as a key competitive differentiator in our business, or does our competitive differentiation arise primarily from the design and marketing of our products? Further: Is our supply chain unique and different from our competitors? If the supplier-facing systems are indeed proprietary, unique, and a source of competitive advantage, then the enterprise may be better off creating a private hub to coordinate the activities of its suppliers and resellers instead of joining an industrywide initiative. For instance, firms like Wal-Mart, Cisco, and Dell consider supply chain management to be a key competitive differentiator. It comes as no surprise that they have, by and large, stayed away from the industry consortia initiatives. On the other hand, automobile companies, aerospace companies, and hotels compete on product design and service quality—sourcing of inputs is not an area where competitive battles are traditionally fought and won. In these cases, it makes sense to collaborate with competitors on sourcing initiatives through the creation of industrywide operating system platforms. Regardless of the strategy adopted by an individual enterprise, the trend is inescapable. Business processes will have to be coordinated across enterprises by the creation of shared platforms that allow information to be shared and synchronized at the level of the business web.

Netsourcing: From Asset Ownership to Resource Access

Modularity and synchronization are key trends impacting the design and development of e-infrastructure. At the same time, the Internet is also revolutionizing the *delivery and deployment* of e-infrastructure. A by-product of a common communications infrastructure based on the TCP/IP, HTML, and HML protocols is the ability to access applications independent of the user's location. Location-independent access in turn means that the applications can reside anywhere and need not be located within the four walls of the enterprise. As we've discussed, this fundamental change opens up vast new possibilities for outsourcing IT applications and operations. Software, hardware, storage, and connectivity can all become services that are accessed over the network from infrastructure "utility" companies. Rather than being owned by the enterprise, they can be *rented* on a subscription basis from the "utility company," much like electricity and water. This is the phenomenon of *Netsourcing*—the sourcing of applications from service providers, over the Net. Today the emerging breed of service providers includes hosting service providers, application service providers, and managed operations providers.

To understand the business logic behind "information utility" companies, consider an analogy of how cooking gas is sourced in India versus the U.S. In Indian kitchens, gas stoves are powered by cylinders of liquefied petroleum gas (LPG). When a cylinder is exhausted, an employee of the gas company stops by the house to deliver a new cylinder. Every cylinder, costing less than $10, is replaced manually in every single home. It's a good thing that labor is cheap in India. In contrast, gas comes over a pipe to homes in the U.S., just like electricity and water. To deliver natural gas, gas companies have built elaborate networks of pipes. For customers, there are no cylinders to own, no spare cylinders to maintain, and no need for gas company employees to deliver gas cylinders to the home. Keeping gas cylinders at home is as quaint an idea in urban U.S. households as digging your own water well or maintaining your own electric power generator. Unless you live in a remote rural area, you simply subscribe to a utility company. You use as much gas as you need, and the utility company bills you for what you use. Most Americans haven't even seen their gas pipes. They don't know how gas flows into their homes and into their stoves. And they don't really care to know. Like good infrastructure, gas supply is cheap and reliable. And it is invisible. It is not something you worry about.

Similarly, without a reliable network, all the software applications, computing power, and networking equipment needed by an enterprise had to be localized within the enterprise. Not unlike the personal gas cylinder. But when enterprises can be connected by high-speed and reliable networks, it becomes more cost effective to outsource infrastructure to utility companies, which are better at running data centers and maintaining applications than the average IT organization within an enterprise can ever be. Even in the consumer world, portal companies like Yahoo! are becoming information utility companies that provide location-independent services to millions of consumers worldwide. Consumers can even use Yahoo!'s servers and infrastructure to store their files, digital photographs, e-mail, calendars, and contact databases. They don't need to *own* all the resources or be responsible for operating and maintaining them. They simply rent services on an as-needed basis.

The emergence of ASPs has been fueled by the promise of lower deployment cost, reduced complexity, increased speed of deployment, and increased flexibility in upgrading software applications. For large enterprises, the primary benefit of Netsourced applications is the reduction of system integration expenditures and the lower cost of ownership. For small- and medium-size businesses, Netsourcing allows access to robust applications that they could not have afforded or maintained on their premises. For startup firms, Netsourcing permits speed of deployment and access to "instant" IT infrastructure, so they can concentrate on building their core businesses. And for small/home office businesses, Netsourcing opens up the possibility of accessing preconfigured integrated IT solutions for managing their operations. While these benefits are powerful, Netsourcing nonetheless faces significant barriers to adoption. These include security and reliability concerns, lack of customized applications, integration problems with legacy applications, and confusion in the service provider marketplace. There may also be significant cultural resistance from internal IT staff who may be reluctant to relinquish control over application deployment and maintenance. It will take time to convince CIOs in large enterprises to outsource mission-critical applications, and it will be a while before service providers can provide the end-to-end solutions that are essential to customize and integrate Netsourced applications with the legacy applications infrastructure.

The Netsourcing ecosystem consists of several categories of participants, and the Netsourcing value chain is complex and multitiered. Starting with the end-customer, the most "visible" layer of Netsourcing participants are the *service integrators*. They bring together applications, professional services, and operations, and they deliver complete, managed solutions to customers. Service integrators started out as service aggregators offering single applications for rent over the Internet. But customers demand integration of applications, as well as services that support the integration and maintenance of applications. As a result, first-generation Netsourcing providers like Corio, USInternetworking, Interliant, and FutureLink are having to evolve from merely offering hosted applications to offering end-to-end integrated applications platforms and managed operations. In fact, the acronym ASP itself presents a very limiting view of service integrators. End-customers don't care about applications. They want to get their business processes to work seamlessly. Therefore, service integrators as a whole need to evolve their business architecture to become business service providers—providers of managed operations, not applications.

Service integrators in turn are customers for *application providers*—independent software vendors that create the software and applications from which solutions are assembled. Application providers create the offerings that the service integrators provide as a service. Increasingly, software vendors are creating hosted versions of their software applications that can be remotely deployed as a service, either by themselves or through service integrators. Service integrators are also customers for *operations providers* that provide the physical facilities for hosting and deployment of applications. These hosting providers, which include Exodus Communications, Digex, NaviSite, and Concentric Network, provide the hardware, communications equipment, and physical plant to end-customers as well as to service integrators. Operations providers are in turn customers for *connectivity providers*, which are at the lowest level, furthest removed from end-customers. Connectivity providers offer the logical and physical connectivity to the network and include telecom companies and Internet Service Providers such as MCI WorldCom and Sprint.

The layered model of the Netsourcing value chain is becoming more specialized as the industry evolves. Service providers are focusing on one or two layers of the multitiered model, and there is intense jockeying for position among the various tiers of providers for a share of the overall services revenue pie. The tiered model for Netsourcing echoes the move to the tiered and modular applications architecture, in that different elements of functionality (the network, the hosting, the platform, the applications, and the end-customer services) are logically separated and can be delivered by independent service providers. Each layer provides its outputs as services to the layer above it, just as each component in a tiered architecture provides its outputs as services to the application layer above it. This similarity means that the tiered model for application delivery is subject to the same integration problems that plague the tiered model for applications design. There are many participants and many handoffs in the delivery of Netsourced services, and these handoffs need to be managed well in order to deliver a seamless customer experience. The service integrators, who manage the end-customer relationship, will be held accountable for the performance of all participants in the Netsourcing value chain.

The Netsourcing marketplace is still in its infancy, but two themes will characterize its continued evolution. The first theme is a shift from Web-enabled applications to Web-native services. The early generations of Netsourcing providers offered retrofitted client/server applications that were never designed to be deployed remotely over the Internet. These applications were not scalable and were not tightly integrated with other enterprise applications. The newer breed of Web-native services have been designed from the ground-up to be deployed over the Internet, with the requisite scalability, reliability, and security. These applications typically focus on specific business processes like accounting, payroll, and procurement. The second theme in the evolution of Netsourcing is the shift from generic "horizontal" applications to customized "vertical" applications that are industry-specific. Horizontal applications are difficult to customize without significant system integration efforts, and the providers of horizontal Netsourced applications lack the domain expertise needed to adapt applications to specific industry situations. In response to the need for industry-specific solutions, a number of industry-specific vertical Netsourcing providers are emerging. Some of these providers are the B2B public exchanges reinventing themselves as marketplace service providers, while others are industry-sponsored consortia initiatives that we discussed earlier in the chapter. We expect this verticalization of ASPs to continue, as the scope of applications moves from generic applications like accounting and operating resource procurement to the core business processes like direct materials procurement, manufacturing operations management, and collaborative design.

Servicization: From Static Applications to Dynamic Web Services

So far we have used the *application* as the unit of analysis in our discussion of e-infrastructure. But the very concept of applications as the building blocks for e-infrastructure is being questioned. Applications are hard-coded blocks of software. While Netsourcing allows applications to be accessed from anywhere, the applications themselves are fixed in their physical location. However, advances in communications protocols now enable a new breed of dynamic and portable *Web services* to be created and delivered over the Internet. Web services are a services counterpart to object-oriented code—self-contained units of functionality that can be transported beyond enterprise boundaries and dynamically combined with other services to create a vast variety of mass customized e-services on the fly. Web services take information automation to a higher level of intelligence—from data-level automation to task-level automation. Web services can operate automatically on behalf of a person or an entity, without human intervention.[15]

To illustrate how dynamic Web services work, consider the process of buying an automobile, which involves several activities, including comparison price shopping, configuring the desired set of options, and arranging for financing. In the Web services world, this process would work as follows: The customer could initiate a Web service for comparison shopping, which would go out over the Web to locate the best price from auto dealers within a specified radius. The lowest-price dealer in turn could respond with a Web service that lets the customer configure the automobile by pulling information from the car manufacturer and aftermarket parts vendors. A Web service for locating a low-cost loan could be fired off in parallel to the comparison-shopping Web service, the output of which could be sent to the dealer as well as the customer by way of a notification of financing approval. This hypothetical scenario illustrates the features of Web services; they can be transported over the Internet, and they can interact and work with other Web services, all in an automated manner. In the Web services model, the traditional *programmed* interactions between people and software are replaced by task-focused interactions that are dynamic and flexible. The Web services model allows enterprises to service-enable their enterprise applications and "open" the applications to make pricing, inventory, customer, and product information available to other Web services, with appropriate security measures to ensure that only authorized Web services are allowed access to the information. Once applications are "servicized," interactions between applications can evolve from the *data* level to the *task* or business logic level. Web services "know" each other and can interact and work together without human intervention. Unlike applications that are hard-coded and fixed in location, Web services are portable, autonomous, and can be customized by service customers.

Web services are made possible by the creation of the Extended Markup Language (XML), a flexible way to create common information formats and to share the format as well as data between applications. In the automobile shopping example, auto dealers and manufacturers would need to agree on a standard way to describe the information about an automobile (make, year, model, engine capacity, etc.) and then describe the product information format with XML. Such a standard way of describing data would enable users to send intelligent agents like Web services to auto dealers' websites to gather data and make price comparisons. In addition to XML, the creation of Web services requires directory services to orchestrate the dynamic combination of Web services, and software platforms to publish, assemble, manage, distribute, and repurpose Web services. Almost every major software vendor has an XML initiative—Microsoft's BizTalk initiative and Hewlett-Packard's e-Speak are examples of initiatives that map traditional applications into Web services. And specialized XML vendors like Bowstreet are creating platforms for Web services automation. These automation platforms allow the IT organization to publish its business processes in the form of Web services, whose inputs and outputs are XML data. Once a business process (like package tracking, credit approval, or product configuration) is described and published in XML, it can be made available for other enterprises and other Web services to use. Web services and enterprises can therefore share and combine business processes into flexible and dynamic business webs. Every business becomes a producer and a consumer of Web services, enabling a new level of flexibility in creating business relationships.

The vision of dynamic business networks enabled by thousands of Web services is compelling, but it requires every participant in the network to agree upon a common set of industry-specific "dialects" of XML that are essential for interoperability of Web services. Industry groups are working furiously toward this goal, and the proliferation of industry B2B consortia will further the creation of industry-specific XML standards. But until these standards become accepted and widely adopted, the vision of Web services cannot be fully actualized. Nevertheless, the concept of Web services starts to raise deep questions. For example: What is an enterprise? What is an application? What is a business process? Our rigid notions of enterprise boundaries, monolithic applications, and hard-coded business process interactions across enterprise boundaries will need to be fundamentally rethought in a world of fluid enterprise boundaries, dynamic Web services, and loosely coupled interactions between businesses. This is an exciting view of the future of business interaction and collaboration.

E-infrastructure has evolved a long way from the archaic mainframe and departmental computing era to the futuristic vision of Web services and hub-centric architectures that are truly network-centric in their design, exploiting the power of open standards to create new levels of collaboration. Several themes are apparent in our discussion of the building blocks and the evolutionary trends in e-infrastructure. The first theme describes a shift from looking inward and thinking in functional terms to looking outward and thinking in terms of relationships with key entities like customers, suppliers, and partners. A related theme is the convergence of the various external faces of enterprise applications into a unified enterprise that presents a unique face to each entity inside and outside the enterprise. The third theme is a shift from linear "chain-centric" views of enterprise applications to a nonlinear "hub-centric" view of enterprise and industry operating systems. The final theme is a shift from rigid applications and assets that are owned to dynamic services and resources that are accessed over the network.

These are the broad-brush themes shaping the future of e-infrastructure. They offer clear guidelines in placing intelligent bets on infrastructure and e-business projects. Placing bets moves us from the realm of technology and infrastructure to the realm of project and portfolio management. So, in the next chapter, we take off our CTO hat and put on our CFO hat as we discuss how to place intelligent bets on e-business initiatives.

6

E-CAPITALIZATION: PLACING WINNING BETS

Since it costs a lot to win
And even more to lose,
You and me bound to spend some time,
Wondering what to choose.

—Jerry Garcia, The Grateful Dead

AN OLD JOKE concerns Sherlock Holmes and Dr. Watson on a camping trip. After a good meal and a bottle of wine, they go to sleep. Some hours later, Holmes wakes up and nudges his friend. "Watson, look up at the sky and tell me what you see."

"I see millions and millions of stars," Watson replies.

"Well, what does that tell you?"

Watson ponders for a minute. "Astronomically, it tells me that there are millions of galaxies and potentially billions of planets. Astrologically, I observe that Saturn is in Leo. Horologically, I deduce that the time is approximately a quarter past three. Theologically, I can see that God is all-powerful and that we are small and insignificant. Meteorologically, I suspect that we will have a beautiful day tomorrow. What does it tell *you*?"

After a moment of silence, Holmes looks over and says, "Watson, you idiot! Someone has stolen our tent!"

To put the joke into context, recall that aberration in recent history when practically every Internet startup seemed destined for capital market success. Not just a modicum of success, mind you, but the kind of success that leads to billion-dollar valuations and induction into the ranks of the Global 2000. With startups promising returns to their investors far in excess of any returns that might be realized through conventional means—like good old-fashioned operating profits—it's no wonder that corporate finance executives came to view equity investments in these startups as a vehicle to maximize shareholder value. Seduced by visions of huge capital gains, corporate investors became swept up in the same euphoria as the venture capitalists and dotcom entrepreneurs. No matter that they may have lacked the expertise and experience ordinarily considered a prerequisite for early stage venture investing, they began to place investments with unprecedented vigor—accounting for 15 percent of all venture investing in 1999, up from a mere 2 percent in 1994. Major corporations soon found themselves as accidental venture capitalists, with sizable equity positions in a range of Internet startups, including some that bore little relevance to their core businesses. And for a while, it seemed, every bet was a sure thing, and every gambler a winner. That is, until the market turned and reality reasserted itself.

An example of a company that temporarily lost sight of its tent, by becoming fixated on the financial returns from e-commerce venturing activities, is Starbucks, the ubiquitous purveyor of coffee. Having long harbored digital dreams, including a vision of creating a chain of cyber cafés, Starbucks invested in four e-commerce startups: Living.com (furniture), Kozmo.com (urban deliveries), Cooking.com (kitchenware), and Talk City (chat/community). "Our research indicates that the revenue opportunities represented by these categories, which is estimated at more than $100 billion, is enormously attractive, given the natural synergies of our core demographics," exulted CEO Howard Schultz, in June 1999.[1] But while Starbucks was busy playing venture capitalist, who was minding the coffee shop? Fast forward to November 2000. Humbled by its mounting investment losses, and admitting to having taken its eye off the ball, Starbucks was singing a different tune. "Our innovation will continue, but we are totally refocused on our core business," Orin Smith, the new CEO, told investors after announcing that charges related to the four investments had nearly wiped out all profit for the fiscal fourth quarter of 2000.[2] All told, Starbucks wrote off more than $58 million, and its stock recovered only after the company promised to forgo any further Internet venturing activities. For every Delta Air Lines, which had the fortune to sell its stake in Priceline.com when times were good, there are many more companies like Nordstrom, which took a $20 million loss on Streamline.com (online grocery delivery), and ValueVision, a cable and satellite broadcasting company that wrote off more than $55 million due to investments in a series of dotcoms that had nothing to do with broadcasting.

For many established companies, the promise of financial returns from e-commerce ventures only served to muddle their priorities.[3] Consider that CEOs have at their disposal a finite number of resource allocation chips for placing their investment bets. These chips are comprised of financial resources, people resources, and time resources. Under pressure to enhance their stock prices, and viewing the soaring market values of the newer companies through the lenses of their own less-than-stellar earnings projections, many CEOs during this period of enchantment came to the logical conclusion: "If you can't beat 'em, join 'em." So they chased the valuations, only to discover, in many cases while in the midst of spinning off what they hoped and prayed would be the next big IPO, that they were only chasing a mirage—always round the bend, but forever elusive.

A rising tide lifts all boats, and in a hurricane even a turkey can fly! But when the winds die down, watch out: That's when the turkeys fall from the sky. And fall they did. By the end of 2000 a large number of finance executives were left shaking their heads in disbelief, wondering what had compelled them to sink so much money into so many unproven business models in the first place. Again, the answer can be traced to two primal human motivators: fear and greed. Fear that they were being left behind, with their core businesses in a vulnerable position, and greed that stemmed from a desire to get in on the money-making action. In retrospect, neither motivator is a good reason to take out the corporate checkbook. In fact, an important lesson to be learned from the dotcom insurgency is the need for a company to temper its reactionary impulses toward moneymaking opportunities, opting instead for a portfolio of e-business bets that are logically related to the firm's core business and are grounded in a solid customer value proposition.

As we've stressed throughout this book, the only safe anchor in a turbulent sea of change is the customer. No matter how attractive the moneymaking opportunity, the primary impetus for investing in any type of initiative should be *customer value proposition engineering*. Venture type activities motivated only out of fear or greed fail to address the reality that a company exists fundamentally to deliver value to its customers through a product and/or service offering. By the same token, an excessively large venture arm focused purely on financial gain, and not necessarily concerned with strategic value-add or learning transfer, may in the big scheme of things be actually performing a disservice. Every investment should advance the company's efforts to create value for its customers—not necessarily today, but in the long run. The extent to which an initiative can be expected to meaningfully impact the customer experience should serve as the key criterion for selecting initiatives.

In formulizing its investment strategy, Starbucks could have drawn some lessons from the e-venturing bets placed by W.W. Grainger.[4] Founded in 1927, Grainger is a large business-to-business supplier of maintenance, repair, and operating (MRO) supplies. The company offers more than 600,000 products through a massive catalog and a network of 574 branch and distribution centers. Viewing the Internet as a logical extension of its reach as well as its offerings, Grainger bet heavily on e-commerce ventures, investing over $150 million by the end of 2000 on a portfolio of ventures that included the following:

- *Grainger.com*, the digital Grainger storefront that offers all of the products in its 3,000-page print catalog. The electronic catalog allowed Grainger to expand the 80,000 items in the paper catalog to over 220,000 electronically searchable listings.
- *OrderZone.com* (now merged with Works.com), a multisupplier B2B online marketplace where companies could purchase a wide range of non-MRO products and services. This initiative was aimed at extending Grainger's reach into the small- and medium-size business market.
- *FindMRO.com*, a Web-based solution for customers looking for discontinued or hard-to-find supplies, typically needed in urgent buying situations like emergency machine repair. In these situations, availability of the item and speed of delivery

are most important, because the cost of down time is far greater than the cost of the part.

- *MROverstocks.com,* a website for customers to buy surplus products using an auction model. Covering 15 product categories and over 140 suppliers, the site gives business customers the opportunity to buy discontinued and excess industrial products at deeply discounted prices, and it allows MRO suppliers to improve their yield from surplus and obsolete inventory.

- *TotalMRO.com,* a Web-based e-procurement solution for large enterprises that allows customers to search, compare, and buy over 3.5 million products from over a dozen leading MRO suppliers.

Three things stand out as we look at Grainger's e-business ventures. First, every e-venture leverages Grainger's set of capabilities around catalog sales and distribution, as well as its long-standing relationships with 1.5 million business customers. Each initiative deepens Grainger's offerings or broadens its reach in the MRO marketplace. Here there is no vague talk of "potential synergies."

Second, a solid customer value proposition underscores every initiative. According to Don Belinski, Group President of Emerging Business at Grainger, all of the company's e-ventures are built around a straightforward value proposition: *being the most convenient and speedy source for companies to buy what they need, when they need it.* While Grainger.com offers greater choice, more convenience, and additional functionality (e.g., search, online help) to Grainger's existing customers, FindMRO.com offers a solution for an unmet customer need (getting their hands on hard-to-find emergency replacement supplies). Similarly, MROverstocks.com responds to a unique buying situation and a unique buying mechanism (surplus inventory sold through a dynamic pricing mechanism). Finally, TotalMRO.com and OrderZone.com ensure that Grainger has a presence in two emerging electronic procurement channels (e-marketplaces and e-procurement platforms for indirect materials).

It is easy to articulate how each of these ventures strengthens Grainger's value proposition of helping customers buy *what* they need, *when* they need it, and *where* they want to buy it.

The third characteristic of Grainger's e-business initiatives is that they differ significantly in their risk/return profile, as a diversified portfolio should. While Grainger.com and TotalMRO.com are logical and incremental extensions of the core business, OrderZone.com was a more speculative and risky venture because it involved a different customer base (small- and mid-size businesses), a different buying mechanism (online marketplace), and collaborating with other MRO suppliers that were equipped with different systems and business processes. However, the OrderZone.com venture had a significant *option value*, because it allowed Grainger to buy an option on playing in the e-marketplace arena, which promised to revolutionize B2B e-commerce in 1999. As it turns out, e-marketplaces did not develop as predicted, and small businesses presented more resistance to change than anticipated. So Grainger had to jettison OrderZone.com by merging it with Works.com, another player in the small- to mid-size online MRO marketplace. This option turned out to be of little value, but it did preserve Grainger's right to play in the e-marketplace arena. So, while not all of Grainger's e-business bets have paid off, the company's diversified and customer-focused portfolio of initiatives gave it a better chance of placing winning bets.[5]

So how can an enterprise think more strategically about its portfolio of e-business investments? To place winning bets, we believe that decision makers need to answer four key questions: (1) How do we increase the range of initial ideas for e-business initiatives? (2) How do we prioritize these ideas in coming up with the set of initiatives to pursue? (3) How do we define the metrics for tracking performance of e-business initiatives? (4) How do we fund different types of initiatives? Answering these questions is no easy task because of the delicate balance e-business leaders need to strike between acting incrementally versus acting radically; between returns and risk; between profits today versus growth tomorrow; between financial payoffs and strategic payoffs; and between short-term wins and long-term wins. Before you make these choices, however, you must maximize the number of chances at bat.

Looking Widely: Maximizing the Flow of Ideas

"The best way to have a good idea is to have lots of ideas," observed the physicist Linus Pauling. In the Net economy, a company needs to sow a thousand seeds of ideas, knowing that relatively few of them will actually germinate into initiatives. In fact, given the expansiveness of today's strategy landscape, the biggest dangers will tend to come not from the obstacles on the road a company has chosen to travel, but from the roads it has failed to explore. Traditionally, strategists have been concerned with minimizing the probability of committing Type I errors: betting on the wrong ideas. The mantra: *Get it right the first time.* This failure-averse attitude is understandable in a humdrum opportunity landscape, where opportunities can be carefully assessed because they are few and far between. However, in times of tremendous change and opportunity, there exists a much greater risk of making Type II errors: failing to place bets that could have won big. Type II errors are much costlier than Type I errors when the opportunity window is narrow and the cost of being late looms larger than the cost of being wrong. This is not to say that strategists should ignore Type I errors. Rather, the win-win strategy would be to minimize Type II errors on the front end while assessing opportunities, and then minimize Type I errors at the back-end while implementing initiatives. The idea flow process should be designed like a funnel, with a very wide mouth at the front-end, and a narrow output at the back-end.

Corporate decision makers charged with placing bets on e-business initiatives should learn from the very different mantra of venture capitalists: *maximize proprietary deal flow.* Ask VCs to name their most important success factors and they are likely to mention their rich sources of proprietary deal flow. Success in the venture world depends heavily on seeing lots of deals, seeing the best deals, and seeing these deals before other VCs see them. VCs work very hard to cultivate sources of proprietary deal flow, which include their portfolio company CEOs, their network of advisers and friends, their contacts with universities and research institutions, and their contacts with the R&D community within large enterprises. And VCs follow a disciplined yet rapid decision-making process to screen deals. So what are the sources of "deal flow" or idea flow in established companies? And how is this idea flow managed?

Ideas, like information, can emanate from many different sources and flow in many different directions in a large organization. Information can flow *vertically,* as top-down communication from management or as bottom-up reporting from the front line. Information can also flow *horizontally,* across functional departments, business units, and geographies. Information can be *imported* into the organization— information pertaining to the market, customers, competitors, and channels, for instance. Finally, information can be *exported* from the organization—sent to channel partners, suppliers, and customers, for instance. These sets of information flows are supported by specific mechanisms. Vertical flows are supported by management control systems; horizontal flows are facilitated by groupware systems and best practice sharing; outward-in flows are supported by market sensing and competitive intelligence systems; and inward-out flows are supported by partner-facing and customer-facing processes and systems. In our discussion of e-infrastructure we emphasized that large organizations can benefit tremendously by streamlining and improving the quality of these information flows.

Now consider where ideas come from in an organization, how they flow, and how these flows can be managed to maximize the range and quality of ideas. Like the four directions of information flow, ideas can also flow vertically, horizontally, outward-in, and inward-out. Ideas can come from senior management and can be diffused downward into the organization. Or they can bubble up from the grassroots level. Ideas can flow laterally across departments and business units. Ideas can be imported from innovative startup firms or from best practice firms. And they can be exported through spin-offs and carve-outs that leverage the firm's capabilities and assets. Each of these idea flow directions should be managed systematically and shepherded carefully. The e-business ventures team, under the direction of executive management, must create pathways to facilitate the efficient flow of ideas and incentives for improving the quantity and quality of ideas. The flow of ideas should be managed like the flow of information—as a systematic business process designed to maximize throughput and quality.

To illustrate how the e-business organization can help centralize and manage idea flow in a large company, consider the "idea broker" role of Boeing Ventures, the ventures group charged with growth initiatives at the Boeing Company. According to Anil Shrikhande, the head of Boeing Ventures, there are three ways in which Boeing seeks to enhance shareholder value: operational excellence in its core businesses; extending the core business into new higher-growth areas like life-cycle sales and support of aircraft; and opening new frontiers through business innovation. The e-business initiatives at Boeing map into these categories. Boeing's individual business units are charged with the responsibility of e-enabling their core business processes and finding ways to leverage their services offerings through e-business. The Boeing Ventures organization is charged with opening new frontiers through a two-pronged approach: *value realization* and *value innovation*. Value realization is the process by which Boeing seeks to unlock the value embedded in its technology, its domain expertise and its human capital. Value realization looks *inward* for seeds of innovation. Value innovation is the process by which Boeing seeks to leverage its expertise and relationships into new arenas, through external partnerships. It looks *outward* for seeds of innovation. While value innovation promotes entrepreneurship, value realization promotes "intrapreneurship."

Value realization at Boeing involves managing *lateral flows* and *upward flows* of ideas by creating an efficient internal market for ideas and an efficient process for managing idea flows within the organization. Lateral flows are ideas that have been created in one part of the organization, but could greatly benefit other parts of the organization, or even the organization as a whole. It may be a product innovation, a process innovation, or a materials innovation. Upward flows are ideas that flow from the company's massive pool of human intellectual capital. To support and fund these lateral and upward flows, Boeing has established a multiyear $200 million pool of money called the Chairman's Innovation Initiative (CII) for new venture ideas from Boeing employees. The Boeing Ventures organization acts as a focal point for reviewing these ideas, making funding decisions, and supporting the ideas as they evolve into ventures. Any individual employee or team of employees can submit an idea in the form of a short outline to the Boeing Ventures organization. If the idea is felt to be promising, the individual or team is invited to write a business plan. Ideas can eventually end up on one of four corporate paths. Boeing could absorb the idea into its core businesses. Or the idea could become a joint venture with Boeing and another party. Or Boeing could launch the plan as a new business. Finally, the idea could be spun off as a stand-alone venture, with the originators of the idea having significant equity stakes in the venture. Boeing hopes that the financial rewards improve the quantity and quality of ideas, while the review process and the support of the Boeing Ventures organization improve the chances of the chosen ideas being scaled into ventures.

Value innovation at Boeing involves trading ideas with the external marketplace by *importing* ideas in the form of venture investments in startup companies, or by *exporting* ideas in the form of external ventures founded by Boeing. An example is Connexion by Boeing, a venture for offering high-speed Internet access services on commercial aircraft. Connexion utilizes Boeing's expertise in the commercial satellite business and the commercial airliner business, as well as the company's relationships with its airline customers. Similarly, Boeing is a cofounder of Exostar, a business-to-business exchange in the aerospace industry. These outward-in and inward-out ventures are also coordinated by Boeing Ventures, which acts as a market maker between Boeing and external partners, investors, and the startup companies in which Boeing might want to invest.

As a stimulator, a clearinghouse, a facilitator, and a coach for managing the idea-to-initiative process, the Boeing Ventures organization performs a function that is crucial for managing growth in any large, multidivisional organization. Without a focal organization like a venture group to manage idea flow, the responsibility for managing growth initiatives tends to become too diffuse. But for a growth-management organization to succeed, it needs to have financial resources. Moreover, no venture organization within a large company can succeed without close and direct interaction with the CEO. New ventures that cut across organizational boundaries simply cannot gain internal traction without executive sponsorship and championing. The ventures organization also needs to have the funds to support promising ideas that come from inside—or outside—the company.

In summary, to maximize the range of ideas and their chances of success, established companies should create a central organization, a well-defined process, and the financial resources to nurture ideas to maturity. Many companies do a good job of managing new *product* creation *within* a business unit. But very few do a good job at managing new *venture* creation that cuts *across* business units. According to Phil Condit, the company's CEO, Boeing "can build a next-generation aircraft with our eyes blindfolded and our hands tied behind our backs. But ask us to do something different, and we are lousy at it."

So, pause and ask yourself: How are ideas for new ventures stimulated and managed in *my* organization? Imagine that you are a junior manager with an innovative idea for a new venture. Would you know where to go with your idea? Do you know if there is a process in place to carry your idea forward? Can you get your idea funded within the company? How long would it take to get it funded? Now, adopt the perspective of a startup company that wants to approach your organization for an investment. Would you know where you would go with your investment proposal? How quickly would your organization make a decision? How clearly are the organization's investment priorities defined and articulated? The answers to these questions might be unsettling when you keep in mind the fact that a leading VC firm sees more than 10,000 plans every year and ends up funding only 20 of them. Do you have this kind of deal flow in your organization?

Sequencing Your Bets:
Exploiting the Power of Flexibility

Having gathered up enough chips, corporate executives need to decide how to place their bets on both growth-focused e-ventures and change-focused internal e-business initiatives. In placing bets, it pays to know that you don't need to place all your bets at one point in time. Rather, you can sequence your bets and preserve your right to play as events unfold. Strategy, after all, is executed as a set of sequential moves, with each move opening up the possibility of making other moves that may ultimately lead to new opportunities. Because strategic investments can create subsequent opportunities that may become available, the investment opportunity itself may be viewed simply as the right to participate in future opportunities—a *call option*, in financial markets parlance.[6] A call option gives its owner the right, but not the obligation, to buy a stock at a given price. If the price of the stock appreciates, the investor will exercise his contract at the striking price and capture the gain.

Similarly, a company that owns a real option has the right, but not the obligation, to make a future decision to invest. For example, Amazon's e-commerce expertise and customer franchise in the books business afforded it real options to invest in other e-commerce markets. It started with music—beating out CDnow, the then-reigning champ, in its first full quarter of selling music titles—and, later, electronics, kitchenware, and even new cars. Or consider, Intuit, whose beachhead into e-commerce through its finance portal Quicken.com eventually paid off in spades (this after having overcome initial resistance from within the top ranks of the organization, including a CEO who was slow to grasp the website's long-term strategic potential). In its first year, Quicken.com generated little revenue—just 5 percent of the $580 million for Intuit's fiscal year ending in July 1998. But that changed as consumers and small business owners gradually warmed up to the idea of using the website to manage their mortgage, insurance, and payroll needs. Meanwhile, margins in Quicken's traditional packaged software began to come under serious pressure due to heavy competition from rival Microsoft Money, which most PC makers could now bundle for a few dollars per license. Within three years of its initial launch, Quicken.com had become instrumental in enabling Intuit to move into new Internet-related businesses. By the beginning of 2001 these businesses were accounting for a third of Intuit's total revenues.

Intuit's experience suggests another important fact in placing bets: errors of omission can be just as dangerous as errors of commission. Not taking a risk *is* taking a risk. Not choosing *is* making a choice. Rarely are employees fired for not making decisions quickly, but they *are* fired for making mistakes. For Intuit, the cost of not moving could have resulted in a lost opportunity to build new revenue streams and new digital businesses that may have ultimately become the company's salvation. Options thinking requires a significant shift in mindset. Simply put, real options afford an opportunity to put a toe in the water, with a line of sight to jumping in much deeper should the seasons change from winter to summer.

Options thinking can also be useful in the context of internal e-business initiatives, by expanding the range of a firm's experimentation and preserving flexibility in placing bets on new offerings, new channels, and new customer segments. Consider the role of options thinking in new product development. Researchers who studied the product development process at Toyota discovered an interesting paradox: By delaying decisions, Toyota is able to speed up projects and make better cars.[7] Toyota designers define a *set* of possible solutions to a design problem, instead of a single solution. And they proceed to explore the entire set of competing design solutions, instead of iterating and refining the single solution. The competing solutions involve multiple teams working in parallel on alternative solutions. The solution set is gradually narrowed, and the final design solution is chosen quite late in the design process. This parallel development process may seem wasteful and inefficient, because it involves spending time and money on alternative solutions, instead of working on refining a specific solution. However, it is actually a very sensible strategy, when you realize how it converts a onetime internal bet into a real option that sequences the bets out over time.

Bets and options both involve making decisions with uncertain future outcomes. A bet is an "all-or-nothing" decision that leaves the decision maker with little flexibility to respond to information that becomes available in the future. Roll the dice, spin the wheel, and see what happens. However, an option allows a decision maker to break up a one-shot bet into many smaller bets that can be sequenced over time. You only place a partial bet at the beginning, and you retain the flexibility to choose what bets to place in the future, once you know more about the future. Unlike traditional product development, where the auto manufacturer would place an all-or-nothing bet on the final design of a new car, Toyota hedges its bets by exploring alternative design options and retains the right to bet on any of them in the future, when it may know more about customer response to these alternative designs. By exploring a large number of prototypes, Toyota is able to explore a broad range of options in the design space, thus increasing the chance that it hits upon the "best" design from among a very large set of possible alternatives. The experimentation strategy allows Toyota to reduce the probability of committing a Type II error early in the game, even at the cost of supporting parallel development efforts. This cost of parallel exploration is the cost of buying a call option on the final design— money well spent when you compare the cost of exploring multiple options at the concept stage against the much higher cost of ending up with a less-than-ideal design much later on in the process. The greater the uncertainty, the greater the importance of sequencing bets to preserve flexibility.

How can the Toyota insight be applied to e-business initiatives? Recall from our discussion in Chapter 3 that e-business presents established firms with far more options than ever before in configuring a business. And e-business presents a diverse range of opportunities and threats by permitting new avenues for business improvement and innovation. As executives pick their way through the opportunity landscape, it is important to explore the opportunity space as widely as possible. In choosing internal e-business initiatives, it is important to experiment broadly, sequence investments in projects, and explore alternative options in parallel. And in exploring external e-business ventures, it is important to place overlapping bets, as well as to place side bets on innovative startup companies that have the potential to disrupt how business is done in the industry.

With the options lens, the logic behind the e-business investments made by W.W. Grainger comes sharply into focus. Again, in placing bets on its go-to-market strategy in the realm of e-business, Grainger was faced with the possibility that its customers would shift their buying from the conventional catalog channel to emerging channels like the Web, online marketplaces, and e-procurement software vendors. It was also faced with the possibility that customers would demand to buy MRO supplies through a dynamic pricing mechanism like an auction or a reverse auction. In anticipation of these possible outcomes, Grainger created a portfolio of option-creating investments to ensure that it would have a foothold in all relevant channels, no matter how the future turned out. Grainger.com allowed it to reach its customers over the Web through a static pricing technique, while MROverstocks.com allowed it to offer dynamic pricing functionality. TotalMRO.com and OrderZone.com allowed it to place bets on the e-marketplace and e-procurement channels. It now seems clear that Grainger.com is a winner, while OrderZone.com was not. The investment in OrderZone.com was the cost of buying an option to play in the potentially lucrative online marketplace arena. As the future unfolds, Grainger now has the flexibility to focus its resources on the channels that turned out to be winners, while letting its options on other channels expire by jettisoning its investments.

The moral of the story: In exploring the opportunity landscape, you need not turn over every last stone. But when a stone does turn over, make sure you own at least part of it and that you have the right and opportunity to own more of it should that stone be later appraised as a valuable gem. To place winning bets, you must convert bets into options and onetime investments into a sequence of investments that preserve flexibility in making future decisions.

Therefore, besides sowing *many* seeds, it is important to sow many *different* kinds of seeds. Just as portfolio managers diversify their investments across different categories (e.g., stocks, bonds, and other financial instruments) and different industry sectors in order to reduce the risk level while maximizing the returns potential, finance executives need to think in terms of a portfolio of e-business initiatives that can be arrayed along a risk-return continuum.

Prioritizing Your Bets: Rating the Portfolio of Initiatives

Despite the elegance of options thinking, there is a key difference between constructing portfolios of financial assets and portfolios of e-business initiatives. While there is practically no limit to the number of financial options a person can own, there *are* significant constraints around the number of initiatives a company can reasonably undertake, because each initiative demands cognitive capital and time capital, in addition to financial capital. Unlike venture capitalists, no investment that a company makes in e-business can be driven by financial returns alone. So it *is* possible to overcommit, by placing too many bets and investing in too many initiatives.

Achieving the fine balance between incremental "income statement" initiatives that focus on the core business and short-term pay-offs, and the more radical "capital appreciation" initiatives that focus on growing the business into new directions over a longer duration, brings us back to the Holmes and Watson joke: How can a company think big thoughts without losing its tent? How can it hit singles that advance the runners along the bases while also looking to hit home runs out of the ballpark? The theologian Austin O'Malley expressed the same idea, albeit less humorously: "If you keep your eyes so fixed on heaven that you never look at the earth, you will stumble into hell."

Hoping to gain entrance into heaven while at the same time prospering here on earth harks back to the problem we explored in Chapter 2 concerning the duality of e-business initiatives. Resolving the duality from an investor perspective requires that e-business initiatives be managed as a portfolio of investments that are balanced in terms of risk, return, and time horizon. While these three dimensions are obvious constructs from portfolio management theory— "Elementary, my dear Watson," in the words of Sherlock Holmes— there are also other *strategic* factors that need to be considered in constructing and prioritizing a portfolio of e-business initiatives.

Also from Chapter 2, recall our discussion regarding the considerations that might be used to influence how a company should go about prioritizing its initiatives. In that chapter, we posed the following questions, designed to help companies better understand their own distinct assets and priorities:

- Do you use a lot of raw materials and components?
- What fraction of your customers is online, and how intense are the interactions?
- Do you have multiple layers of resellers and many different types of channels?
- Do you spend a lot of money on new product development?
- Are you a "knowledge factory"?

Clearly, the answers to these "Know thyself" questions should be combined with the risk-return questions we explore in this chapter. With that in mind, we propose the following factors for prioritizing the portfolio of e-business initiatives:

Anticipated payoff The anticipated payoff from the initiative is an assessment (often subjective) of the ratio of the payoff to the investment that is needed for the initiative. Theoretically, this becomes the ROI for the project. But there are several problems in measuring ROI for e-business initiatives that we will elaborate on later. Suffice it to say that an informed assessment, updated periodically as the project evolves, is probably better than trying to figure out the ROI to the third decimal place.

Time to payoff Some e-business initiatives may begin to bear fruit within a matter of weeks, while others may require investing for a long time before making any payoff—not unlike the fabled Chinese bamboo that must be fertilized every day for years without showing any outward signs of life and then one day, in the fifth year, skyrockets through the soil and quickly grows to a height of eighty feet. While initiatives that pay off sooner may be preferred to those that pay off later, there may be a trade-off between the time to payoff and the magnitude of the eventual payoff. After all, low-hanging fruit is not the sweetest fruit. Therefore, the importance given to achieving payoffs quickly is a function of the management's time horizon and its preference for a "bird in the hand today" versus "two in the bush tomorrow." However, projects that have a short time to *initial payoff* should be unambiguously preferred to those where the initial payoff is much further into the future. The reason: Initial payoffs build confidence that the project is on track to produce returns.

Scope of impact How broad is the scope of the audiences that will be impacted by the initiative? Will the beneficiaries be one department, related departments, multiple related and unrelated departments, the entire enterprise, or the entire value network? For instance, an enterprise portal project, by definition, impacts the entire enterprise, so its scope of impact is very broad. Similarly, an e-procurement initiative may have an enterprisewide impact for a multidivisional firm. On the other hand, an initiative to set up an e-commerce site for a specific business unit may be limited in scope to only the business unit.

Competitive differentiation Another important consideration in choosing initiatives is the extent to which the initiative will set the enterprise apart from its competition. Is it a "game-changing" initiative, or a "table stakes" initiative that will preserve competitive parity but not do much for competitive differentiation? Implementing a plain vanilla e-procurement initiative, for instance, might enable the enterprise to stay in the game but not change the game in terms of competitive advantage. But creating a new way to go to market, or a new offering that taps into a new customer segment, may greatly impact the company's competitive position.

By the same token, as we've discussed, a company would not want to participate in a joint venture that revolves around its own proprietary strengths. For example, in the insurance industry, Allstate's core competencies are its claims underwriting and risk management capabilities. These involve relatively complex processes that are out of reach of most stand-alone dotcoms, leaving them to contribute to only a small part of the overall business model: presales prospecting. They identify potential buyers for insurance coverage and Allstate underwrites the risk. A company should keep its proprietary business know-how close to its chest and refrain from partnering along that dimension. Therefore, while Allstate might be persuaded to join a consortium to buy office supplies or computers, under no circumstances would it participate in an industrywide claims processing platform, where it would compromise a primary source of differentiated value. Similarly, DaimlerChrysler's core competencies are in its ability to create new designs and coordinate activities across the assembly line, and not in its ability to source raw materials. As such, it stands to reason that the company would join an industry consortium geared to raw material and component purchases but not product design and assembly.

Trialability While initiatives with a broader scope of impact are obviously preferable to those with a narrower scope, it is also important to assess whether the initiative is monolithic and in need of being implemented in a "big bang" manner, or whether it can be piloted on a small scale and then scaled across business units, product divisions, and departments. For instance, an ERP system whose implementation requires that the entire enterprise participate at the same time is a classic "big bang" initiative. The risk of failure with such projects is much higher than with those that can be tried out locally and then gradually scaled across the enterprise. Consider an innovation management platform piloted by a brand team at GM. If found to be successful, the initiative could be easily extended to dozens of other brand teams at GM, as well as to GM's dealers, suppliers, and customers. Initiatives with higher trialability allow the enterprise to preserve flexibility, by buying an option on whether to scale the initiative. On the other hand, "big bang" initiatives are all-or-nothing bets with limited option value.

Capability risk Every new e-business initiative will require the sourcing or development of new capabilities. But some initiatives might rely mostly on capabilities and resources that are available in-house or for which resources have already been identified and tapped. In these instances, the enterprise has a high level of confidence that it will be able to bring the capabilities required for success to bear on the initiative. On the other hand, other initiatives may push the enterprise into entirely new capability directions, and they may involve a significant capability risk. For instance, a dynamic trading platform may present a significant capability risk if the procurement decision makers and the IT organization have limited experience in dealing with spot markets and robust exchange platforms.

Adoption risk While capability risk allows you to assess whether you can take the horse to water, adoption risk allows you to assess whether the horse will drink! Adoption risk is the "human risk" inherent in any new initiative. It measures the extent to which the initiative will face barriers and hurdles to acceptance from internal constituencies, as well as from external business partners. Adoption risk may stem from a disruption in established behavior patterns of the audiences impacted by the initiative, a misalignment of incentives between the sponsor and the users of the initiative, or from the technical complexity and time demands of the initiative. For instance, a sell-side e-commerce initiative may face angry resistance from the sales force or from channel partners who view it as a threat to their margins. On the other hand, an e-procurement initiative may be immediately welcomed, because it may be seen to benefit all users without creating any strong conflicts of interest.

Integration risk E-business initiatives often create new systems that need to be integrated with legacy systems. The deeper the level of integration required by the new application, the greater the risk that the initiative will run into implementation hurdles. For instance, an e-learning application for training the sales force or customer service reps does not require deep integration with the ERP system, so the integration risk is low. On the other hand, an e-commerce initiative demands deep integration with the ERP system, in order to provide customers with real-time information on products, prices, and order status. In this case, the integration risk is considerably higher. Integration risk is a function of the number of integration points that exist between the e-business initiative and the legacy applications, and the likely level of difficulty posed by each point of integration.

These considerations constitute the dimensions along which a portfolio of e-business initiatives can be assessed. However, the question remains: How are each of these dimensions to be weighted relative to one another? The answer: Let your strategic priorities do the talking. The members of the leadership team should come up with a weighting scheme for the evaluation criteria that reflects their risk tolerance, their preferred time horizon for payoffs, their attitude toward cost-saving versus revenue-enhancing initiatives, and their overall attitude toward being an e-business innovator versus a follower.

All of these factors can be organized into a simple visual tool, such as the one shown in Figure 6-1. The visual snapshot arrays the payoff-related factors on the top half of the circle and the risk-related factors on the lower half. This visual snapshot may be refined by including additional criteria or by weighting different criteria. To evaluate the entire portfolio of the project, the same dimensions can be used to create a simple spreadsheet with different projects rated on a comparative basis, based on the considerations outlined above, the priorities articulated by senior management, and the ratings assigned to each initiative by the e-business team. Producing such a spreadsheet would result in a unified and relative assessment of all e-business initiatives in the pipeline. Further, it could serve as a "living" planning document, because it can be continually updated as the future unfolds and priorities evolve.

Choosing Pathways to the Future:
Capabilities as Options

So far, we have discussed how an enterprise can choose among e-business initiatives at *one point in time*. This is a cross-sectional view of placing bets and prioritizing initiatives. However, the enterprise

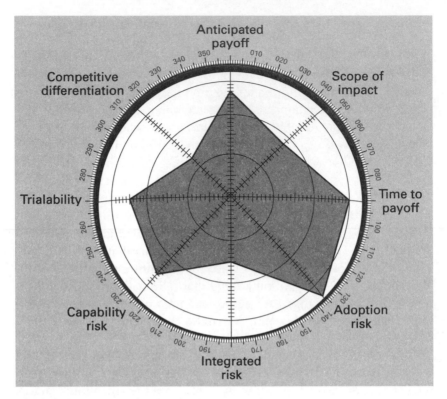

Figure 6-1
A visual tool for evaluating e-business initiatives

also has to make choices on how to *sequence* initiatives over time. Each initiative is a stepping stone on the pathway to the future. Clearly, the sequence in which the stepping stones are arranged will affect the ease with which an enterprise can proceed along its pathway. The reason is simple: e-business initiatives are interdependent. They often require similar capabilities, similar partnerships, and similar technologies. Therefore, it stands to reason that the initiatives you engage in early on will influence the paths that will open up for you in the future—a concept that economists call *path dependence*. Strategic e-business initiatives are connected in far more intricate ways than a "portfolio." As such, they should be viewed collectively as a family of initiatives with a cumulative logic that is shared across initiatives. Just as siblings in a family share the same gene pool, e-business initiatives can share technology, teams, relationships, assets, and capabilities. They must be managed as a family, by understanding the common strands that tie them together and exploiting the power of commonality to create leveraged growth opportunities. Such is the notion of *platform think-ing.*[8]

Because the interconnections that run across initiatives also run across time, it can be helpful to array the portfolio of initiatives along a time axis. Having done so, it becomes easier to itemize the stores of capabilities and knowledge that are required for each initiative, and which will be generated by the initiatives. The options logic becomes relevant here in that capabilities, relationships, and assets are not deployed at one point in time, because all e-business initiatives are not implemented at the same point in time. By realizing that the initiatives can be sequenced over time, it becomes obvious that each initiative can serve as a platform from which to launch future initiatives.

The options logic suggests that in prioritizing a portfolio of e-business initiatives, it is important to see initiatives not only as *options-creating investments*, but also as *capabilities-creating investments*. Each initiative creates capabilities. The firm has the ability, but not the obligation, to leverage these capabilities for future initiatives that may require them. The capability set provides a firm with a *platform of options* for launching future initiatives.[9] The key implication: In evaluating any e-business initiative, inventory the set of capabilities and relationships the firm would need to assemble, and then think about the *option value* of each capability for undertaking future initiatives. The initiatives that demand capabilities and relationships that have high option value should be moved earlier in time, because these capabilities can be redeployed in many different ways and can become launching pads for a rich set of subsequent initiatives. Conversely, initiatives that demand fairly unique capabilities with limited redeployment potential should be pushed further back in the timing sequence, because of their limited option value.

Consider the following scenario: A consumer products company has a choice between investing in an online market research system that would survey customers and produce reports in an automated manner, and investing in a marketing communications system that would allow it to quickly create and distribute multimedia TV-style advertisements as outbound e-mail attachments. The potential payoffs of the two initiatives are comparable. But the option value of the capabilities that would be created by the two initiatives are quite different. The by-product of the marketing communications system would be the creation of a capability set and the infrastructure for creating and distributing streaming media applications. After carefully thinking about all of the other ways in which these capabilities might be leveraged, the firm realizes that an e-learning initiative currently under way could use the streaming media capabilities for sales force training. Similarly, the outbound rich media e-mail attachments could be sent as product demonstrations for prospective clients. Essentially, streaming media and automated outbound communications turn out to be capabilities with a lot of leverage potential. On the other hand, the online marketing research system would involve using an outsourced services provider, which would not transfer the infrastructure or the proprietary software for distribution and statistical analysis of marketing research data. From the "capabilities as options" perspective, the marketing communications initiative wins hands down.

A highly instructive exercise for e-business executives is to visualize the ideal end-state of their e-business infrastructure and capabilities. Having envisioned this ideal, they might then ask: What are the sets of e-business initiatives that we will need to undertake in order to get there? Next, they should list the capabilities, assets, and relationships that each initiative would require and look at the extent to which these capabilities, assets, and relationships are common across initiatives. Those that have the greatest proportion of common capabilities, assets, and relationships should be the ones sequenced first in the queue. The mapping between initiatives and capabilities is illustrated in Figure 6-2. In this example, there are five initiatives that may constitute the end-state, and seven capabilities required across all of these initiatives. The "leverage index" can then be defined as the number of times the capabilities created for one initiative is used across other initiatives, divided by the number of new capabilities created for each initiative. For instance, Initiative 1 requires the creation of three new capabilities, each used an average of 3.7 times across the intended family of initiatives. In contrast, Initiative 2 requires the creation of five new capabilities, each used an average of 2.4 times. Initiatives 3, 4, and 5 do not require the creation of new capabilities. In this hypothetical case, Initiative 1 should be completed first, because it generates capabilities with the highest leverage potential. Initiative 2 should be next,

	Initiative 1	Initiative 2	Initiative 3	Initiative 4	Initiative 5
Capability 1	✔		✔	✔	✔
Capability 2		✔	✔		
Capability 3	✔	✔		✔	✔
Capability 4		✔			
Capability 5		✔	✔		✔
Capability 6	✔			✔	✔
Capability 7		✔	✔		✔
Leverage index (# times used/ # capabilities created)	11/3 = 3.7	12/5 = 2.4	NA	NA	NA

Figure 6-2
Using leverage potential to choose the sequence of e-business initiatives

and Initiatives 3, 4, and 5 should follow, because they rely entirely on capabilities developed for the first two initiatives.

Clearly, this example is simplistic and needs to be refined along many dimensions. For instance, all capabilities do not require the same amount of money, time, and effort to acquire, so the leverage potential of a capability needs to be tempered by these factors. In addition, it is not just capabilities that need to be considered in the matrix, but also assets and relationships. And not all capabilities may be reused in their entirety in future initiatives, so we need to allow for "degree of reuse" for each instance of redeployment of a capability. However, the basic insight is sound: Sequencing decisions for e-business initiatives should be based on the *leverage potential* of the capabilities, assets, and relationships created by each initiative.

Similar to the notion of sequencing initiatives within a portfolio is the notion of sequencing investment phases within an initiative. To this point, a Turkish proverb says: "No matter how far you have gone on the wrong road, turn back." The proverb summarizes perfectly the notion of *reversibility*. Here the idea is to minimize the upfront commitment of resources in order to be able to cut the losses should it become necessary to step on the brakes farther down the road, by scaling back the project, or altogether abandoning it. For instance, rather than spend $8 million on infrastructure in Phase 1 and an additional $2 million on user testing in Phase 2, a more risk-sensitive approach might be to do the user testing on the front-end (e.g., by using static HTML or paper prototyping techniques rather than dynamic database-driven interfaces) and delay the infrastructure investment decision until after the user testing has been completed. Ask yourself: To what extent can we sequence out our investments?[10] As much as possible, arrange the various phases in such a way so as to put the *learning options* up front and push the irreversible commitments into the future.

By expanding the envelope of its capabilities, an organization will find that the envelope of its opportunities also expands. This phenomenon speaks to the importance of coordination. The e-business leader needs to set up camp at the center of the organization, from an outpost where she can constantly scan the extended enterprise for all of the different initiatives that are underway, all the while identifying common characteristics and leverage points. The objective is to identify connections and relationships that may not be so obvious at first glance.

With respect to our example of a marketing department that builds a turnkey system to create TV-style advertisements as outbound e-mail attachments, for instance, not everyone would realize that such an initiative involves a highly leverageable set of capabilities that could be put to good use by practically every department in the company. Therefore, the e-business leader must be someone who can readily see the connections and connect the dots. Unlike the CFO, who is traditionally thought to limit his portfolio thinking to only one dimension (how to optimize ROI), the e-business leader needs to be able to think across boundaries, to identify and exploit the power of platform thinking.

Measuring Payoffs: The Problems of ROI Thinking

In the 1997 Oscar-winning movie *Jerry Maguire*, a star athlete repeatedly states his demand: "Show me the money!" His sentiment is echoed far and wide by corporate stakeholders, particularly finance and IT executives, whose natural tendency is to use familiar metrics like return on investment (ROI) and total cost of ownership (TCO) as their standard yardsticks for evaluating the performance of e-business initiatives. But while these yardsticks have been commonly employed for evaluating the payoffs from traditional IT initiatives, they don't always measure up when used to evaluate e-business initiatives.

With respect to ROI, the first problem is the letter I—the denominator. Not all costs can be fully anticipated in advance of implementation. For instance, the costs associated with developing a Web-based application may not include additional costs for analytics (e.g., data warehousing), or for globalization (e.g., website localization). Invariably, e-business initiatives involve continual layering of functionality to the initial applications, as the applications become more refined and sophisticated. It is difficult to know up front how many bells and whistles will be added, and what these bells and whistles will look like. As we indicated in Chapter 2, the ladder of e-business initiatives gradually reveals itself as you climb from rung to rung and progress from generation to generation. For such open-ended initiatives, the investment picture becomes even fuzzier.

The second, and more disconcerting, problem with ROI is the measurement of the letter R—the numerator. We have repeatedly emphasized in this book, particularly in our discussion of e-strategy, that e-business initiatives are systemic in nature. As such, they will always produce a host of unintended consequences and unanticipated returns. The effects of practically any enterprisewide e-business initiative will ripple through various parts of the organization and affect many different business processes. The pathways that link cause and effect in e-business are multistranded, making it difficult to isolate the returns and measure the value of individual initiatives, as if they existed in a vacuum. An investment that e-enables a specific business process may eventually deliver even larger benefits to another part of the corporate ecosystem. It can be a daunting task to try to artificially partition all of the benefits. ROI seeks to measure results in isolation. But e-business thwarts this effort by making the *entire* business system more efficient or effective. Remember: Value is often nonlinear. As long as the initiative adds value for customers, it will ultimately show up as a holistic measure. Even point efforts will tend to affect the system as a whole. In our conversations with e-business leaders across a broad spectrum of companies, we have found little evidence of ROI being measured, or even being measurable, before the project has gotten underway.

Another problem with the letter R: The returns refer only to dollars, whereas not all e-business outcomes are readily convertible into hard currency, at least not in the short term. For example, the value of a CRM initiative will manifest itself as improved customer loyalty and increased customer satisfaction, but these outcomes can be difficult to quantify in terms of dollars and cents. They are *softer measures*, reported on rating scales in qualitative terms. Unfortunately, most finance executives have a predilection for focusing on the hard and ignoring the soft. The intangible is assumed to be unimportant. "If you can't measure it, you can't manage it," declared the management guru Peter Drucker. That hard-to-measure and intangible outcomes tend to get discounted is just one of the biases of ROI thinking. This bias toward measurability is dangerous, however. Why? Because if the payoffs for an e-business initiative are very easy to measure in terms of dollar impact on the bottom line, chances are it's an incremental initiative that will produce cost savings and efficiency outcomes but will not likely lead to new revenue streams and transformational outcomes. As e-business initiatives evolve and become increasingly sophisticated, their impact tends to shift from the bottom line to the top line, from cost minimization to revenue enhancement.

A related problem: It is difficult to compare initiatives that produce very different types of outcomes on an apples-to-apples basis, using dollars as a common denominator. Consider a scenario in which the corporate purchasing department argues for an SCM solution, claiming it will reduce inventory in the supply chain from 40 days to 10 days. Meanwhile, the marketing department, vying for the same money, makes the case that what the company really needs is enterprise CRM software that will improve customer satisfaction by 20 points on a 100-point scale. At this point the CIO chimes in, declaring that the organization would be better served to deploy a competitive intelligence system that reduces its response time to competitive activity from six days to three days. Now, how should a decision maker compare 30 days of inventory reduction to 20 points of customer satisfaction to three days of competitive response improvement? How can the expected value of these three different initiatives be measured relative to one another? All dollars are green, but not all initiatives are easily converted into dollars.

Recall the four sets of e-business outcomes that we discussed in Chapter 1: cost reduction, revenue expansion, time reduction, and relationship enhancement. These outcomes represent three distinct units for measuring results. Cost reduction and revenue expansion are measured in terms of dollars. Time reduction is measured in terms of time, and relationship enhancement is measured in subjective terms, e.g., customer satisfaction. In truth, the time reduction and relationship enhancement outcomes are merely short-term measures, to be used for intermediate tracking. Long term, every successful initiative, including those aimed at relationship enhancement and time reduction, would eventually impact the top or the bottom line. Just as every initiative eventually touches the customer, often after meandering through a series of intermediate points, the route to achieving dollar results can also be indirect.

This isn't to suggest that the business case ought to focus only on the nearest interim step. It also doesn't mean that an analyst should lose sleep trying to calculate those *eventual* quantitative measures. Because the return estimates can never be accurate, an analyst's time is better spent assuring stakeholders that the initiative at hand is grounded in a concrete value proposition. The lesson is to think broadly and think softly. Think systemically about measuring returns, and remember that getting a precise financial measure of the returns can be elusive for two reasons: (1) It can be difficult to visualize and identify all of the returns, and (2) it can be difficult to convert the returns from apples and oranges into dollars.

Traditionally, as we've said, IT infrastructure projects have been also measured based on total cost of ownership (TCO), an acronym that reflects a cost minimization mindset. While the T hits the bull's-eye insomuch that it advocates a broader view of costs—after all, owning a server farm entails not only actual hardware acquisition but also ongoing maintenance and systems integration—the C presents a significant shortcoming in the context of e-business. Why? Because while IT initiatives tended to focus on trying to reduce operating costs and make operations run more efficiently, an e-business initiative that focuses purely on cost savings will never create radically new revenue streams. In general, it's better to think about new value propositions that can create new ways of serving customers. Furthermore, don't let the numbers become an end unto themselves. While a company might crow about the $20 million that it saved by streamlining its customer care center, a way to save even more money would have been to shut it down! The point being that a company can save money in any number of ways, including firing all of its employees—but has its actions created happier customers? The lesson: *Don't get stuck at the bottom line. Rise to the top line.* Getting stuck at the bottom line means staying focused on cost savings, whereas the real opportunities for customer value creation invariably lie in revenue (top line) enhancement.

Because ownership should focus not on cost reduction but on value creation, TCO might be more aptly labeled TVO (total value of ownership). For that matter, ROI might be better restated as RCS (return on customer satisfaction). Even supply chain initiatives can be better seen through the lens of RCS—after all, improving process visibility allows customers to track their orders, and reducing inventory allows them to receive their orders more quickly. Again, the acid test for every e-business initiative should be: How does this benefit our customers?

From Payoffs to Milestones: Using Adaptive Metrics

In many parts of the developing world, where the pace of life is somewhat less frenzied than, say, in midtown Manhattan, trains tend to run late. One day an unknowing tourist, frustrated that his train was now running two hours behind schedule for departure, marched into the office of the station manager to complain. "But if not for that schedule in your hand," replied the station manager, "how would you even know that your train is running two hours late?"

Despite our assertion that a limited metric like ROI is a flawed approach to measuring payoffs, it is still important to use metrics to *track performance* and *measure progress* of e-business initiatives. These metrics, however, act more like milestones along a journey, rather than measures of attractiveness of the final (and fixed) destination. Therefore, instead of measuring performance in terms of a *break-even point*—or any other fixed point, for that matter—we strongly recommend the adoption of a rolling plan, with rolling milestones, rolling objectives, and rolling metrics—what we call *unfolding* or *adaptive metrics*.

To illustrate the notion of adaptive metrics, consider an anecdote about Albert Einstein. As the story goes, Einstein was administering an exam to one of his graduate classes when a student called him over and said, "Excuse me, Professor Einstein. The questions on this year's exam are exactly the same as the questions on last year's exam. And we all had a copy of last year's exam." To which the great scientist looked back at the student and said: "That may well be, but this year the answers are different."

Similarly, while the overriding objective of an e-business initiative in terms of what it aims to accomplish does not generally change over time, the metrics for measuring its progress along the journey *should* evolve over time. While this thinking may at first seem counterintuitive, one need only consider that a great deal of Einstein's thinking is counterintuitive!

Therefore, in response to the question, "Should we throw all metrics to the winds and completely forget about ROI?" the answer is a resounding "No!" In reality, measurements need to be framed in terms of milestones, and they need to be adaptable, flexible, and broadminded. Be short-term in the measurement and long-term in the vision. Just as the ladder that leads to e-business transformation reveals itself over time, there is no point in trying to put metrics in place for the whole project. Rather, simply have them in view for the next phase, and adapt them as it comes into view and becomes better defined. Focusing on the journey instead of the final destination ensures a better chance of actually reaching that final destination.

Also, drop your financial yardsticks and take a step back. In the beginning, progress can be measured using a host of intermediate metrics, such as time metrics (e.g., launch dates), usage metrics (e.g., number of customers or suppliers using an application), performance metrics (e.g., on-time deliveries or site up-time), or relationship metrics (e.g., customer satisfaction or channel partner satisfaction). And these metrics can be sequenced, just as milestones are sequenced in a long journey. For instance, in developing a partner-facing application for partner relationship management, the first milestone might be the launch date for rolling out the first set of application modules. The next milestone might be the number of partners using the site. And a third milestone might be the transaction volume accruing through the website or the improvement in productivity of leads generated for partners through the site. Only after this latter stage, when the site functionality is robust, partners are using the site, transactions are flowing through the site, and financial results are measurable, does it become possible to start talking about the *financial* payback from this project, using traditional point measures like ROI. In the interim, make sure that all milestones are tracking progress toward the final goal. Because progress toward this goal may require progress on many different dimensions of the initiative, the milestones also have to be multidimensional. In this example, the final goal might have been making it easier for partners to do business with the company—but, again, the ability to track that return may entail several intermediate steps.

In explaining the use of adaptive metrics with respect to Sears Online, Alice Peterson recalls that the

> milestones became more sophisticated as we went along. The first milestone was "make your release date." In other words, get all of the major appliances and brands online, e-commerce-enabled, by May 15. We didn't say anything about the qualitative aspects. Just get it up, make it functional, and make the date. After that, we started to get more sophisticated with the milestones. We said, "Now, we want to achieve x amount of visitors, y amount of conversion rate, and z amount of customer satisfaction." So we started doing more and more measuring as we went along.

Adaptive metrics unfold over time, leading closer and closer to a final goal. In the early stages of the project, you may not even know what measures will be important at the end, because the nature of the project itself may change as the project evolves. The idea is to have a living and flexible measurement scheme, to respond to a living and flexible plan, while continuously tracking toward a defined goal. The new mantra: *fixity in vision but flexibility in measurement*.

To this point, recall the Spiral Model for Software Development that we discussed in Chapter 2. At first, an initiative may be narrow in scope. But as it becomes layered with more and more functionality and features, it grows increasingly sophisticated and complex. Conversely, the metrics and milestones may be fuzzy at first but become more and more focused over time. The metrics become more precise, winding inward in the spiral, while the application itself becomes more functionally complex, winding outward in the spiral. Over time, the project team will have more sophisticated functionality but more precise measurements. Picture the metrics as a fuzzy target that becomes better defined over time, whereas the initiative itself is like painting on a canvas that becomes increasingly broad.

Payoffs from Venturing:
From Earning Payoffs to Learning Payoffs

In evaluating the performance of internal e-business initiatives, we argued that financial goals are an inadequate metric, because they are one-dimensional. A similar case can be made for measuring the performance of external venturing initiatives. Measuring financial returns alone is a simplistic way to measure payoffs from e-business ventures, because the motivations for corporate venturing should be strategic as well as financial. With this in view, it may be wise to insert the letter L before the word *earning* in measuring payoffs from venturing. The real upside may not come in the form of capital appreciation, but by way of knowledge enhancement.

Consider Kraft Foods. Over the past couple of years, the largest packaged food company in the United States has established strategic partnerships with several online grocery delivery services, including Webvan, NetGrocer, and Peapod. From Kraft's point of view, these relationships have less to do with the prospect of making money or increasing revenues through a new channel than with the opportunities to participate in learning about online shopping behavior, online marketing, and electronic promotions. Even if the online grocers crash and burn, as many of them already have, Kraft has learned a great deal about how the Internet will (or won't!) affect consumer shopping for frequently purchased packaged goods. Kraft's other investments include Food.com, a Web-based take-out and delivery service, and EthnicGrocer.com, an e-retailer of ethnic consumer products. "From the Food.com investment, we hope to learn more about consumers' take-in food experience," explained Paula Sneed, the head of Kraft's e-business group. This learning is important, because Kraft's core business has forever been focused on making ingredients for home cooking. But with the number of meals prepared outside the home having now surpassed the number of meals cooked at home, Kraft needs to forge deeper links with restaurants and take-out establishments. These channels are becoming important customers for Kraft. Food.com gives Kraft a window into a consumer trend and a channel important to its future, at a relatively low cost.

Similarly, through its investment in EthnicGrocer.com, Kraft hopes to get a better understanding of ethnic consumers, guerrilla marketing techniques, and Internet-based supply chain management. While ethnic consumers represent an important growth market, their low density has prevented food manufacturers like Kraft from being able to create mass-marketed products for ethnic consumers and distribute them in mainstream grocery stores. But the Internet allows ethnic audiences dispersed geographically to be aggregated to a scale where it may be viable to create and market such products nationwide. Whether this will be a successful approach remains to be seen, because of the difficulties of scaling an e-commerce business. But instead of spending tens of millions of dollars to find out by itself, Kraft has bought a front-row seat in the war room of a startup company that is fighting hard to find out. Similarly, Kraft has a lot to learn about the way startup companies, starved of marketing dollars, use creative guerrilla marketing techniques to stretch their promotional budgets. Using event marketing, permission-based e-mail marketing, word-of-mouth referrals, and creative co-marketing arrangements to build their customer base on a shoestring, startup firms like EthnicGrocer.com cannot behave like mass marketers because they have never had the resources to do so; yet their unconventional go-to-market techniques can have significant implications for large companies like Kraft. To put things in perspective, if Kraft could shave off only ten prime time 30-second TV spots by improving the productivity of its marketing dollars, it would have paid for its $5 million investment in EthnicGrocer.com.

So, even if the startup pioneers end up with arrows in their backs, they can nonetheless provide valuable learning grounds for established companies as they seek to understand the new possibilities of e-business. By going along for the ride, these companies stand to gain a new perspective on their core businesses. Whether any of Kraft's venture investments ever make money may be almost beside the point. At the end of the day, the learning payoff may be orders of magnitude higher than any financial upside the company may have hoped to realize. Investments that are failures from an earnings standpoint may pay off handsomely from a learning standpoint, and companies that view their strategic investments in startups as only financial investments may be missing the boat.

Not that the financial investment should ever be viewed as a complete loss. After all, a company that owned a 10 or 20 percent stake in a failed startup need only consider the money it saved by virtue of not having been the primary investor. Had the experiment been conducted in-house, with the company contributing all of the resources, the cost could have been many times higher. So, even if a company ends up losing a few million dollars from a minority interest in an external venture, one that it knew from the start to be highly speculative, the figure pales by comparison to the amount the company *could* just as easily have lost had it instead taken a majority or 100 percent interest.

As we've suggested, a key difference between earning payoffs and learning payoffs is the risk of write-offs. Earning payoffs have a downside that encompasses the entire investment in a venture. However, the learning payoff rarely presents a complete write-off. Even failures can teach valuable lessons about what works and what doesn't. For instance, while online grocery shopping may have failed, Kraft, through its association with online grocery shopping firms, has learned valuable lessons about how to communicate with consumers online — knowledge that it can leverage into other efforts, such as its Kraft Interactive Kitchen site. Similarly, whether or not e-retailing ultimately succeeds, Kraft can still learn valuable lessons for managing its own direct marketing efforts, including Gevalia coffee and FamousMarkets.

Experienced corporate venture investors recognize the importance of learning payoffs relative to earning payoffs in managing equity investments in startup firms. According to a recent report by the Corporate Executive Board, firms like Dell, HP, UPS, and 3M consider their financial goals satisfied as long as their venturing investments produce returns that exceed their cost of capital.[11] Beyond this, the success or failure of the investment is determined by the value of the learning payoffs.

Of course, the corporate venturing group also needs to strike a balance between the earning payoff and the learning payoff. Should a disproportionate amount of attention become focused on the earning payoff, the group could begin to look like a poor man's venture capital firm — "poor" because it would be acting like a traditional venture capital firm while lacking its depth of experience and capabilities. With too little attention paid to the earning payoff, the venturing group could end up making investments that lose money, inviting negative reactions from stakeholders.

The upshot: Option value correlates with more than just financial profitability. It also plays a role in what the company learns and how it uses that knowledge to create further opportunities for leverage. Again, the financial risk of investing is that the company loses a certain amount of money, but the learning risk is never absolute, and every failure can teach at least a few valuable lessons about what works and what doesn't. In truth, an investment may generate enough knowledge to fill an encyclopedia, but it may be *useless* knowledge in the context of the company's value creation activities. It may be knowledge that can never be redeployed, in which case the investment was no more than an unfortunate detour down a blind alley.

Defining and Measuring Learning Payoffs

With the importance of learning payoffs in view, it stands to reason that the risk and return assessment for a corporate venturing group considering equity investments in startups should include learning-related criteria. And what criterion should be used for measuring intellectual capital gains? Certainly, it should revolve around both the quality and quantity of the insights that the company would capture, and to what extent these insights could be utilized to make existing operations more effective or to discover new value propositions. The link between what has been learned through external venturing activities and how that knowledge has impacted the company's core business operations is a touchstone that every corporate venturing group ought to hold dear.

Some questions to consider: What are the dimensions that we will learn on? How valuable is this learning likely to be? What are the chances that we won't learn much of value at all? What are the chances that we will be able to transfer this learning successfully to our core business? And how can we maximize our learning payoffs? These questions are complicated by the same problem we faced in assessing payoffs from internal e-business initiatives: Learning payoffs are "soft," and their dollar value is often hard to pin down. What is the value of an insight? What is the value of learning that changes the corporate culture? What is the value of discovering a threat to the core business through an investment in a disruptive startup? The value of learning payoffs is difficult to quantify, but the payoffs are valuable nevertheless.

We suggest that instead of attempting to place dollar metrics on potential learning payoffs, corporate venturing executives establish a concise list of criteria on which the learning payoffs would be measured subjectively, and then use these criteria consistently for evaluating investments and tracking performance of corporate venturing investments. An illustrative list of criteria is shown in Table 6-1. As this list suggests, learning payoffs can be defined on a set of strategic "learning windows" that offer insights on emerging technologies, business architectures, distribution channels, customer segments, and business practices. Corporate investors should think of themselves as outsiders looking through these windows into the future, borrowing eyes and ideas from innovative startups.

This is the strategy that Accenture (formerly Andersen Consulting) is adopting through its Accenture Technology Ventures arm, which has invested in an extensive network of over seventy technology and e-commerce startup companies. The value that Accenture brings to these startups is the benefit of its deep domain expertise in implementing enterprise applications in a vast array of businesses, as well as its extensive relationships with Global 2000 clients. However, the startups in turn provide Accenture with a knowledge base that it can leverage to grow its core business. For instance, from its investment in e-infrastructure companies like Asera, Jamcracker, and Rivio, Accenture can keep abreast of the latest developments in modular e-business platforms, e-services, and software delivered as services. Similarly, through its investment in MarketSwitch, a marketing optimization solutions firm, Accenture's customer relationship practice can help its clients evaluate and implement the latest advances in marketing automation and optimization. The network of startup investments leverages Accenture's $8.9 billion core business into new practice areas and strengthens its value proposition for its own clients. Without these windows into the future, Accenture's core business would eventually atrophy.

It's important to realize that learning payoffs don't come to those who sit on their hands or in their caves. We have heard some corporate venture capitalists described as "passive investors," given their minority financial stakes in startup companies and their lack of involvement in these companies' day-to-day operations. A passive stance toward managing the startup is understandable, but a passive stance toward *learning* is inexcusable. There is no such thing as a *passive learning investor.* Your financial payoffs will show up as checks in the mail, but you have to work actively to generate your learning payoffs. To fully capitalize on learning opportunities from their venturing activities, companies need to put people and processes in place for capturing and disseminating the learning and for tracking the learning payoffs from investments. Some tips for maximizing learning follow.

Create formal learning screens   Using the dimensions suggested in Table 6-1, evaluate every potential investment on a consistent set of learning criteria. Investments should be approved using a financial payoff threshold as well as a learning payoff threshold. These thresholds should be independent hurdles to be met. A superior financial payoff should not compensate for a subpar learning payoff. For every investment that does pass the screens, the key learning criteria that formed the basis for the approval should be highlighted in the investment approval document, so the learning performance of the investment can be appropriately tracked.

Table 6-1
Learning Payoff Windows from Corporate Venturing Investments

Learning windows	Description	Examples
Technology window	Access new e-infrastructure technologies to improve existing business processes	Investment in XML technology startup as a window into supply hub technology
Opportunity window	Insight into new or underserved customer segments, or market opportunities that leverage existing customer relationships	Investment in startup targeting small-business customers as a window into SME segment
Channels window	Learning about emerging go-to-market channels to serve existing or new customer segments	Investment in B2B e-commerce startup as a window into e-marketplace channel
Business architecture window	Learning of innovative and disruptive business architectures that threaten the core business	Investment in free telephony provider to learn about the threat to core telephony business
Cultural window	Transferring entrepreneurial culture and business practices to established companies	Learning about partnering from startup companies well-versed in building extensive value networks
Outsourcing window	Ideas for improving asset productivity by outsourcing business processes as services	Investment in application service provider startup to identify opportunities for managed operations outsourcing
R&D window	Sourcing new technologies and new products and buying options on new developments	Investments in promising early-stage research companies to improve new products pipeline

Get board observer rights   Every investment that a corporate venturing group makes should have a condition that it be granted observer rights to attend the board of directors meetings. Observer rights allow corporate investors to stay closely connected with the startup's management team and other investors, and give them a ringside view of what the startup is learning through its trials and tribulations. Board observers should make it a point to attend as many meetings as possible. And board observers should be active listeners.

Appoint relationship managers   Every venture investment made by a corporate venturing team should be managed by a point person, someone charged with managing the relationship and the transfer of learning. This person may be a representative from the corporate venturing team with board observer rights or an operating manager. For instance, the CIO or a member from the technology team should manage an investment in an e-infrastructure technology startup, while the Vice President of Purchasing may be a more suitable candidate to manage the relationship with a B2B e-marketplace startup. The relationship manager becomes a focal point for the learning transfer between the startup and the corporation, not unlike hunters bringing big game back to the cave.

Track learning payoffs   It is not enough to make investments on the basis of anticipated learning payoffs and then to forget about them. The performance of every strategic investment should be monitored periodically on a set of learning-related metrics. These metrics might include the number of people exposed to the startup's technology or team, the number of ideas or initiatives generated as a result of the investment, the progress made on identifying new customers or new offerings attributable to the investment, and a record of best practices that have been gleaned and then implemented as a result of the relationship. If the learning payoffs start to drop off, the investment should be reviewed for exit, or it should be retained only as a financial investment.

   To facilitate learning transfer, the corporate e-business team also needs to create tight integration between its external ventures group and its internal "enabling group"—which, after all, are two sides of the same coin. One side lives and breathes change, which means energizing the core. The other side lives and breathes growth, which means searching out new business opportunities. An organism that grows has to change, while an organism that fails to change will be unable to grow. For this reason, the groups should interact closely with each other. By drawing the relationship managers from the core business and using them to forge linkages between the individual investments and the operating units, the overall agenda of creating tighter links between the growth-centered e-venture organization and the change-centered e-enabling organization can also be furthered.

Creating the E-Business Case

A bumper sticker reads: "If technology is the answer, then what is the question?" A first step in creating the e-business case is to define the problem and not the solution. Customers don't think in terms of solutions. Rather, they think about what hurts and the pain they feel. Words may escape them if asked to articulate a solution focused on supply chain optimization. But they won't hesitate to complain about the shortcomings of their current systems around shipping and receiving: "Our supplier base stinks. It takes us forever to get orders in."

The value a company delivers is only the means to the ends that its customers seek. For example, no customer wants DSL or cable modems, per se, but millions of customers are happy to pay twice what they would for a dial-up connection in order to enjoy streaming video and faster downloads of their favorite websites. In creating a business case, think in terms of the end-goal for customers. In the case of the aforementioned SCM solution, the end-goal might be expressed as: "We ship 60 days after we receive the order from our customer. We need to reduce it to 30 days."

In addition, the e-business case should recognize the value being created not only for the company and its customers, but for all of the trading partners, as well. Failure to anticipate the ways in which the initiative would benefit other companies might result in undercounting the value creation potential, and it may also impact their willingness to contribute to the effort. Finally, value might be viewed in terms of how the initiative would position the firm competitively—preempting competition, either defensively or offensively.

In summary, consider the following "e-business case checklist":

- What problem is being solved?
- What business processes are being targeted?

- What audiences will be affected?
- What business impact can be expected?

Having defined the problem, processes, audiences, and impact, the next step is to select the implementation team and technology partners that will help construct the e-business solution. At this point, also determine the level of outsourcing and the approach for managing the interface between the internal IT department and any external partners. Given the go-ahead, would the internal IT team be building the technology platform, doing the project management, or doing some of both? Next, come to an agreement on prototyping and testing strategy. Feedback and validation should be solicited from sample groups of target users throughout every stage of the development process, the more the merrier. Even if the initiative involves the construction of a large-scale, complex application, there are always opportunities to chunk it down and prototype it with a live audience. When prototyping, don't strive for perfection. The name of the game is "fast and dirty." Everyone involved should understand that a prototype is simply an approximation of the offering along a particular dimension. It need not exemplify the full-blown end-product. Each stage should simply present one discrete aspect of the user interface or database architecture for testing the various functionality and usability issues. The need to solicit external validation of an initiative while it still remains a work-in-progress can't be emphasized enough. Building a mammoth initiative over many months in a vacuum is a surefire recipe for disaster. Always think *reversibility*. A team of programmers can hunker down in their cubicles and crank out code for months at a time, only to emerge one day to discover, as did Rip Van Winkle, that the world has changed.

In "marketing" an e-business initiative from the "bottom up," present metrics that are relevant and context-specific. Rattling off random benchmarks and all-purpose statistics gleaned from market research reports can undermine the cumulative logic behind undertaking the initiative in the first place. Also, in the search for compelling, relevant success stories, realize that in fact there may simply not be any. That being the case, the initiative would need to be sold at some level as purely an act of faith—which of course is how investment dollars have always been raised, at least ever since Christopher Columbus convinced Queen Isabella of a shorter route to the Indies! More recently, Warren Buffett, discussing his early days as a money manager, recalled:

"The first investors just believed in me, and the ones who had faith stayed on, but you couldn't get my Aunt Katie [to participate] if you came at her with a crowbar."[12]

In truth, it may be that corporate executives have witnessed few compelling success stories around e-business, and even fewer of immediate relevance to their firm's particular business situation. Certainly, the aftermath of the dotcom insurgency, when CEOs emerged from their bomb shelters to discover legions of Internet startups lying in pieces on the ground, gave no reason to snap into action. Moreover, as we've suggested, it may be that every company in their industry that has taken the plunge, has—despite their upbeat press releases—only lost a boatload of money. That being the case, it's understandable that a CEO might question the urgency to join the club.

A word to the wise: Don't present a skeptical CEO with the Mother of All Business Cases, and don't ask the gray-haired board of directors to sow only Chinese bamboo seeds. Instead, as we suggested at the start of this chapter, plan a series of surgical strikes and quick wins to establish confidence. There is no better way to tunnel through the brass and marble walls of cynicism and disinterest than to show short-term gains. Also, in taking the value proposition to the top of the mountain, it may be helpful to don the robe of a zealot. Preach the merits of the earning *and* learning payoffs. Proselytize to the unconverted about the cornucopia of customer benefits. Speak with conviction and religious fervor—but not in foreign tongues! Be passionate but not fanatical.

One by one the dominoes will fall. If they don't fall by selling the faith, then they will fall by showing real, honest-to-goodness results. The results need only hint at the larger possibilities on the horizon. After all, what is being sold is not so much an e-business initiative, per se, as it is a vision for the company's future wealth. Of her experience in selling the vision for Sears Online, Alice Peterson recalls:

> In 1998, when it looked like less than one percent of total company sales over the next year would likely, even under the best circumstances, come through the Internet, it was easy for people to say, "You're not gonna scare me." So we had to say, "Okay, you know in 1960 this is what we should have been thinking vis-à-vis Wal-Mart, and we didn't, and look what happened by 1980. Now we're building a lot of what's going to happen by 2020. We therefore need you to decide how we're going to maintain and deepen relationships with customers." So we may have used some scare

tactics early on. But after we started getting successes, it was easier to point to the momentum and results, and we could start to make comparisons to other programs. For example, I compared our Internet results to the Sunday circular. You know, we print those god-awful Sunday newspaper inserts that nobody reads. Yet they're like heroin; people can't get off of them. Survey after survey, customer research can't justify the expense. By contrast, I had very tangible evidence of what the Internet was producing.

Finding the Money: Funding E-Business Initiatives

We have offered several tips for placing winning bets on e-business initiatives. But before you gamble, you must have a pot of money! For every e-business organization, the $64 million question is: How do initiatives get funded? Who pays for the $25 million SCM initiative, the $35 million CRM implementation, and the $4 million knowledge management prototype? Do these expenditures come out of the CEO's discretionary budget? The corporate e-business budget? The CIO's budget? Or do the business units pick up the tab? If they do, which business units should pay, and how much? Faced with the realities of managing numbers quarter by quarter, and e-business initiatives that need to be funded from operating cash flows, finding the money for them demands creativity and careful planning.

At the early stages of the corporate journey into e-business, the initiatives tend to be small and don't require substantial human or financial resources. These early initiatives often arise within individual departments or business units, and the managers who champion these localized initiatives often beg, borrow, and steal from their department heads to secure funding and people for their projects. However, this ad hoc funding approach quickly reaches its limits, as initiatives become broader in functionality scope and grow in scale. The early funding is rather like the angel funding that seeds a startup company—small investments from friends and family that help the startup to get off the ground until it can attract institutional capital from professional investors. Just as a startup firm eventually needs to tap into institutional capital with deep pockets, internal e-business ventures need to tap into the internal capital market for sources of capital that are sufficient to scale the venture beyond its early manifestation. However, venture capitalists in turn have a set of limited partners with even deeper pockets who invest in their funds. But in a corporation, there are no limited partners. Corporations need to raise their own capital for funding their internal initiatives.

Funding approaches for initiatives will differ based on the *scope*, and the *sponsor*, of the initiative. To simplify matters, we will distinguish between *enterprise-led* initiatives and *department-led* initiatives. Those that are enterprise-led are "top-down" initiatives that are sponsored by the executive team, in cooperation with the e-business organization. These initiatives typically span the entire enterprise in their scope, are too big to be funded by an individual business unit, require cross-business-unit cooperation in implementation, and tend to be transformational in their impact. Funding responsibilities for enterprise-led initiatives lie with the corporation as a whole or the corporate e-business organization. In contrast, departmental initiatives are "bottom-up" and sponsored by a business unit or a department. They tend to be localized in scope and in their implementation requirements, although they may eventually be extended to other departments or business units. Funding responsibilities for departmental initiatives lie with the sponsoring business unit or department or the e-business team at the business unit level.

Funding for enterprisewide e-business initiatives has to be budgeted at the enterprise level as an investment in business improvement and development. If the initiative will result in a hit to earnings in the short or medium term (as many initiatives do), it is the responsibility of the CEO and the CFO to "sell" the growth story to Wall Street. For instance, Grainger's investments in e-commerce initiatives are bleeding valuable earnings from its bottom line and have hurt its stock performance. But they have also given Wall Street reason to believe they will eventually translate into higher growth and new revenue streams. The same idea was echoed by Mike Winkle, the head of corporate strategy at R.R. Donnelley & Sons Company: "Wall Street does not see a compelling growth story in our core business of putting ink on paper. This is a mature business, and it will grow slowly, if at all. Our e-business initiatives, while consuming cash in the short to medium term, make for a far more compelling growth story for analysts." In other words, when using earnings and operating cash flow to fund large corporate e-business initiatives, the CEO and CFO need to ensure that they communicate the top-line and bottom-line impact that the initiatives will have in the longer term, so that equity analysts and investors can put the short-term hit to earnings in perspective. Of course, there is a limit to investors' patience, and they can grow weary of the growth story if the promised payoffs from e-business do not materialize. Even masters of selling the growth story like Amazon are being questioned about how long it will be before they "show the money" to investors.

A company needs to avoid the possibility of what might be fittingly called a "margin call"—basically, a situation in which Wall Street pulls the plug on the company's valuation, catching it at a low point in terms of cash flow. Such are the perils of going out on a limb: It might snap. One approach a company might take to funding its enterprisewide e-business initiatives without having to risk "drawing its margins" is to find *matching cuts* in expenditures that offset the investments in e-business initiatives. In this way, the initiatives can become almost neutral in their net impact on earnings.

The natural question that arises: Are these cuts not possible anyway, so that earnings could actually be *increased* by cutting expenses, as opposed to investing the savings in e-business investments? Not quite. The cuts become more palatable inside the organization if the affected employees see that the money is being spent in order to make the company stronger in the long run. Edward Liddy, the CEO of Allstate, articulates the logic behind matching cuts with a simple analogy, which tells the story of a family that wants to buy a new car but will also soon have a graduating high school senior they want to send to college. Because the family can't afford to do both, it comes to the only sensible conclusion: Pay the college tuition and postpone buying the car for a few years. "The family tightened its belt, and it was happy to make the sacrifice because it was for a good cause. We did something similar at Allstate when we announced our Good Hands Network initiative for customer relationship management. As part of the initiative, we announced that we would be closing call centers and laying off people, to cut costs. However, we also emphasized that we would be using these savings to invest in a state-of-the-art multichannel customer contact center. This made the internal selling task to 50,000 Allstate employees much easier than if we had just announced layoffs and cutbacks." In other words, when you tell people what you're going to cut, also show them where and how you're going to invest. By putting these together, the morale within the firm is improved because you are showing people a better tomorrow. In essence, you're telling them that you've got to skip a meal today so you can eat three meals tomorrow.

A variant of the enterprisewide funding approach is the funding of initiatives that are sponsored by the corporate e-business organization. In this case, the e-business organization may create an internal marketplace to "sell" its initiatives or services to individual business units which can be implemented through a process of *charge-backs*. The notion of charge-backs dates back to the origins of modern civilization, in the form of *taxation*. Just as citizens pay taxes to the federal government, which in turn provides them with a set of common services, charge-backs are an internal pricing mechanism that has long been employed by IT organizations as a way to support staff functions that have no budget for such services. The idea is to allocate the funding required by the staff function across all of the operating units that do have P&Ls, in some equitable proportion. The allocation may be based on the volume of actual resources consumed or on the relative sizes of the different business units. In the context of e-business initiatives, the e-business organization can use charge-backs as a mechanism to fund initiatives it feels might benefit multiple business units, like a knowledge management or an e-procurement initiative.

Having identified the initiative, the e-business organization may "market" it to heads of individual operating units and ask them to contribute to a common pool of money that will be used to fund the project. The e-business organization serves as a matchmaker between external technology and consulting vendors who will implement the initiative and the business units that will be users of the initiative. By involving multiple business units in the project, the costs and the risks involved in large initiatives can be spread across several different entities. Further, by aggregating demand across multiple business units, the e-business organization can negotiate better terms from the implementation partners, by being able to present them with multiple "customers" within the enterprise. The same logic of shared risks, shared costs, and shared rewards can be applied across enterprises, and it is the motivating logic behind the formation of B2B consortia by established industry players.

Charge-backs need to be handled with care, however, because multiple customers and multiple sponsors are involved. And these customers have differing preferences, differing risk profiles, and differing visions for what they want the initiative to accomplish. Their different end-goals may translate into different functionalities and time frames for the initiative. For instance, in implementing an e-procurement platform, one business unit might argue strongly for a reverse auction functionality because it routinely buys large quantities of commodity raw materials that are best sourced through a buyer-initiated auction. Another business unit, which manufactures engineered parts, may argue that collaborative design functionality is absolutely essential from its point of view. While these debates are inevitable and cannot be eliminated, the spirit of collaboration can be greatly enhanced by involving technology as well as representatives from all sponsoring business units, so they all have a voice in the decisions and feel a sense of ownership in the joint initiative.

At times, the e-business organization may go further than charge-backs and become a "reseller" of services that are created by initiatives it sponsors and operates. In this case, the e-business organization becomes a profit center, managing its own P&L and selling its services to internal customers. For instance, at Cordis Endovascular, a medical device company owned by Johnson & Johnson, the e-business organization serves as an internal consulting arm that can be said to earn its keep. The e-business team at Cordis constantly looks for opportunities to improve internal business processes. Having identified an opportunity, it then enters into a risk-and-reward-sharing scheme with the various business units. For example, members of the team identified an opportunity to use wireless handheld devices, such as the Palm VII, to improve the effectiveness of the field sales force in their interactions with physicians. They created a business case for the initiative that documented the current productivity of the sales reps and calculated the productivity improvement that would be needed to meet the sales targets for the following year. Next, they asked the business units how much productivity increase they could squeeze out of the sales reps in the next year without the wireless detailing application. Finally, they promised the business units an additional productivity increase beyond this amount, given their willingness to implement the application. If the promised productivity increase is indeed accomplished, and if the e-business team and the business unit agree upon all the other parameters that contribute to productivity so they can isolate the incremental effect of the application, these targets can be used to define the risk-and-reward-sharing scheme. A proportion of the savings can be charged back by the e-business organization. This explains how the e-business organization might fund itself. This performance-based charge-back scheme aligns incentives of the e-business organization with the objectives of the business unit. Both have an incentive to deliver on the agreed-upon results, and the e-business organization gets paid for the quantifiable value it creates.

Initiatives sponsored by individual departments can also use the charge-back scheme, but in the reverse direction. If a sponsoring business unit or department feels it has an initiative that will benefit other business units or the enterprise as a whole, the unit can approach the e-business organization with the initiative for corporate funding. The sponsoring business unit should typically be asked to put up "founder's equity" of between 20 and 40 percent of the overall funds, as well as resources to implement the project at the departmental level. The balance of the funds would be subsidized by the corporate entity through the e-business team. These funds should be sufficient to implement the initiative at the business unit level. Once the initiative is shown to be viable, it can then be offered by the e-business organization to other business units, which are then asked to pay in terms of charge-backs. These charge-backs accrue to the corporate entity and the sponsoring business unit, in proportion to their "ownership" of the internal venture. In case the internal venture is spun off or carved out as a separate entity, the returns accrue through capital appreciation to the corporation and the sponsoring business unit. This coinvestment mechanism allows the sponsoring business entity to access capital beyond its own limited financial resources from the corporate level. Conversely, it allows the corporate entity to ensure that the sponsoring business unit has sufficient "skin in the game" to make the project a success.

The coinvestment approach between business units and corporate parent relies on equity investments by the corporate entity in department initiatives. There is another variant of this mechanism: a debt mechanism called the *corporate bridge loan*. This is an internal variant of "borrowing from tomorrow to fund today." In this mechanism, a sponsoring business unit or department may approach the corporate entity for funding of an initiative that it promises will result in cost savings or revenue enhancements. For instance, it could be a customer relationship management initiative that promises to migrate a significant proportion of the customer support calls to the Internet, which would consequently reduce customer support costs by 20 percent within the next 12 months. Now, suppose that this projected 20 percent cost savings amounts to $20 million from $100 million overall budgeted spending on customer support for the following year. Based on these estimated savings as "collateral," the corporate entity could advance $20 million to the business unit as a bridge loan for the project. The bridge loan would be payable in terms of a reduction in the following year's budget. If the business unit achieves its stated goals on savings, the loan pays for itself because the reduced costs compensate for the reduced budget. And if the business unit fails to deliver, the corporate bridge loan gets "called" anyway, by a reduction in the budget, leaving the business unit to find ways to deal with the reduced budget. This mechanism forces the business unit to put its money where its mouth is, while being able to access resources beyond its reach for e-business initiatives.

In summary, e-business initiatives can be funded through a variety of mechanisms at the corporate or the department level. At the corporate level, the initiatives can be funded by finding matching cuts, by selling the growth story, or by finding external partners willing to co-invest. Initiatives sponsored by the corporate e-business organization can be funded through a charge-back mechanism or by converting the e-business organization into an internal consulting services organization. Initiatives sponsored at the department level can be funded through equity co-investments by the corporate parent or by corporate bridge loans. The single theme that runs through all these mechanisms is the need to create an efficient internal capital market for financing e-business initiatives. The mindset has to change from a "tax and spend" approach, which characterized the way traditional IT projects were funded, to a "shared risk and reward" approach that aligns incentives toward the common goals of increasing productivity and creating value for customers.

Recall the 1970s hit "The Gambler," in which Kenny Rogers sang, "You got to know when to hold 'em, know when to fold 'em, know when to walk away and know when to run." In dealing with e-business transformation, corporate executives need to become gamblers. Of course, the extent to which they gamble, and how they play their cards, depends largely on their appetite for risk. But any way you slice it, being a gambler is a dicey business! Therefore, not only do they need to place intelligent bets in order to maximize their odds—hence the notion of options thinking—but at the same time they need to keep their day jobs, which means also staying focused on operating profits. As we've said, CEOs have a finite number of chips with which to place their bets, the most important of which are people. How people should organize for e-business, and how the e-business organization should be structured and managed, is the topic of our next, and final, chapter.

7

E-ORGANIZATION: RALLYING THE PEOPLE

You must be the change you wish to see in the world.
—Mahatma Gandhi

The reason men oppose progress is not that they hate progress, but that they love inertia.
—Elbert Green Hubbard

AN ANIMAL FABLE, from a collection of fables in Sanskrit literature known as the *Panchatantra*, tells of how a flock of ringdoves saw tragedy narrowly averted. According to the fable, a hunter sets a giant snare in a spreading banyan tree and scatters grain to catch the attention of the birds. Spying the grain from high in the sky, the flock of ringdoves swoops downward and soon becomes trapped in the hunter's net. As the hunter, wielding his mighty club, approaches the birds, they begin to panic and flap their wings in desperation. White Wing, the leader of the flock, says to the rest of the ringdoves, "We must not panic, my friends. There is a way to escape from this terrible fate, but we must all agree to work together. The net is too large and too heavy for any one of us to lift. But if we all fly upward at the same time, I'm sure we can lift the snare and carry it away." The other ringdoves quickly agree. When White Wing gives the signal, the birds all fly upward at the same moment. As the hunter watches in amazement, the birds raise the net and disappear into the afternoon sky.[1]

The fable of the ringdoves offers valuable lessons about the critical role of *people* in e-business transformation. As with any change initiative, e-business demands changes in the way that organizations look, think, and interact. Changing an organization involves changing the attitudes, behavior, and roles of all its individuals. Only by aligning the actions of individuals toward a shared vision can established companies escape the mental models that imprison their thinking, much like the net that imprisoned the ringdoves. Alignment of actions, in turn, demands strong leadership. Like White Wing in the fable, the CEO needs to act as a catalyst, a champion, and a cheerleader for change. The fable also points to the importance of centralizing strategy while decentralizing execution in the management of change. While vision and strategy need to flow from the top, implementation and actions should emanate from all parts of the organization.

Ironically, the "softer side" of e-business transformation—the role of people, organizational structure, and leadership in the process—is actually the harder side to manage. Yet, surprisingly, the organizational aspects scarcely receive the attention they deserve. While digital strategy books are replete with discussions of Coase's Law (transaction costs), Moore's Law (processing power), Metcalfe's Law (network dynamics), and Gilder's Law (bandwidth expansion) as empirical generalizations that define the network economy, these laws often meet their match in another law that determines the fate of e-business initiatives.[2] It is Paul's Law, which states: *You can't fall off the floor*. A fear of falling may well present the greatest impediment to e-business transformation.

E-business requires fundamental changes in how people think and act. Unfortunately, few people naturally embrace change. Instead, they tend to follow Newton's first law of motion, which is to say that they tend to remain at rest or in uniform motion unless compelled to change by the action of an external force. This natural tendency to resist change, also known as *inertia*, is exacerbated by the fact that deeply held corporate cultures often reward the status quo by not encouraging risk-taking. Most successful firms have deeply ingrained mental models of "how we make money" and "how we do business." Abandoning the comfort of the existing way of doing things in the uncertain hope of a better tomorrow is not a prospect most people relish. The writer Marilyn Ferguson summarizes the challenge: "It's not so much that we're afraid of change or so in love with the old ways, but it's that place in between that we fear. It's like being between trapezes. It's Linus when his blanket is in the dryer. There's nothing to hold on to." Our mental models are like Linus's blanket, offering a false sense of security in times that demand true change.

Consider the traditional role of the IT department, where the key responsibilities have long centered on network availability and mission-criticality—"make sure the data center doesn't blow up" and "keep the machines running smoothly." For years, the IT staff was expected to funnel every ounce of energy into overseeing the robustness, redundancy, security, integration, and maintenance of standard-issue technologies, which usually delivered only marginal advances in terms of efficiency and effectiveness. The mindset was geared to incremental improvements, not transformational changes, and *risk* was not a word that CIOs normally wanted to hear. Contrast this mindset with the role the modern CIO is expected to play. Nuke your data centers and move them outside the firm to hosting companies. Outsource mission-critical enterprise applications. Place bets on emerging technologies that are far from mature and robust. Take risks, rock the boat, think different. These are heretical thoughts for traditional-minded CIOs.

Equally discomforting thoughts are reverberating throughout other departments. Marketing needs to approach decision-making less as a subjective art and more as a fact-based science. Purchasing needs to move from personal and manual procurement to technology-enabled systems. HR could evolve from being a staff function that exists as a cost center to a shared services organization that exists as a profit center. The sales force needs to master Internet-based selling tools, and it needs to organize around customers, not products. Engineering needs to involve partners, customers, and suppliers as members of an extended team in the collaborative design of new products. And manufacturing needs to become virtual, orchestrating manufacturing operations without owning and operating actual factories.

So how do we move the organization toward these new and unfamiliar ways of thinking and acting? How do we translate e-business vision into aligned action? How can we ensure that e-business initiatives will be embraced, not resisted, by the rank and file? How do we beat the odds, which suggest that most change management initiatives in large organizations are destined to fail? As we've suggested, the key is to think systemically about the multifaceted organizational issues that surround e-business, and to realize that every e-business initiative involves the creation of a *sociotechnical system*—the "technical system" (technology, procedures, rules, etc.) affects input, transformation and output, while the "social system" (the people) determines how effectively and efficiently the "technical system" is used. E-business success requires alignment of technology with multiple organizational dimensions, both "hard" (structure and staffing) and "soft" (culture and incentives).

The Seven Steps to Organizational Nirvana

Even greater than the number of books devoted to e-business transformation are those that posit theories about how organizations change, and what obstacles prevent them from changing.[3] One model that has gained widespread acceptance for explaining organizational excellence is the classic 7S *model* proposed over twenty years ago by consultants at McKinsey & Company.[4] We draw inspiration from this model, noting that it offers another testimonial to the power of the number seven! The 7S model contends that organizational excellence demands superior fit among seven different dimensions:

1. Strategy: the plan for allocating the organization's resources to achieve its goals
2. Systems: the administrative procedures, routines, and information systems that characterize how work is done in the organization
3. Structure: the way the organization's units relate to each other, including formal reporting and authority relationships
4. Staff: the numbers, levels, and types of people employed in the organization
5. Style: patterns of behavior of key managers in achieving the organization's goals; how managers relate to employees
6. Skills: distinctive capabilities of key personnel or the firm as a whole
7. Shared values: the significant meanings, guiding concepts, values, and aspirations, often unwritten, that go beyond the conventional formal statement of corporate objectives

Strategy, systems, and structure are the "hard" dimensions, while the remaining four are the "soft" dimensions. The basic message underlying the 7S model is that high-performance organizations are distinguished by the amount of attention they devote to the "soft" S's, the degree of fit among the seven dimensions, the clarity of shared values and goals in guiding the organization. While the 7S model provides a useful checklist of the organizational issues that drive excellence, it falls short of articulating how the dimensions relate to each other and how they can be sequenced into a logical set of processes.

Our model—also, of course, comprising seven dimensions— defines the processes involved in managing organizational change associated with e-business transformation (see Figure 7-1). While our model draws some ideas from the 7S model, it goes well beyond merely offering a checklist of dimensions to think about in explaining organizational performance. The dimensions in our model are logically related *processes* that flow from the e-business vision and strategy. They define the steps that need to be taken to convert the vision into reality. The vision and strategy define the goals that the company seeks to achieve and the set of strategic choices it needs to make in order to reach these goals. With the ends and the means serving as anchors, the seven organizational processes that constitute the model are:

1. Catalyzing: initiating change from the top by creating a culture that embraces change, and a shared e-business vision that energizes the organization

2. Diffusing: communicating the e-business vision broadly and deeply inside and outside the organization, and creating a sense of urgency around e-business

3. Motivating: creating incentive systems that promote acceptance of change and experimentation, and a culture of sharing

4. Skilling: educating individuals about new processes, systems, and business practices. Creating mentoring programs that overcome the fear of the unknown and resistance to change

5. Externalizing: marketing change initiatives externally to partners and suppliers, and making investments in partners and suppliers to increase commitment and loyalty

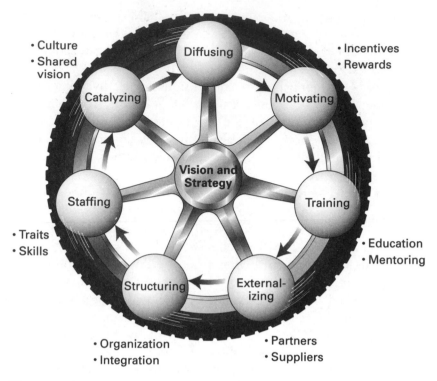

Figure 7-1
Seven organizational processes in e-business transformation

6. Structuring: defining roles and responsibilities for the
e-business organization; managing the vertical tension of
centralization versus decentralization, as well as the horizontal tension of separation versus integration of the e-business
organization

7. Staffing: recruiting the leader and the members of the
e-business team, and defining the skills and the personality
traits of the core e-business team members

Taken together, these processes ensure that the organization is
aligned with the vision, strategy, and infrastructure we have discussed
in earlier chapters and that every individual becomes a willing participant and enabler of change.

Catalyzing: Lighting the Spark

As we stated in the opening chapter, e-business transformation is not the job of a middle manager. The systemic nature of the changes dooms to failure any localized efforts championed by middle managers. Instead, the context for change needs to be established by the CEO and the senior management team. Several CEOs told us of their own "Welch moments," named after the mercurial CEO who launched GE's e-business crusade in 1999. For instance, Phil Condit, CEO of Boeing, explained that he became convinced of the enormous significance of e-business after learning that more than half the cost of doing business at Boeing comes from interactions—moving information around inside the organization and between Boeing and its customers and suppliers. He realized that, just as the Industrial Revolution had transformed the business landscape by automating the manufacturing and transportation of goods, the e-business revolution could make Boeing's business dramatically more efficient by automating these information flows.

In truth, the epiphany can come in any number of ways: by individual meditation, by a pilgrimage to the Meccas of e-business, or by way of a "guru" or other force from inside or outside the organization. For Ernest Deavenport, CEO of Eastman, the road to Nirvana could hardly be missed, relentlessly championed as it was by CIO Roger Mowen. For many CEOs, the catalyst came in the form of suppliers and customers insisting that their partners get connected and become e-enabled. By now, of course, most CEOs managing the helms of large companies have made the appropriate noises about the importance of e-business in their communications to investors and external stakeholders. That said, there is a difference between *espoused values* and *enacted values*—what people say, as opposed to what they actually do. Consider the Japanese proverb: "If you really want to know a man, look at his feet, not his mouth." People have a natural tendency to tune out the empty pronouncements that emanate from the corner office if they see much talk but little action. The CEO's conviction about the need for change has to run deep, and it has to be visceral. When talking about e-business, CEOs must sound as though they *mean* business. This may require some acting. Because while few CEOs remain outright intimidated by the specter of e-business, it's nonetheless important to acknowledge a basic fact of life: Many of the individuals who inhabit the executive suites of Corporate America belong to a generation that did not grow up with computers and may be uncomfortable with anything even remotely related to IT. To help remedy the situation, CEOs, as well as all other senior executives, should be encouraged to experience e-business firsthand. Jack Greenberg, the CEO of McDonald's, credits his exposure to best-practice companies like Cisco and Dell for the perspective that he needed to push the frontier on e-business transformation within his own company. CEOs have much to gain by touring the actual facilities of companies that are ahead of the curve with respect to their e-business activities. As a variation on the theme by author Tom Peters of *management by walking around*, CEOs might also embrace the notion of *management by surfing around*. This can simply mean spending more time online, exploring relevant websites as a way to broaden their perspectives and raise their Net IQ.

Having come to see the light, CEOs need to work closely with their inner circle of senior managers to develop a shared vision before communicating the vision more broadly to the entire organization. The sequence of events is important. If the CEO's direct reports and heads of business units are not well-versed with the vision and fully energized about its implications, they will undoubtedly fail to transmit the requisite level of enthusiasm to their staff. A shared vision establishes common cognitive ground. It creates a common understanding for what e-business means in the context of the company's own priorities. The shared vision is a map of the direction and intended destination, even if the exact details of the journey have yet to be defined. At this early stage, what matters most is the communication of strategic intent, and not the tactics of implementation. Strategic intent can be stated clearly and concisely in a set of guiding principles, such as those outlined by Eastman:

- Focus on the customer—create customer-centric e-business solutions that make it easy for customers to do business with us. Invest in technologies and capabilities that bring real value to customers.
- Hold a portfolio of investment options and build a network of partnerships.
- Leverage intellectual capital, industry knowledge, relationships, brand, and customer base.
- Build the company's profile as an "eBrand."

Eastman's guiding principles clearly define the company's *goals*—"make it easy for customers to do business"—as well as its *strategy*—hedge risk, build partnerships, and leverage assets, relationships, and capabilities. The vision is articulated consistently throughout all of the company's external and internal communications. Similarly, W.W. Grainger's vision "to become the most convenient place for customers to buy what they need, when they need it, and how they want to buy it" has guided that company's channel-centric e-business efforts. And Boeing's vision of "operational efficiencies in the core business, value realization from intellectual assets embedded in existing businesses, and value creation from new frontiers and entirely new businesses" clearly defines a three-pronged approach that has become the bible for that company's e-business strategy.

For any company, the word *shared* needs to move front and center. While the initial realization that e-business holds the key to the company's future success may originate with the CEO, the broader scope of the vision has to be jointly formulated with the other members of the executive team in order to arrive at a shared understanding of the company's goals and aspirations.

To this end, an immersion exercise can serve as an excellent vehicle. An intensive off-site retreat lasting two or three days, the exercise is designed to create a shared understanding among the key executives about emerging trends, opportunities, and competitive threats. The exercise is composed of facilitated dialogues, in which experts point to best practices and offer ongoing analysis, and after which executives should leave with cognitive alignment around the organization's strategic direction. The main objective is to answer the question: *So, what do we do about it?* At the end of the discussions, the executive team should come away with half a dozen or so initiatives that it deems to be priority areas.

The exercise should involve the *entire* senior management team, including the CEO, whose participation demonstrates commitment and seriousness of purpose. The development of the e-business vision cannot be relegated to a subset of departments or functional units. Because the impact of e-business reaches every part of the organization, every operating unit and functional area needs to become an owner of the shared vision. The exercise should feature presentations by external experts, including consultants, academics, and leaders from best-practice firms, as well as the internal technology team. The presentations should be designed to expose the senior management team to disruptive and innovative business architectures, technology trends, organizational design trends, and best practices for managing organizational change.

In conducting these immersion exercises, we have often found that a dose of good old-fashioned fear can be a powerful lever for opening the minds of senior managers. After all, change involves unfreezing deeply held attitudes and beliefs. To unfreeze an attitude, it helps to present senior managers with concrete scenarios that outline how their core businesses could come under attack, threatening their very survival. Even better, the participating managers can be asked to create their own threatening scenarios—an exercise we noted in Chapter 3, in which we told executives to imagine their "worst nightmare competitor." When freed from the constraints of their legacy businesses, managers can become very creative about concocting "destroy your business" innovations.

While fear can help unfreeze old attitudes, opportunity can help to focus the process of freezing new attitudes. This step of identifying opportunities should be the focus of the exercise's next phase. Participating managers, with help from external facilitators, should work to define a set of guiding principles and priorities for e-business. These principles and priorities constitute the shared vision.

Diffusing: Communicating the Vision

"There is nothing more difficult to take in hand, more perilous to conduct, or more uncertain in its success, than to take the lead in the introduction of a new order to things," wrote Niccolò Machiavelli in *The Prince*. And certainly few "new orders to things" are as difficult, perilous, or uncertain from the perspective of an established company than the organizational challenges of e-business transformation. The CEO and senior management can serve as catalysts for initiating change, creating the push from the top. But the challenge still remains: How do you get the attention of every person in the organization, especially people who are focused on the lines of business and operating results? Like any "new order to things," e-business needs to be diffused systematically throughout the organization. Diffusion requires that the senior management team communicate in a frequent and consistent manner, and from a unified front. In addition, every operating unit and functional department should have its own designated evangelists who also communicate the need for change and champion specific change initiatives.

As we've suggested, communication should go well beyond pronouncements. Actions speak louder than words in building internal momentum for change, even if they are merely symbolic, and little actions can go a long way in communicating the message of seriousness. Call it *the big shadows of little actions*. For instance, following a meeting one day with his executive team, Phil Condit announced that he would henceforth use only e-mail to communicate with them and the entire Boeing organization. And while this might seem like a trivial move, for some senior managers who had never before used e-mail it created initial discomfort. Soon enough, however, they grew accustomed to it, and now the entire senior management team relies on e-mail for nearly all of its internal communication needs. Similarly, when Phil Condit caught wind of the latest streaming media application under development by the company's IT staff, to display a ticker tape with breaking news and stock prices, he immediately signed up as a beta user. Due to the extent to which their actions are scrutinized by the rest of the organization, the CEO needs to lead by example. At Allstate, Ed Liddy ate lunch every week for a year with the e-business steering team, whose accomplishments he never ceases to praise before both internal and external audiences. Why? Because, just as fear can be used to open people's minds to e-business, another human emotion—pride—can help sustain their enthusiasm. To that end, flattery goes a long way. So, it's important to not only celebrate early successes, but the individual heroes responsible for those successes.

Communication also goes beyond describing the goals and outcomes of e-business. Beyond defining *what* the organization seeks to achieve and become, communication should also stress *when* these changes need to happen. Because change needs to come faster than the time that the organization usually takes to react to new initiatives, the CEO needs to convey a general sense of urgency focused on producing results. One tactic: Draw a line in the sand, by publicly announcing dates by which certain milestones must be met. The public communication of dates creates stretch goals in time and sets a deadline that motivates the team toward defined milestones and goals.

Milestone thinking does not come naturally for most established companies. Large companies tend to be *budget companies*. Budgets are the metronomes that play in their heads and the lifeblood that flows through their veins. By contrast, startup companies tend to be *milestone companies*. Generally, they march to the beat of a different drummer. Their moves are measured in milestones, not budgets. All things being equal, whenever a budget company competes against a milestone company, the latter comes away with a distinct competitive edge. Why? Because budgets create artificial clock speeds. One of the greatest artificial clock speeds hangs on the wall: the calendar. Think about it: monthly staff meetings, quarterly announcements, yearly planning retreats, three-year rolling plans. These metrics are purely time-based—e.g., an annual budget cycle always requires a fixed amount of time: one year. This is equivalent to saying: "I'm on a journey, and I'm going to measure my progress based only on the amount of time that has elapsed. My progress has no correlation to how far I actually travel or what I accomplish along the way."

Speed is measured in distance per unit timed. To increase its speed, a budget company needs to gauge not how much time has elapsed, but what it has accomplished during that period of time. It needs to operate as a milestone company—on *execution time*, which is *not* calendar-specific. How quickly a company can hit a milestone is a function of how fast its rocket ship can fly. To fly faster, budget companies must speed up their calendar time to Internet time. This may mean annual budgets and plans formulated on a quarterly basis and monthly planning meetings that take place every week! With milestone thinking, the resources allocated to a project are contingent on hitting the milestones, not on hitting the calendar date. In budget thinking, resources are constrained and time is fixed. In milestone thinking, resources and time are completely elastic, whereas achievements are fixed. Budgets are backward-facing, framed with the past as a reference point. Milestones, on the other hand, are forward-facing. A milestone looks only to the future and communicates a strong sense of urgency about getting to that future.

So communication of the e-business vision has to include a clear statement of milestones and deadlines. Also, communication should be directed to all stakeholders, internal as well as external. In the world of e-business, it is important not only to do things, but to be *seen* doing things. After all, the battle for mind share among investors and potential employees is fought and won well before the battle for market share even begins. Investors, analysts, journalists, prospective customers, and even competitors are watching closely to see if the company "gets it," and if it has a credible e-business strategy and implementation plan. It is no coincidence that companies like Dell, IBM, Cisco, Schwab, Enron, and GE get profiled in almost every article, magazine, or book that deals with e-business. They have all either written their own thought leadership books or have been profiled extensively as thought leaders in others' books. Their CEOs never pass up an opportunity to evangelize their initiatives in public forums, constantly touting their vision and claiming thought leadership in the race to define the e-business innovation frontier. Building the "corporate brand" should be a deliberate act of strategy. As e-business becomes one of the defining dimensions for competitive advantage, external communication of the firm's e-business vision is fast becoming an essential element of building the corporate brand.

In summary: Communicate frequently and consistently. Communicate through actions. Communicate desired outcomes, as well as milestones. And communicate externally to build the e-brand. Remember: The opportunity to catalyze e-business change comes only once. Blow it through a false start, or by crying wolf, and it may be impossible to ever regain the lost organizational momentum.

Motivating: Paying People to Play

"Call it what you will," declared Nikita Khrushchev, "incentives are what get people to work harder." Granted, the old Communist risk/reward profile more often embodied the spirit of "you pretend to work and I'll pretend to pay you." Nonetheless, Khrushchev's basic point was right on the money: Incentives shape behavioral outcomes. By failing to carefully think through these issues, a company can end up creating incentives that are perverse and set itself up for failure.

A Hindi fable tells of a king who instructs his people to save now while skies are blue, in case a day should ever come when skies turn gray. To get the ball rolling, the king orders that a deep well be dug. He then decrees that every subject throughout the kingdom line up before the new well with a full cup of milk and pour it in. The next day, eagerly expecting to behold a rich pool of white milk, the king peers into the well only to discover that it contains nothing but water. Not a single drop of milk. What happened? Human nature happened. Everybody thought their actions would go undetected and be of little consequence if they substituted water for milk. After all, everybody else, presumably, would be adding only milk.

Different versions of this fable play out every day across Corporate America, particularly with respect to e-business initiatives that demand collaboration and shared contributions. One version we know of concerns a consumer goods manufacturer that deployed a knowledge management system for its sales force. Underlying the initiative was the hope that the sales reps, always on the road, developing their own unique knowledge, would share their tricks of the trade with the rest of the team. A database that captured best practices around selling could then be used to boost overall productivity, or so it was thought. For their part, however, the sales reps scoffed at the idea of "doing knowledge management." All asked the same question: What's in it for me? With this, senior management came to realize that the issue at hand was a matter of *incentives* and that the sales reps' refusal to volunteer their competitive advantages could be easily overcome by simply putting the right incentive structure into place. So, the company proceeded to create incentives based on the actual volume of content that each of the sales reps contributed to the database. Of course, the only problem with this approach was that quantity had no correlation with quality, and soon people were filling the repository with everything but the kitchen sink. Obviously, this defeated the very purpose. Finally, the company got it right, by realizing that the problem was indeed incentives-based, but that the solution was tied not to individual incentives but to *team incentives*. Thereafter, some part of the sales reps' compensation package would be linked to the results produced not by individual sales reps, but by the sales force as a whole. Lesson learned: Incentives are what get people to work harder only if they are the right kind of incentives.

Clearly, the CEO who issues an edict to "Go out and do e-business" should not expect that everyone will actually cooperate. The nature of e-business initiatives is such that everyone needs to come together and everyone benefits. But this can also set off the tragedy of the commons as everyone seeks to reap the benefits, but nobody wants to be the first to act. The key, therefore, is to redo incentives at a high level. For example, while it may not be feasible to reward direct knowledge creation, a company *can* reward the *outcome* of knowledge creation. Stock options are a physical alignment force, and they should be used to reward the entire sales force based on group performance. The secret: Move away from rewarding the means to rewarding the ends, and from rewarding individuals to rewarding groups. At a higher level, this approach creates a self-policing mechanism; participants know which of their colleagues is shirking.

In designing incentives, it is important to look beyond those that are purely monetary. People are motivated for a variety of reasons, money being only one of them. While employees expect to be paid equitably and are always in search of the financial upside, there are many other mechanisms that get them out of bed in the morning. These include social recognition, human capital, learning, marketability, and power. To varying degrees, all might factor into their overall job satisfaction. Organizations ought to realize that presenting employees with the opportunity to participate in e-business ventures within the company can become a reward in itself. Just like channels, people have hybrid motivations, and companies may lose some people whose objective function is a corner solution. In this case, a corner solution is money only, whereas a hybrid solution includes less tangible incentives, such as higher visibility, access to the CEO, and human capital enhancement.

How does a company create incentives for people to support internal, enabling initiatives that would seem to be a world apart from their day-to-day areas of accountability? How does it persuade people to embrace change management initiatives? How does it convince line managers in operating units to support and give resources to new ventures that would seem to fall outside of their jurisdiction? One way is by offering employees performance-linked options, indexed not to how the stock behaves relative to the market, but to the extent to which the company meets internal goals for revenue and profit growth. The performance-linked options become vested based on growth metrics set by the firm—e.g., deliver 10 percent compound growth, and the initial batch of options will vest; deliver 11 percent compound growth, then another batch will vest. Rewards can be linked purely to the growth of the company, with no connection whatsoever to the performance of the stock price. Performance-linked options motivate all employees to think about how they could contribute to meeting the performance objectives that would lead to the vestment of their options. This can create a very powerful internal pull to find new sources of growth and profits, and new ways to create value. Having primed the pump, the e-business organization need only sell employees on the fact that e-business tools will accelerate progress in that direction. They simply need to be shown that e-business can become one of the most salient levers and promising paths to achieving their goals. Forget about selling them on e-business; instead, sell them on the outcome. In this way, e-business becomes a means to an end, not a goal unto itself. Whereas e-business initiatives traditionally tend to get pushed, this approach converts the push into a pull. Before long, people will come knocking on the door, asking to participate in an e-business initiative.

While strategies are formulated in executive boardrooms and at senior management levels, people in the trenches are often left to wonder what they stand to gain by following the latest marching orders. And while it's easy to complain about the inertia that the average line manager feels with respect to adopting new technologies and redesigned business processes, deeper reflection might reveal that there is no real incentive for them to stick their necks out. Therefore, managing incentives simply means stepping into other people's shoes and addressing the issue of WIIFME—"What's In It For Me?" In many cases, the risks are clear while the rewards are ambiguous. Just as software developers should adopt a user-centered approach for software design, executives should adopt a user-centered approach for incentive design. This means acquiring a genuine understanding of the needs of *all* of the people within the organization, in order to be able to flip the aforementioned equation: *Make the rewards clear and the risks ambiguous.* Why should people want to participate? What makes it worthwhile from their perspective? Sit down with them and ask them, in essence, "What can we do for you?" and "How can we make your lives better?" Then proceed to sell them concrete proposals. Few people are interested in e-business for the sake of e-business. But every last sales rep would perk up his or her ears were you to say, "You know, I can make you 30 percent more productive," as would the purchasing organization given the comment, "I've done a study and think I can cut down your inventory from 40 days to 25 days." Don't sell the message in abstract terms. Instead, sell an initiative in concrete terms. Sell something with which employees can identify and that makes salient the WIIFME factor. Don't sell e-business theory. Instead, sell employee value propositions. And don't call it "e-business." Instead, call it "a tool kit." Take the problem-solution approach: Here's what's broken, here's how you can fix it, and here's the benefit that you will derive.

Given all that we have said about incentives, there will still be employees who are unable to get past the WIIFME factor. For them, implementing technology initiatives requires change, and any threat of change will automatically be confronted with inertia. In truth, some of the people whose collaboration is absolutely critical to make initiatives a success are the people who are the least technology savvy and have the most deep-seated fear of the unknown. A company can purchase and install technology on every single desktop, but if it hasn't thought through all dimensions of the sociotechnical systems, then people may simply ignore it. As we've said, e-business is everybody's job—but, like *quality*, it can end up being nobody's job.

Training: Bringing People Up to Speed

"Tell me and I'll forget; show me and I may remember; involve me and I'll understand," or so goes a popular Chinese proverb. Even if a company can overcome the inherent resistance to change when introducing new software, it may still fail to get adoption if people are not adequately trained to use it effectively. To think that people learn if left to their own devices, or if forced to attend instructor-led "telling" sessions, is wishful thinking. Consider even the most basic types of software, such as the word processor or spreadsheet. Chances are, you have stumbled your way through the learning process, making mistakes and creating workaround solutions for problems, because you never knew how to effectively use the hundreds of sophisticated features, or to even know all the features that exist. Now think about your corporate intranet, your marketing automation software, or your knowledge management applications. Are these applications being fully exploited? Not likely. In reality, most e-business applications are used well below their potential, because insufficient thought was given to the process of bringing people up to speed.

Consider the adoption of courseware at Northwestern University. A new software platform was announced to faculty members, along with a set of training sessions designed to familiarize them with its features and functionality. Most faculty members skipped the training sessions, claiming they were too busy. While there may have been some truth to this claim, there was another likely factor that kept them from attending: their egos. Many faculty members dismissed outright the notion that they could be "students" who needed to be "taught" in a classroom setting. As a result, few faculty members ended up using the software, despite its obvious value. It was not until support reps sat down with members one-on-one to help them put their courses online that the faculty as a whole began to warm up to the courseware platform. Software is experiential in nature. And despite the move toward user-friendliness, software is still hard to use.

As this story suggests, training can be especially difficult to carry out when the users are senior managers who are loath to admit their ignorance of IT. Having always acted as teachers and mentors, senior managers are often unwilling to acknowledge that they might have something to learn from their juniors. However, reverse mentoring is exactly what senior managers need to do. Consider the adoption of reverse mentoring at GE, where Jack Welch ordered his top 600 or so managers to reach down into their ranks for mentors who could help them visit competitors' websites, order their own products online, and gain a deeper knowledge of the customer benefits that websites can deliver. According to Welch, "e-business knowledge is generally inversely proportional to both age and height in the organization."[5] With the CEO leading the way, more than a thousand executives quickly signed up for "e-mentors," some for assistance with such basic tasks as how to use Yahoo!

"You teach best what you most need to learn," observed the author Richard Bach. To *really* teach people about the possibilities of e-business, it pays to make learners into teachers. At Cisco, John Chambers requires that each of his senior managers gain a deep understanding for how Internet technology can be used to create a competitive advantage in each of the company's business areas, including public relations and legal services. According to Chambers, senior managers need to integrate the Net into their planning, thinking, and day-to-day operations. And how does he ensure that they do? As part of the project, each corporate function has to benchmark its Internet capabilities against those of outside organizations considered thought leaders within that particular function. For example, the legal department would look at such areas as self-service tools to assist in contract generation and approval and assess whether Cisco lags behind, is even with, or is ahead of the benchmarked competition. The twelve heads of functional areas spend a day with the CEO presenting their initial plans, and they then provide extensive updates of their progress on the plans every quarter. The amount of progress they make factors into their overall performance evaluation.[6]

Externalizing: Bringing
Partners and Suppliers Along

Imagine gazing through a pirate's telescope. The tube sections are perfectly aligned, and yet the distant image is dark and blurry. When questioned, each section of the telescope says, "I did my part, I amplified light, I took it to the next level." But obviously there was a disconnect somewhere along the way, because each section was concerned only with its own local perspective and not with that of the end-user. Similarly, in implementing an e-business initiative, a company can deliver superior work but still fail to get the initiative off the ground without the participation of its partners. Just as incentives need to be properly aligned internally with employees, so, too, must they be aligned externally with partners.

For this reason, an argument can be made for subsidizing the acquisition costs of hardware and connectivity systems owned by partners, without whose cooperation and participation the company's own systems can never be optimized. This retools the age-old notion of "vendor development" for the information age. To successfully outsource manufacturing, firms have traditionally invested in upgrading vendor systems, business processes, and quality control systems, and at times they have even financed capital equipment for vendors and partners. The same philosophy extends to the creation of partner-facing and supplier-facing infrastructure. Investment in upgrading partners' business processes and infrastructure is an important step in ensuring end-to-end integration of interenterprise business processes. Moreover, these investments also contribute to increased partner and supplier loyalty, and increased reciprocal dependence because partners are motivated to adopt technology platforms and standards compatible with those of the firm. However, these investments do demand a rationalization of the partner and supplier base, because you cannot spread your investments too thinly. A company needs to invest in only a few strategic partners and suppliers and make sure it gains their loyalty and trust.

As with employees, partners and suppliers can be arrayed on a bell curve in terms of their attitude toward technological change. There are early adopters who take a proactive stance toward e-business, and there are laggards who will hide behind channel conflict and margin erosion to resist e-business initiatives. Given the importance of word-of-mouth among the partner and supplier base, it is very important to pick early adopters as the initial target for piloting e-business initiatives, so they can become proponents of change for the rest of the partner population. When Herman Miller was piloting its new partner relationship management system, it chose a small sample of "progressive" retailers that demonstrated receptivity to new technologies and open-mindedness in their discussions of potential channel conflict issues. Furthermore, even for these early adopters, Herman Miller initially chose new accounts previously held by competitors to pilot the system, so that channel conflict concerns would be minimized at the outset. Once the numbers were in, the dealers had validation that the new system would more than compensate for the lost transactional fees due to direct handling of transactions by Herman Miller, by generating new leads for installation and maintenance service contracts. The results could be used as evidence for convincing other dealers to adopt the initiative. Instead of rolling out the initiative broadly to the entire dealer population, and by carefully picking early targets, Herman Miller ensured that the adoption curve worked in its favor, not against it.

Special challenges arise in working with *competitors as partners* on collaborative initiatives for procurement and supply chain management. In consortia ranging from Covisint in automobiles to Exostar in aerospace and Elemica in the chemicals industry, the threat of the tragedy of the commons is very real. The sponsors of these consortia are firms that have traditionally competed with each other, and so they may find it difficult to create the level of trust essential to making partnerships work. History teaches us that consortium initiatives are destined to collapse if partners fail to assign their best people to the team and do not shelve internal efforts that compete with the consortium initiative. To create the necessary level of commitment, partners in these situations should agree to follow the simple mantra: *burn your bridges*. Consider the ChoiceParts consortium initiative in the automobile parts business, a collaborative venture between ADP, CCC Information Systems, and Reynolds & Reynolds, which has adopted a policy of punitive damages for any partner that does not kill competing internal initiatives. All partners have to commit to the consortium as their only ongoing initiative for managing procurement of auto parts. The consortium buys out all competing internal initiatives. If any competing initiative is discovered in violation of this agreement, the guilty partner is forced to surrender its entire equity stake in the joint venture. Strong medicine? Yes, but in the absence of natural trust, and given all the possible conflicts of interest that can arise, it may be the only way to keep people honest.

Structuring: Managing Centralization/Decentralization and Integration/Separation

With the strategy, culture, and incentives in place, the next step in the process is to define the structure of the e-business organization and its role relative to other parts of the organization. This means confronting two basic design dilemmas:

* Centralization versus decentralization of the e-business organization
* Separation versus integration of e-business from the core organization

Achieving balance on these two dimensions is an ongoing challenge—one made more difficult by the fact that the balance needs to constantly adjust over time as the e-business organization matures.

Centralization Versus Decentralization

Democracy is a wonderful idea, but it can sometimes run amok. This is especially true in multidivisional companies, where employees at the grassroots level, on their own little pieces of turf, start their own decentralized e-business initiatives. The HR department may create a website for self-guided retirement benefits management; the public affairs department may create a website with investor information for the media; the marketing department may build a customer communications application; the packaging department may create a website for linking to suppliers. These websites typically have disparate standards, platforms, and user interfaces. Moreover, the sites are often limited in terms of functionality and scalability.

The lack of coordination across these websites can only mean that, at some stage, the "identity and standards police" are called in to take action. Often precipitated by the announcement of a corporate e-business strategy, the standardization police dictate that all business units and departments adopt common standards, platforms, and a consistent look-and-feel. The logic relates to the need to present a unified face to customers and partners. In reality, however, a move to centralization has the potential to create significant resentment because of the time and effort people have already invested into developing decentralized initiatives. The important question: How can a company manage the balance between centralization and decentralization across different levels in a classic multidimensional, multigeographical, multibusiness unit organization?

The first lesson is to realize that the central elements of any e-business application are the technology infrastructure, the business logic, and the user interface. The right balance of centralization versus decentralization is different across these layers. Specifically, the degree of centralization should progressively reduce as you move closer to the customer end of the application and away from the infrastructure end of the application. Why? Because the customer-facing organization has the best understanding of what the user interface should look like and how the applications should be customized to end-user needs. The customer-facing organization should be free to adapt the presentation layer to respond to the needs of their customers, as well as to add their domain expertise to the application. Conversely, the last thing you would want to decentralize is infrastructure. So the solution is to create a "sandbox," and give people freedom to play in it. Each decentralized application should conform to a set of standards of look-and-feel, and should be based on a common technology platform. However, users should be free to customize the interface and add content to the application. Think of the infrastructure as the vessel and the content as the wine. The vessels should be standardized, but the content that fills the vessels should be controlled locally by departments and business units. Allow users to manage content and context, but not platforms, servers, databases, and licenses for enterprise software. Infrastructure should be centralized and pushed to the core, while content and context should be decentralized and pushed to the periphery.[7]

This mixture of centralization and decentralization is reminiscent of a federal government structure, where some powers are decentralized and rest with local governments, while other powers are centralized and rest with the federal government. In the e-business analogy, the "federal government" should control infrastructure, standards, and platforms—the "core"—while the "local governments" should control all aspects related to customers, content, and customizability. This is the secret to managing the centralization-decentralization paradox. Moving to one extreme, where infrastructure and user intelligence are decentralized, is wrong. So, too, is moving to the other extreme, where everything becomes centralized. The trick is to decouple the user intelligence from the infrastructure intelligence, so that infrastructure intelligence can be centralized while user intelligence can be made modular, decentralized, and customizable.

Consider another analogy from the political system: the use of "subsidy schemes" as incentives for adopting corporate standards. For instance, a company can still allow its employees to continue to use their own standards and platforms, but it could make them pay a much higher freight for doing so—subsidizing their initiatives if they play within the sandbox, but penalizing them if they want to go outside the sandbox. In other words, make it expensive, but not impossible, to deviate from the standard by offering a better deal and better support to business units if they adopt the corporate standards. The subsidy scheme will sway most people to eventually fall into line, but without coercion on the part of the corporate IT organization.

Another issue related to vertical organization: Should e-business initiatives be financed at the business unit level or at the corporate level? The advantage of conducting initiatives at the corporate level is the ability to learn across business units, to spread the cost of the initiatives across multiple business units, and to cut across business unit or departmental boundaries. On the other hand, it may be difficult to get buy-in for corporate e-business initiatives from the operating units. Whether e-business initiatives are financed at the business unit level or at the corporate level generally depends on the nature of the initiative. As we discussed in Chapter 6, those initiatives that are too far-reaching in scope and too large an investment to be supported by a single business unit should be financed at the corporate level. On the other hand, if a business unit sponsors the initiative, then it *should* be managed at the business unit level. Every business unit should have an e-business leader who works closely with the business unit operations but also participates in the corporate e-business steering committee. The steering committee should be responsible for setting overall priorities for the company, making decisions on corporate standards and funding, and coordinating e-business activities across business units.

Separation Versus Integration

Another issue in managing organizational structure is the horizontal tension—the degree to which the e-business organization should be separated from the parent company or integrated with the operating units. Recall our discussion in Chapter 2, where we compared the evolution of the "distance" between the e-business organization and the core organization to a sapling that at first grows separately but is subsequently grafted on to the roots of the old tree. Revisiting this argument, the approach to managing separation versus integration should be to create a separate organization at first, for focus and direction, and then to gradually integrate most of the e-business initiatives into the core organization. Consider how the process has evolved at Kraft Foods. According to Paula Sneed, initiatives had been proliferating long before her appointment to head the e-business organization. Human Resources had created HR Online; the packaging group had created an application to send color labels and images to packaging suppliers; the marketing department had created the Kraft Interactive Kitchen and was participating in several trials with online grocery vendors; and the purchasing group was working on supply chain initiatives. But these efforts weren't integrated, and few of them were getting any traction. In response, the CEO formed an e-business team to act as a central point of focus, not only for coordinating these internal efforts, but also for making external investments and entering into partnerships with startup companies.

In general, individual departments and business units have neither the due diligence skills nor the time to evaluate partnering opportunities. The e-business group is much better equipped to scan the landscape, to review and screen proposals for partnering, and to structure partnerships in a variety of areas that may benefit specific business units or departments. So, for *internal* initiatives, the e-business organization should play the role of matchmaker, adviser, coordinator, and facilitator. For *external* and *cross-business unit* efforts, the e-business organization should serve as a home for projects that would otherwise be orphaned by business units needing to focus on their quarter-by-quarter priorities. But while this scenario suggests a way to get started, what is the "steady state" degree of separation? Is the e-business organization a temporary entity that should eventually be folded back into the business units as they become more experienced at handling vendors, alliances, and productivity-enhancing initiatives? Some would argue that as the IT organization becomes more externally focused and develops capabilities around doing due diligence, then the business units, in collaboration with the IT organization, should take over in managing those e-business initiatives that are aimed at enabling the core business.

We agree, but only partly. Certainly, we think that the e-business organization's catalyzing role should diminish over time. Its objective should be to give the business units fishing poles, not fish, so that e-business initiatives can gradually become part of their day-to-day operations. This has been the trend at companies where e-business has evolved to a higher level. For instance, at Boeing, the business units are responsible for all e-business initiatives that focus on "operational excellence." The Boeing Ventures group handles only growth-oriented external ventures. Similarly, at Eastman, the "enable Eastman" initiatives are gradually being pushed down to the business units.

In the end, the role of the e-business organization depends on two dimensions: the scope of the initiative, and the *intended outcomes* of the initiative (see Figure 7-2). The e-business organization can play any of the following roles:

- *Matchmaking role.* For strategic e-business initiatives focused on productivity improvement, the e-business organization can serve as a matchmaker between emerging technology vendors and the CIO/IT organization by scanning, doing due diligence, and presenting promising technology vendors to the IT organization. This is especially true for new and emerging areas of technology that may not be familiar to the CIO—nontraditional partner-facing and customer-facing applications, for instance. Over time, this role tends to diminish, as technology evaluation and due diligence on new technologies become part of the IT organization's responsibility. At Eastman, the e-business team evaluated technology vendors like eCredit.com and Moai Technologies, even though these technologies would help *enable* its core business, not create new revenue streams.
- *Venturing role.* For growth-oriented strategic initiatives, the e-business organization can play a classic venturing role, either as a co-investor in a startup or as a cofounder of startups. These ventures are geared to finding new revenue streams and top-line growth.
- *Coordinating role.* For department-led initiatives, the e-business team can play a coordinating role to ensure that

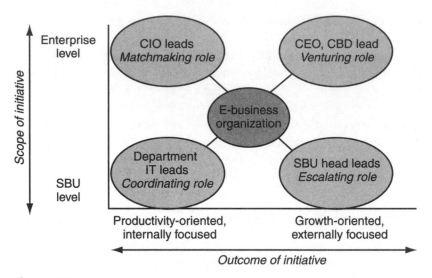

Figure 7-2
The roles of a mature e-business organization

different business units are using similar technologies, working on standardization of platforms and vendors, and "cross-leveling" learning and best practices across business units. This is a "lateral" communication and knowledge management role.

• *Escalating role.* Growth-centric initiatives can come from departments, too, but they often need to be escalated to the corporate level for funding, or for finding co-investors. Here, the e-business organization can facilitate *vertical* coordination—making sure ideas are nurtured and that funding at the business unit level is complemented by corporate funding, as needed. Our discussion in Chapter 6 regarding corporate bridge loans and coinvesting mechanisms are examples of the escalating role.

Over time, the role of the e-business organization moves *upward* and *outward,* as illustrated in Figure 7-2. It becomes more strategic as the departmental level projects get pushed down to the departmental level, and more externally focused as the internally focused initiatives become the budgetary responsibility of the business units.

Staffing: Hiring the E-Business Team

The e-business team typically starts out as a temporary SWAT team, assembled with the assignment of figuring out what the company's e-business strategy ought to be. Over time, this SWAT team evolves into an e-business organization, with a leader at the helm who takes on the role of "e-business czar." Who should this leader be? Paradoxically, selection criteria of the e-business leader should not weigh heavily in favor of the candidate's technology expertise, or even knowledge of e-business. In this context, personalities count for more than functional backgrounds. Even in organizations where the CIOs are leading e-business efforts, these CIOs tend not to come from technology/IT backgrounds. Roger Mowen, the CIO charged with spearheading Eastman's e-business efforts, is a self-taught techie, with a 30-year background in manufacturing and sales. Jim Yost, the CIO at Ford, spent 26 years in Finance and is an engineer by training.[8] And Gary Vanspronsen at Herman Miller has a marketing background. Given the customer focus, a significant proportion of e-business leaders tend to be drawn from marketing and other customer-facing roles.

Personalities that can rally people around the cause should be the number one consideration. These individuals also need to be able to empathize with employees' concerns and reservations about technology and its impact on their jobs. Selecting technologists to lead the venture carries forward the myth that e-business is about technology, when in fact it's mostly about organizational change. The person leading the organization should possess *referent power* and, to a much lesser extent, *expert power*.[9] Referent power arises from people's identification of the e-business leader as a role model, while expert power involves following the person who knows best. Today, expert power around e-business transformation is limited, of course, since nobody can claim to have more than a few years of experience under her or his belts.

When it comes to leading the e-business organization, find people who are well liked, well respected, and highly credible. Find people who can act in a way that is visionary and inspirational, and who understand the barriers, inertia, fears, and political issues that would impede adoption of these initiatives. In short, find people who can cut through the thickets.

The Role of the CIO: Wearing New Hats

While e-business initiatives should generally not fall directly onto the plate of the CIO, the CIO should nonetheless contribute in meaningful ways to the overall e-business effort, alongside the CEO and e-business team. To contribute in meaningful ways, however, requires a reassessment of the CIO's role and relationship with the CEO, which traditionally has been distant, at best. A recent study by the recruiting firm Korn/Ferry finds that only 15 percent of CIOs interact with the CEO more than once a month, with most interactions limited to budget approvals and occasional project updates. With technology becoming a key driver of competitive advantage, however, the CEO needs to understand the major technology decisions, and become actively involved in making these decisions. This ultimately means forging a tighter relationship with the CIO. To this end, the e-business leader can play a valuable mediating role, improving communications between the business leadership and the technology leadership within the organization.

The e-business leader also needs to make sure that the CIO and IT organization become involved as a partner in the e-business projects and initiatives that may fall outside the traditional scope of the CIO. This is important for two reasons. First, the IT organization has deep technology expertise and a deep understanding of the legacy systems that is invaluable in integrating new e-business applications and technology platforms. Lacking this depth of expertise, the e-business leader may find it difficult to evaluate the merits of the various technology solutions. More important, the IT organization has ownership over the enterprise systems, and it can place hurdles in the way of implementation of new initiatives if it has not been involved in the decision-making process. So, while the IT organization may not be the most favorably disposed toward change and innovation, it *should* be a partner in change, alongside the e-business team and the CEO.

Traditionally, the CIO has played an *inward-facing* role, managing the infrastructure and internal technology operations. However, with the increasing importance of *outward-facing* applications, CIOs need to augment this role with an outward-facing role that requires them to evaluate and bet on new technologies and new startup firms that can help their companies to gain a technology-based competitive advantage. Traditionally, this role has been associated with the Chief Technology Officer (CTO). While the CIO keeps internal operations running, the CTO looks outward for emerging technologies. The CIO focuses on stability and mission-criticality, while the CTO focuses on experimentation and innovation. In many established companies, especially those that are conservative users of technology, the CIO has also acted as the CTO. Regardless of whether the CTO and the CIO are the same person, the two *roles* need to be performed. The inward-facing role is important for improving the effectiveness of today's infrastructure, while the outward-facing role is important for discovering innovations for tomorrow's infrastructure. Enlightened CIOs are really a CIO, a CTO, and a venture capitalist all rolled into one. And they evolve a symbiotic relationship between themselves and the e-business leader, collaborating on the evaluation of new tools, new technologies, and new venturing opportunities. Over time, the boundaries between the roles of the CIO, CEO, and e-business leader become increasingly blurred. Eventually, these individuals should all become members of a cross-functional team responsible for managing enabling technologies, and for maximizing the impact of these technologies on the bottom line as well as the top line.

We the People

While many of the steps involved in managing organizational change may sound like motherhood and apple pie, in practice these are the steps that most often get ignored. In this chapter, we have put forth a systematic framework for thinking about the multifaceted organizational issues in the context of e-business transformation.

What does an organization that has undergone this transformation look like? In what ways is it different in form, function, and culture? We summarize the key differences between the traditional organization and the e-organization in Table 7-1. The traditional organization is hierarchical, inflexible, risk-averse, and optimized for stability. With the implementation of the seven steps for organizational change, it evolves into an organization that is decentralized, flexible, and optimized for speed. The organizational change that e-business engenders may be the most valuable, if not entirely anticipated, consequence of e-business transformation.

In this chapter, we began by discussing the role of the leader as a catalyst and cheerleader. The CEO needs to see the light first and then become the evangelist for a shared vision of what e-business means for the organization and what it plans to do about it. This

Table 7-1
From the Traditional Organization to the E-Organization

Dimension	Traditional culture	E-culture
Design goal	Maximize stability and efficiency	Maximize flexibility and speed
Decision-making process	Numbers-driven. Analytical and quantitative	Qualitative and quantitative. Intuition combined with analysis
Role of partnerships	Limited, antagonistic relationships with suppliers and channels	Extensive network of technology, marketing, manufacturing, channel, and startup partners
Role of leadership in e-business	CIO leads, limited involvement of CEO	CEO and e-business team lead, partnership with CIO
Role of teamwork and knowledge sharing	"Hoarding" of knowledge, limited internal and external sharing of knowledge	Extensive sharing of knowledge inside the company; and externally with customers, partners, and suppliers
Role of mentoring	Limited, one-directional only	Extensive, top-down as well as reverse mentoring
Role of experimentation	Low, try to minimize risk. "If it ain't broke, don't break it"	High, see risk as opportunity. "Nothing ventured, nothing gained"
Locus of decision making	Decisions are centralized	Decisions made by those closest to customers

vision needs to be transmitted throughout the organization, through words as well as actions. In transmitting the vision, it also helps to climb down from the rarefied atmosphere of the corporate boardroom and adopt the perspective of all the individuals in the organization by asking a simple question: What's in it for them? This empathy inevitably leads to the design of incentive systems that reward team- work and innovation and that may even spur employees into asking for ways in which they can exploit the power of e-business as a means for improving their own economic lot.

The same empathy argument applies to externalizing the vision to partners and suppliers, by creating incentives that make them want to play and by making investments in upgrading their technology infra- structures. Finally, as we discussed, the e-business organization needs to be structured in a way that strikes a balance between centralization and decentralization, and between separation and integration. Its roles and responsibilities as a mediator, coordinator, investor, and knowl- edge manager need to be defined clearly, as does its relationship with three important constituencies: the CEO, the heads of operating units, and the CIO. Only by creating alignment among all of these interre- lated dimensions can an established company effectively rally the peo- ple around e-business transformation.

E-ENLIGHTENMENT: REVISITING THE JOURNEY

IN HIS SERMONS and teachings, dating from the sixth century B.C., the Buddha often spoke of "a path which opens the eyes and bestows understanding, which leads to peace of mind, to the higher wisdom, to full enlightenment, to Nirvana!"[1] While it would be foolish for us to pretend that this book delivers "full enlightenment" around e-business transformation, hopefully we have at least been able to provide a useful perspective on the journey that a company must travel to move from where it stands today to where it wishes to be in the future, given the expanded set of possibilities and tools that e-business affords.

Our main goal has been to give people a compass. Why a compass? Because the hurricane force winds that sweep across the business landscape can be extremely disorienting. Buffeting us in every possible direction, the waves of change can make our heads spin and cause us to lose all sense of direction. As a result, we might be easily led to believe that e-business is about technology, which it isn't. Or that e-business is about IPO-driven capital appreciation, which it also isn't. Or we might be inclined to jump on the latest bandwagon, only to see it plunge off the nearest cliff. A compass is the antidote to disorientation. It can put us back on the right path by taking us in the general direction of improved business performance and customer satisfaction—which *is* what e-business is all about.

Paradoxically, the right path may well be the same path the company was on before it happened to lose its way. To this point, the French have a saying: *Le plus çe change, le plus çe le même chose*. The fundamentals of business *do* remain the same, no matter how much the landscape seems to change beneath our feet. Hence our attempt in this book to take the "e" out of "e-business" by arguing that to focus on the "business" part and not the "e" part is to focus on the end and not the means. "E" is the means; business is the end. The ends are invariant and deceptively simple. As always, firms win by creating superior value for their customers and by producing superior returns for their shareholders. E-business is simply an effective means to these ends. It creates value by either improving the bottom line (enabling the core business), or by finding new revenue streams (leveraging the core business into new directions).

Enabling change and finding growth: These are the key value drivers of e-business. And the ultimate compass in this journey? Nothing other than the customer value proposition. No matter the exact nature of the e-business initiative, one question should always command everyone's complete attention: *How does this initiative strengthen my existing value proposition, or create new value propositions, for existing and prospective customers?* If this basic question can't be answered satisfactorily, then go no further.

In developing our ideas, we have attempted to resolve paradoxes that force myopic views and to reconcile dichotomies commonly seen as irreconcilable. Disintermediation versus reintermediation. Offline channels versus online channels. External venturing versus internal venturing. Separation versus integration. Spin-off versus spin-in. Earning versus learning. Growth versus change. Centralization versus decentralization. In our view, these all are false dichotomies that can be ultimately transcended. Overcoming the paradox of duality and finding unity in opposites is a recurrent theme in this book. For instance, we exposed substitution and "plus-one" thinking as a myth in managing channels, arguing that channel redesign is about reallocation of functions across all channels, not about substitution of channels. We also showed how the organizational debate on centralization versus decentralization hides the possibility of centralization of infrastructure and decentralization of user intelligence. And we proposed that learning payoffs in venturing are nothing but earning payoffs delayed in time, through their impact on the core business.

In our discussions, we also emphasized the systemic nature of e-business and the power of modularity in enabling business innovation. For instance, we argued that strategy is not about components, but about architecture; it is not about the pieces of the business, but about the scheme that puts the pieces together in creative ways. We said that business innovation arises from creative combinations of capabilities, resources, and relationships. Similarly, in our discussion of e-infrastructure, we highlighted the evolution of modular and component-based architectures, where the emphasis shifts from manufacturing to assembly and from hard-coded applications to configurable Web services. The same idea of componentization and reconfiguration extends to the synchronization of channels and the creation of hybrid channel systems. In the world of business, value lives in modularity and in orchestration.

Another theme that runs through our discussion is the blurring of boundaries and the breaking of silos. The theme manifests itself in many ways: the breaking of functional boundaries within the organization in the creation of cross-functional applications and the real-time enterprise; the breaking of enterprise boundaries by the creation of interenterprise business processes; the breaking of linear chains and sequential processes by the creation of networks of businesses and synchronous processes. The theme transcends several different chapters, which admittedly are the "content silos" that we were forced to erect in writing this book. At one point we even toyed with the idea of doing away with the linear and sequential concept of *chapters*, to emphasize the fact that some ideas and concepts form a nonlinear pattern that cannot be artificially compartmentalized. However, our publisher thought otherwise—and besides: boundaries can be useful as long as we recognize that they are crutches and not legs.

Using the metaphor of a ladder, we made the case that e-business should not be seen as a fixed target or a one-step process. Instead, we argued for a rapid series of evolutionary steps that start with limited, local, and modest initiatives and gradually evolve into enterprisewide and large-scale initiatives. And because the upper rungs of the ladder come into view only after the lower rungs have been climbed, the metrics that measure progress and define success need to evolve and adapt as the initiatives evolve. For this reason, e-business initiatives demand fixity in vision but flexibility in implementation, and thus the emphasis on thinking in terms of options, not bets; platforms, not portfolios; and flexibility, not commitment.

It is no coincidence that we saved our discussion about the "softer side" of e-business for the last chapter. Strategy and technology need to bow at the altar of organization, because what ultimately makes e-business happen, or not happen, rests on the "people component." E-business represents a fundamental change in attitudes and behaviors, from the CEO to the front line. Before a company can rally the people, it needs to think systemically about aligning the various organizational dimensions.

We have also tried to strike a balance between the short-lived euphoria touched off by the dotcom revolution and the dotcom-bashing that has more recently come into vogue. The fact that much experimentation ends in failure does not mean there are not deep lessons to be learned. Internet startups paved the way for established companies to move faster, think more creatively, and execute more effectively. E-business can usher in myriad opportunities to instigate change. It can become a rallying point for change—and what is the usual rallying point? A near-death experience. But why wait for another company to nearly steal your lunch before deciding to enact radical change? E-business teaches us to find the companies that are playing in our spaces but are playing by a different set of rules. Moreover, it teaches us that *any* company can make up a new set of rules.

At the close, we might explain the concept of *strategic insight,* as in our subtitle, "Strategic Insights into E-Business Transformation." In our view, strategic insight is nothing but a penetrating view of the obvious. It is a nugget of wisdom, a lens that allows you to see differently. Insights are intuitive, not analytical. In fact, we have eschewed analysis in favor of *synthesis*—by emphasizing patterns and themes over facts and details. We have tried to stay at a high level so as not to lose sight of the big picture. Moreover, we have tried to offer sense-making frameworks that not only present a meaningful interpretation of the current state of e-business, but answer the question: So what? In our view, strategic insights should have the capacity to move us from knowing what is happening to knowing why it is happening and predicting what might happen in the future.

Our journey begins where it ends. Marcel Proust captured the essence of this statement when he wrote that "we don't receive wisdom; we must discover it for ourselves after a journey that no one can take for us or spare us." A Punjabi proverb conveys the same idea: "If you want to see heaven, then you have to die yourself."

Notes

Introduction

1. The capacity of the short-term memory is thought to be seven chunks of information. See G. Miller, "The Magic Number Seven, Plus or Minus Two: Some Limits on Our Capacity for Processing Information," *Psychological Review*, 1956; 63, 81-97. Also see R. L. Atkinson, and R. M. Shiffrin, "Human Memory: A Proposed System and Its Control Processes," in *The Psychology of Learning and Motivation*, Vol. 2., K. W. Spence and J. T. Spence (eds.) (London: Academic Press, 1968).

Chapter 1

1. Kevin Kelly, *New Rules for the New Economy: 10 Radical Strategies for a Connected World*, (Viking Press, 1998).
2. Nick Carr, executive editor of the *Harvard Business Review*, coined the term *leveragable advantage*.
3. The term was introduced in the book *Digital Capital: Harnessing the Power of Business Webs* by Don Tapscott, Alex Lowy, and David Ticoll (Harvard Business School Press, 2000). Many companies are adopting the term to describe a value network of meshed entities—suppliers, distributors, service providers, infrastructure providers, and customers—that use the Net as the basis for business communications and transactions.
4. Consider the way that a company brings products to market. It is a complex, iterative process that involves interactions among functional departments and also among many external entities. The whole process could be transformed by an innovation management solution such as that being developed by Chingari.
5. For a description of Intel's approach to next-generation microchip design, see Albert Yu, *Creating the Digital Future: The Secrets of Consistent Innovation at Intel* (The Free Press, 1998).

Chapter 2

1. Barry Boehm, "A Spiral Model of Software Development and Enhancement" in ACM *Software Engineering Notes*, August 1986, 14–24.
2. Peter F. Drucker, *Post-Capitalist Society* (Harperbusiness, 1994), 57.
3. James M. Utterback, *Mastering the Dynamics of Innovation*, (Harvard Business School Press, 1996).
4. Clayton M. Christensen, *The Innovator's Dilemma* (Harvard Business School Press, 1997).
5. Clayton M. Christensen and Michael Overdorf, "Meeting the Challenge of Disruptive Change" *Harvard Business Review*, March–April 2000.
6. A NewCo refers to consortia that have been capitalized with a line of sight to a liquidity event, as distinguished from a coop, which follows a utility company model. For a detailed explanation, see the article "Dangerous Liaisons" by Mohanbir Sawhney and Julia Acer, *Business 2.0*, October 26, 2000.
7. "Online Banks Can't Go It Alone," *Business Week*, July 31, 2000, 86–87.

Chapter 3

1. Gary Hamel calls this "business concept innovation." For an excellent description, see Chapter 3, "Business Concept Innovation," in Gary Hamel, *Leading the Revolution* (Harvard Business School Press, 2000).
2. For more details, see the article "Spark Innovation Through Empathic Design," Dorothy Leonard and Jeffrey Rayport, *Harvard Business Review*, November–December 1997. Also see the overview of the process of contextual inquiry in Hugh Beyer and Karen Holtzblatt, *Contextual Design* (Morgan Kaufmann Publishers, 1997).
3. For an excellent discussion of the resource-based view of competition and the ambiguity in labeling resources, see John Fahy and Alan Smithee, "Strategic Marketing and the Resource Based View of the Firm," *Academy of Marketing Science Review* [Online] 99 (10).
4. For a fuller description of these dimensions of intellectual capital, see Thomas A. Stewart, *Intellectual Capital: The New Wealth of Organizations* (Bantam Books, 1998). An excellent exposition of the mechanisms for converting human capital (tacit knowledge) into structural capital (explicit knowledge) can be found in Ikujiro Nonaka and Hiro Takeuchi, *The Knowledge-Creating Company: How Japanese Companies Create the Dynamics of Innovation* (Oxford University Press, 1995).
5. These ideas of MetaMarkets are described in detail in the book *MetaCapitalism: The e-Business Revolution and the Design of 21st-Century Companies and Markets*, Grady Means (editor) and David M. Schneider (John Wiley and Sons, 2000).

6. The value network has been given various labels, including the "value net"—David Bovet and Joseph Martha, *Value Nets: Breaking the Supply Chain to Unlock Hidden Profits* (John Wiley, 2000)—and "business web," Don Tapscott, Alex Lowy, and David Ticoll, *Digital Capital: Harnessing the Power of Business Webs* (Harvard Business School Press, 2000). Bovet and Martha define a value net as a dynamic, high-performance network of customer/supplier partnerships and information flows, which parallels the systemic and dynamic aspects of our definition but is limited to the vertical dimension. Tapscott et al. define a business web as a "distinct system of suppliers, distributors, commerce services providers, infrastructure providers, and customers that use the Internet for their primary business communications and transactions."

7. Kevin Kelly, "New Rules for the New Economy: Twelve dependable principles for thriving in a turbulent world," *Wired*, September 1997.

8. "Destructive Behavior," *CIO Magazine*, July 15, 2000.

9. Interview with Mike Winkel, Executive Vice President of Strategic Planning at R.R. Donnelley.

Chapter 4

1. Database integration, upon which the promise of synchronization depends, was first made real in the form of enterprise resource planning (ERP) applications, which predate the commercial Net by at least a decade. When ERP first appeared on the scene, the primary expectation was that now there was a tool by which to enable data currency and integrity. The idea that information could be captured in one part of the organization and made accessible in all other parts in an internally consistent manner was nothing short of revolutionary. Before ERP, data was divided into nearly as many silos as there were employees. The democratization of databases is dangerous, especially where version control is concerned. But with ERP the database was one. Every view, be it finance-driven or marketing-driven, simply became a query to the database. As we discuss in Chapter 5, ERP stands as the precursor to everything e-business. The Net delivers a radical improvement over the original ERP applications in two important ways. First, the Net enables real-time processes as opposed to batch processes. Second, whereas ERP had a shorter reach, limited to internal operations, the Net reaches out to the extended enterprise—and beyond.

2. "Matters of Style," *ASEE Prism*, 6(4), 18-23 (December 1996), discusses the principles and applications of four learning style models (Felder-Silverman, Kolb, and models based on the Myers-Briggs Type Indicator and the Herrmann Brain Dominance Instrument).

3. Because the pure price segment in financial services saturates at somewhere between and 13 and 17 percent of the market, companies like

GEICO and E*Trade that compete on price point with a single product offering quickly tap out the market on people who want automobile insurance or stock trades. The pure play is a limited play. It generally attracts a low net worth selection of customers, putting margins under enormous pressure. These types of companies tend to hit a ceiling on market size and a floor on price point.

4. Consider Charles Schwab, which learned the hard way about the importance of internal consistency when it launched its online brokerage service. Initially, Schwab tried to prevent its online customers from using the support and services that it provided to its "regular" customers, who paid more to interact with brokers. This discrimination provoked a violent reaction from Schwab's online customers, forcing it to offer the same services to all its customers. By now most companies know better. "We're the only ones who offer you an agent no matter how you come to us," crows Allstate in its TV ads. Indeed, every service offering from Allstate has the same price tag and the same set of benefits attached to it, regardless of which channel provided the entryway.

5. This example draws from the article "3M: Glued to the Web," *Business Week*, November 20, 2000, and from a case study on 3M by the Corporate Executive Board in its report "Great Leap Forward: Launching E-Business at the Large Corporation," Working Council for Chief Information Officers (Corporate Executive Board, 1999).

6. This insight is discussed more fully in the article "Making New Markets," Mohanbir Sawhney, *Business 2.0*, May 1999.

7. Personal interview with Anurag Wadhera, ex-brand manager, Procter & Gamble.

8. John Naisbitt, *Megatrends* (Warner Books, 1982).

9. Sources: Motion Picture Industry Association's 1999 U.S. Economic Review, Paul Kagan & Associates, and the Video Software Dealers Association.

10. See the wonderful discussion on opposites and duality in Chapter 2, "Half of It," Ken Wilber, *No Boundary* (Shambhala Press, 1979).

11. Brian Greene, *The Elegant Universe: Superstrings, Hidden Dimensions, and the Quest for the Ultimate Theory* (W.W. Norton & Company, 1999).

12. For a thorough discussion of channel design, see Louis W. Stern, Anne T. Coughlan, and Adel El-Ansary, *Marketing Channels*, 5th edition (Prentice Hall, 1996).

13. Mathematically, a *corner solution* dictates that the optimum point for a curve lies at the end points, as opposed to an *interior solution*, where the optimum point can lie at any intermediate point on the curve.

14. The closest that gasoline has come to being sold over the Net is the "name your own price" for gasoline promoted by Priceline.com. Will consumers spend valuable time to bid for a few dollars off a tank of gasoline? More

important, will gasoline marketers provide bulk discounts that will make the Priceline.com concept workable? Time will tell, but we aren't too convinced.

15. "Home Depot Tells Vendors to Stay Off the Net," *Industrial Distribution*, September 30, 1999, 21.

16. "How PC Makers Are Reprogramming Themselves," *Business Week*, October 30, 2000.

17. "Let's Get Physical," *Inc. Magazine*, October 15, 2000, 168–169.

Chapter 5

1. For a detailed discussion of business process redesign in e-business, see Ravi Kalakota and Marcia Robinson, *e-Business 2.0: Roadmap for Success* (Addison Wesley, 2000). For a technical overview of enterprise application integration, see David S. Linthicum, *Application Integration: e-Business-Enable Your Enterprise* (Addison-Wesley Information Technology Series, 2000). For a strategic overview of Net-enabling the enterprise with a detailed case study on Cisco, see Amir Hartman, John G. Sifonis, and John Kador, *Net Ready: Strategies for Success in the E-conomy* (McGraw-Hill, 2000).

2. See Regis McKenna, *Real Time: Preparing for the Age of the Never Satisfied Customer* (Harvard Business School Press, 1997).

3. Firms offering relationship management systems include DoubleClick, MarketFirst, E.piphany, Responsys, MarketSwitch, PostMasterDirect.com, and Paramark.

4. Firms offering customer interaction management systems include E.piphany, Siebel, Silknet, Quintus, and Synchrony.

5. Firms offering partner relationship management systems include Channelwave, Partnerware, Pivotal, Webridge, Click Commerce, Intershop, and Asera.

6. For a discussion of how and what businesses buy, see the classification scheme proposed in the article "E-Hubs: The New Business-to-Business Marketplaces," Steven Kaplan and Mohanbir Sawhney, *Harvard Business Review*, May-June 2000.

7. Firms offering enterprise portals include Portera, Epicentric, Webridge, and Netscape. Traditional software vendors like IBM, Oracle, Siebel, and Microstrategy are also rolling out their own versions of enterprise portals.

8. An excellent discussion of component-based architectures can be found in Peter Fingar, Harsha Kumar, and Tarun Sharma, *Enterprise E-Commerce* (Meghan-Kiffer Press, 2000).

9. This discussion draws from the white paper "Asera eService," *Architecture Review*, December 2000.

10. For a detailed discussion of the "synch-and-stabilize" model, see M. A. Cusumano and R. W. Selby, *Microsoft Secrets: How the World's Most*

Powerful Software Company Creates Technology, Shapes Markets, and Manages People (Free Press/Simon & Schuster, 1995), 187–326.

11. For a management-oriented discussion of the bullwhip effect and how to overcome it in the context of supply chains, see Hau L. Lee, "Creating Value Through Supply Chain Integration," *Supply Chain Management Review*, September–October 2000.

12. "Competition and Collaboration—The Future of B2B," white paper, Atlas Commerce, May 5, 2000.

13. See a detailed discussion in the report "The Rise of the Industry Operating System," Goldman, Sachs & Company, November 8, 2000.

14. The different evolutionary stages of a B2B consortium are outlined in detail in the article "Dangerous Liaisons," Mohanbir Sawhney and Julia Acer, *Business 2.0*, October 26, 2000.

15. The evolution of Web services is described from one company's perspective in the white paper "Web Services: Computing's Fourth Wave," Frank Moss, Bowstreet, Inc.

Chapter 6

1. "Starbucks to Create New Lifestyle Portal; New Internet Subsidiary to Be Formed," press release, June 30, 1999.

2. "Starbucks Sees Profit Plunge on Charges for Web Holdings," *The Wall Street Journal*, November 16, 2000.

3. In the case of Starbucks, then-CEO Howard Schultz had scored big wins with some of his early dotcom investments. His streak of "beginner's luck" undoubtedly served to whet his appetite, setting the stage for the coffee roaster's subsequently bullish stance on external venturing activities.

4. Sources: Carolyn M. Brown, "Tales of a Cyber Pioneer," Gartner Group, October-November 2000; "W.W. Grainger & Company," case study by Anthony Paoni, Kellogg Graduate School of Management, 2000; company presentations and press releases.

5. Early results indicate that Grainger's e-business portfolio is doing well in terms of actual revenues, with overall Internet sales expected to be between $350 million and $400 million in 2000, up from $102 million in 1999. Its flagship site Grainger.com was expected to generate over $280 million in revenues in 2000. Almost 9 percent are incremental revenues from first-time customers or existing customers who bought more than expected, based on historical trends.

6. For a discussion of the value of flexibility and the concept of real options, see Thomas E. Copeland and Philip T. Keenan, "How Much Is Flexibility Worth?," *McKinsey Quarterly*, 1998, 2; 38–49.

7. For an interesting discussion of how designers at Toyota pursue a broad exploration of solutions by thinking about "sets of design alternatives" that

lead to "excessive numbers of prototypes," see Allen Ward, Jeffrey K. Liker, John J. Christiano, and Durward K. Sobek II, "The Second Toyota Paradox: How Delaying Decisions Can Make Better Cars Faster," *Sloan Management Review*, Spring 1995.

8. For a discussion of how platform thinking can be used to guide strategic decisions on diversification and growth, see Mohan Sawhney, "Leveraged High-Variety Strategies: From Portfolio Thinking to Platform Thinking," *Journal of the Academy of Marketing Science*, Volume 26, No. 1, 1998.

9. See Marc H. Meyer and Alvin P. Lehnerd, *The Power of Product Platforms* (The Free Press, 1997).

10. For a discussion of flexibility and commitment in strategy, see Pankaj Ghemawat, *Commitment: The Dynamic of Strategy* (The Free Press, 1991).

11. *Corporate Venture Capital: Managing Equity Returns for Strategic Returns*, Corporate Executive Board, May 2000.

12. "The Berkshire Bunch," *Forbes*, October 1998.

Chapter 7

1. Adopted from "White Wing's Escape," Arthur W. Ryder (trans.), *The Panchatantra*, (University of Chicago Press, 1956), 214–217.

2. These laws (Moore, Coase, Metcalfe, and Gilder) are the conceptual foundation for many recent technology and digital strategy books, including Don Tapscott, David Ticoll, and Alex Lowy, *Digital Capital: Harnessing the Power of Business Webs* (Harvard Business School Press, 2000); Larry Downes and Chunka Mui, *Unleashing the Killer App: Digital Strategies for Market Dominance* (Harvard Business School Press, 1998); and George Gilder, *Telecosm: How Infinite Bandwidth Will Revolutionize Our World* (Free Press, 2000).

3. The change management topic has spawned hundreds of articles and dozens of books in the academic as well as the popular press. These include: John Kotter, *Leading Change* (Harvard Business School Press, 1996); Jeanie Daniel Duck, "Managing Change: The Art of Balancing," *Harvard Business Review*, November–December 1993; Rosabeth Moss Kanter, "Moving Ideas into Action: Mastering the Art of Change," *Harvard Business School Note*, 1988; Rosabeth Moss Kanter, *The Change Masters: Innovation and Entrepreneurship in the American Corporation* (Simon & Schuster, 1985). More recent books on change management in established companies include: Jeffrey Pfeffer and Charles A. O'Reilly III, *Hidden Value: How Great Companies Achieve Extraordinary Results with Ordinary People* (Harvard Business School Press, 2000); Rita Gunther McGrath and Ian MacMillan,*The Entrepreneurial Mindset* (Harvard Business School Press, 2000); Gary Hamel, *Leading the Revolution* (Harvard Business School Press, 2000).

4. The McKinsey 7S framework was presented in the article "Structure Is Not Organization," R. Waterman, T. Peters, and J. Phillips, *Business Horizons*, June 1980, 14-26. Also see the classic book *In Search of Excellence: Lessons from America's Best-Run Corporations*, Tom Peters and Robert H. Waterman, Jr. (New York: Harper & Row, 1982), and the article, "Dealing with Structure and Systems," James Brian Quinn and Henry Mintzberg, in *The Strategy Process* (Prentice Hall, 1988).

5. Claire Tirstram, "Turning the Tables," *Red Herring*, August 2000; Matt Murray," General Electric Mentoring Program Turns Underlings into Web Teachers," *The Wall Street Journal*, February 15, 2000.

6. Carol Hildebrand, "The Art of the New Deal," *Darwin Magazine*, June 2000.

7. A detailed argument for this trend is presented in the article "Where Value Lives in the Networked World," Mohanbir Sawhney and Deval Parikh, *Harvard Business Review*, January 2001.

8. "Who's in Charge of IT?" *Information Week*, October 16, 2000.

9. For details of different forms of power in organizations, see B. H. Raven and J. Z. Rubin, *Social Psychology* (2nd ed.) (Riley, 1983).

Epilogue

1. Ephanius Wilson, *Sacred Books of the East* (The Colonial Press, 1900).

INDEX

ABOUT THE AUTHORS

Mohan Sawhney is the McCormick Tribune Professor of Electronic Commerce and Technology at the Kellogg Graduate School of Management, Northwestern University, and the Director of the Center for Research on Technology, Innovation, and E-Commerce at the Kellogg School. The author of several influential articles in publications like *Business 2.0, California Management Review, Harvard Business Review, Financial Times* and *Context Magazine,* and recently named by *Business Week* as one of the 25 most influential people in e-business, Mohan is an internationally renowned consultant, teacher, and speaker. He serves on the advisory boards and board of directors of several technology and e-commerce startup firms and advises many Global 2000 firms on e-business strategy. His MBA course *Technology Marketing* and *TechVenture,* and his executive course *Winning Strategies for e-Business* are some of the most popular courses at the Kellogg School. He is a Fellow of the World Economic Forum, a Fellow of DiamondCluster International, and a Charter Member of The Indus Entrepreneurs (TiE). Mohan can be reached at mohans@nwu.edu.

Jeff Zabin is an independent writer and speaker based in Evanston, Illinois. He is a research fellow with DiamondCluster International, a premier business strategy and technology solutions firm, a co-founder of an e-business thought leadership network, called nMinds, and a strategic advisor to several technology and e-commerce companies. With extensive experience analyzing markets of rapid change, and developing strategy innovations, he consults to both startups and Global 2000 firms. A returned Peace Corps volunteer, Jeff began his career in educational publishing, at Houghton Mifflin Company, where he eventually came to direct a division's electronic production activities. Jeff can be reached at zabin@7s2n.com.

For more information, please visit us at www.7StepstoNirvana.com.